WILT THOU GO ON MY ERRAND?

WILT THOU GO ON MY ERRAND?

Journals of Three 18th Century Quaker Women Ministers

SUSANNA MORRIS   1682 – 1755
ELIZABETH HUDSON   1722 – 1783
ANN MOORE   1710 – 1783

Edited by Margaret Hope Bacon

Pendle Hill Publications
Wallingford, Pennsylvania 19086

Cover Art, Maps, and Illustrations
by John Davis Gummere

John D. Gummere is a painter and illustrator living in
Philadelphia. He studied at the Pennsylvania Academy
of the Fine Arts.

Library of Congress Cataloging-in-Publication Data

Wilt thou go on my errand? : journals of three 18th century
    Quaker women ministers : Susanna Morris, 1682-1755;
    Elizabeth Hudson, 1722-1783; Ann Moore, 1710-1783 /
    edited by Margaret Hope Bacon.
        p.   cm.
    Includes bibliographical references and index.
    ISBN 0-87574-921-6 : $16.00
    1. Morris, Susanna, 1682-1755. 2. Hudson, Elizabeth,
1722-1783. 3. Moore, Ann Herbert, 1710-1783. 4. Women,
Quaker--United States--Diaries. 5. Women clergy--United
States--Diaries. I. Morris, Susanna, 1682-1755. II. Hudson,
Elizabeth, 1722-1783. III. Moore, Ann Herbert, 1710-1783.
IV. Bacon, Margaret Hope.
BX7793.W55   1994
289.6'092'273--dc20
[B]   94-21187
                                                            CIP

CONTENTS

INTRODUCTION

From its birth in mid-seventeenth century England, the Religious Society of Friends has liberated both men and women from socially prescribed roles. Its men have been freed to be tender, loving, nurturing, and peaceful; its women to be strong and assertive. Partnerships between men and women within marriage, within the church, and within the many reform movements that Quakers have undertaken have been traditional. There is very little structure and hierarchy within Quakerism; decisions are made on the community level through an earnest seeking of God's guidance. Early Friends believed that Christ as an Inward Teacher was available to each person who earnestly sought Him. While this belief holds true for many Friends today, it is more often expressed by the statement: there is that of God in everyone. Belief in the equality of all people flows from this central tenet.

Beginning in the mid-seventeenth century, Quaker women joined Quaker men in the task of spreading the Truth, as they called their belief in the ready availability of Christ, up and down the British Isles, overseas to the continent of Europe, and to the new American colonies. Because Quakers had no paid ministry, the role of these traveling ministers was vital in establishing new Quaker meetings and in providing spiritual ministry and nurture to existing Quaker groups.[1]

At first Quaker ministers were self-selected. Men and women who felt the stirrings of the Holy Spirit within them would begin to speak to the informal groups of seekers who had banded together to worship in silence, waiting for the word of God to be expressed by one of their number. They

1

also preached to the men and women of their towns and villages. Since Quakerism imposed no set doctrine, other than a close adherence to the inward voice of Christ, there were many variations in this early ministry.

Some of the new recruits to the Children of the Light, as they at first called themselves, came from Ranters, individuals in the extreme left wing of the Puritan movement who believed that there should be no stops in one's individual religious expression. James Nayler, one of the early leaders of Quakerism, a brilliant writer and thinker, was said by some to have had Ranter tendencies. In 1656 a group of followers gathered around him and appeared to be challenging the leadership of George Fox. After an imprisonment during the summer of 1656, he appeared confused, and in October he allowed his enthusiastic followers to conduct him into the town of Bristol on a donkey, saying "Holy, holy, holy" and behaving as though he were himself the Christ. This incident brought further persecution to the Quakers and caused the leadership to decided to establish more order by setting up small local meetings charged with overseeing the conduct or "conversation" and preaching of members. There then evolved a system for recognizing ministers and releasing them for service outside the meeting community. Women as well as men were so recognized. When they traveled in the ministry, they took with them minutes from their local meeting testifying to the soundness of their "conversation," or integrity, as well as of their message.

Thus, from 1670 onward, Quaker women were recognized and recorded as ministers, almost two hundred years before Antoinette Brown became the first ordained woman minister in the United States. Their pioneering experiences in dealing with almost universal disapproval of women preaching outside of the Society of Friends, and their efforts to pursue their calling as full-time Quaker ministers and yet play roles

2

as daughters, wives, mothers, and aunts make their stories of contemporary as well as historic interest.

To understand the traveling Quaker women ministers and their journals, it is necessary to touch briefly on the theology of early Quakerism. George Fox, considered the founder of the movement, discovered, after a long period of religious search, that he did not need priests or sacraments or churches, but that he could have direct contact with Christ as the Inward Teacher. Through the Inner Light of Christ, it was possible to discern and rise above sin and slowly, through many inward baptisms, to return to the state of innocency of Adam and Eve. Arriving at this state was no sudden rebirth, but a lifelong process. As one became cleansed of sin, one became dead to the old self and able to serve as a channel of God's Holy Spirit. Self-will and intellectual ideas which had no root in experience, or "airy notions" as Fox called them, were the enemies of this process.

In that original state of innocence, Fox believed, man and woman had been created as helpmeets to one another. In the Fall, man had been placed over woman, but now that it was possible through Christ to reverse the Fall and regain the original state of perfection, men and women should again be helpmeets to one another. Fox's first convert was a woman, Elizabeth Hooten, a grandmother, who became a spokesperson and traveling minister for the new society. Another important convert, Margaret Fell, was Fox's partner in nurturing the new group, and sometime after the death of her husband became Fox's wife in a marriage remarkable for its equality. Both Fox and Fell wrote treatises arguing for a woman's right to preach and prophesy, rejecting every biblical injunction against it.[2]

The concept of serving as a channel for the Holy Spirit meant that nothing, not one's social status, wealth, gender, age, nor role in the community, mattered as much as one's role as a conduit for God's will. In the Quaker meeting, the servant was on the same footing as her master; women as men. As William Penn once wrote: "Sexes made no difference, since in Souls there is none."[3]

This belief in equality was a cornerstone of early Quaker thought. It preceded the peace testimony for which Friends are now widely known. When asked to enroll in Oliver Cromwell's New Model Army, Fox said, "I live in that life and power that taketh away the occasion for all wars."[4] By this he meant he was already living in the state of Eden, having overcome the lusts of the world, a state in which there was perfect equality among persons. Later when he traveled in the New World and met the Native Americans and the black slaves, he began to realize that these people too must have within them the Light of Christ, and hence were equal in the sight of God. He did not see the full implications of this insight, but later generations of Quakers became famous for their peaceful relations with the Native Americans and their advocacy of the abolition of slavery.

Other left-wing Puritan sects gave some latitude to women, but Quakers did so on a larger scale and a more permanent basis. While most of these other groups disappeared, Quakerism has remained a small but vital religious voice until today.[5] Very early Quakers institutionalized the revolutionary concept of women's equality in several respects: the establishment of separate women's meetings for business, the recording of women ministers, and the development of a marriage ceremony in which the partners take each other on the basis of equality.

In the separate meetings, women developed their talents for speaking, for raising money, for keeping minutes, for writing epistles, and for influencing their brethren. Some meetings were more successful in this than others. For reasons that are not yet clear, the women's meetings in the

American colonies apparently developed more fully than their counterparts in Great Britain. In their travels, the Quaker women ministers relying on the guidance of God, met many obstacles and came to demonstrate to both men and women what devotion and heroism women were capable of. Returning from these travels to take part in the separate women's business meetings, the ministers further reinforced the women's growing sense of their own powers, at the same time that they elevated the status of women in the wider Quaker community. Without the traveling women ministers, it is conceivable that the women's business meetings would not have flourished. The two were symbiotic. Together they developed the testimony for equality which has been a mark of Quakerism and a contribution of Quakers to the larger society. It is no accident that a significant number of the leaders of the nineteenth-century women's rights movement in the United States were Quaker.[6]

It cannot be claimed that Friends were always successful in living out their basic concept of equality—racial, gender, or otherwise. Sometimes the biases of the dominant culture have seeped in. As the Quaker movement was gaining a foothold, the right wing of Puritanism was developing a strong emphasis on masculine-dominated hierarchy. Each man was adjured to rule over his wife and children. At its best, however, Quakerism has been a model for a new form of social organization, attempting to exist in the midst of a structure hostile to its basic tenets of peace and of equality.

Quaker women were among the Valiant Sixty who carried the Quaker message up and down the British Isles, and Quaker women were the first to bring the Quaker message to London, and to the American colonies: Mary Fisher and Ann Austin to the Massachusetts Bay colony in 1656, and Elizabeth Harris to Virginia and Maryland at the same time. Mary Fisher, a young servant, later made a trip to preach to the Sultan of Turkey; while Mary Dyer, one of the pioneer women ministers, was one of four Quakers hanged on Boston Common for defying a law banning Quakers. Elizabeth Hooten visited the American colonies three times and was stripped, whipped from town to town, and abandoned in the wilds for her efforts to preach Quakerism in Puritan Massachusetts.

The right wing of the Puritan movement, as exemplified in the settlers of Boston, were opposed to women's preaching as a form of antinomianism which they saw as a threat to their patriarchal theocracy. Jeannette Gadt in "Women and Protestant Culture" has suggested that it was a fear of women, "out of their place," which most alarmed the Boston Puritans and caused them to persecute the Quakers. The early Quaker women ministers who visited the colony were searched for signs of witchcraft. There was a rumor that Mary Dyer was a witch, and had given birth to a monster.[7]

By the end of the seventeenth century, the days of persecution which the Friends had suffered were over, and the movement entered into a period of consolidation and of impact on the world. The establishment of Pennsylvania as a Holy Experiment, a place where both Friends and Catholics, Mennonites, Presbyterians, and Anglicans could experience religious freedom, was an important aspect of that impact. In several of the American colonies, the Quakers became prominent in both government and business; some grew wealthy. Instead of defending themselves from imprisonment, the chief problem now was to keep their movement spiritually alive. Wealth and status tended to undermine the simplicity of the Quaker way of life, while the religious tolerance that Friends practiced meant that their children were exposed to the children of "the world's people" in schools and in the communities. The minutes of Quaker meetings in the first half of the eighteenth century are full of concern

6

about worldly styles of dress and of behavior creeping into the youth of the Society.[8]

To counteract this, the Friends relied on meeting discipline and on the ministers who exhorted them in meeting, and who traveled from meeting to meeting, visiting isolated and backsliding groups. Beginning around 1750, a large number of reforming ministers began traveling under concern to awaken Friends to the need for a tighter discipline. One aspect of this crusade was to make sure that the complete parallel system of business meetings for men and women on the preparative, monthly, quarterly, and yearly meeting level, advocated by George Fox, was in place, and that select meetings for ministers and elders were held quarterly and yearly. Thus we find Mary Peisley (1717–1757) of Ireland, traveling in North Carolina in 1753, much troubled that the Quarterly Meeting was not select, while Susanna Morris, on her third trip to England, rebuked English Friends in 1752 for their "too frequent use of strong drink and tobacco" and for their justification of defensive war. Later, in 1753, she appeared in London Yearly Meeting to urge the establishment of a women's yearly meeting, a goal to which reformers on both sides of the Atlantic bent their efforts for many years.[9]

Many of the larger meetings had one or two local ministers who preached in their home meetings, clerked preparative meetings and monthly meetings for business, and attended the select meetings quarterly and yearly of ministers and elders. A few of these ministers felt themselves called to travel in the ministry in their quarterly meeting, covering a geographic area the size of a county, or through the yearly meeting, covering a regional area. Others ministers began to visit other yearly meetings, and some of these felt the missionary call to go overseas. Between 1685 and 1835, according to one list, some 141 American ministers traveled to the British Isles, Europe, or both, several of these making the trip two, three, or four times. Another list places the number of British Friends coming to the American colonies, and later the United States, between 1656 and 1843, at 185. Of the American ministers, forty-seven or 34 percent were women; of the British, fifty-three or 35 percent.[10]

The traveling ministers attended or "took" as many pre-parative (local), monthly, quarterly, half-yearly and yearly meetings as they could fit in. Both men and women some-times visited and prayed with all the families belonging to a particular meeting. Most of them also appointed meetings with non-Friends, speaking from the town hall or town square. It made traveling slow; many of the women who went over-seas spent three to five years away from their families.

As a result of their shared experiences, the traveling min-isters developed a sense of camaraderie with one another, as evidenced in the journals. Attending Uxbridge Monthly Meeting before London Yearly Meeting in 1753, Susanna Morris, a minister from Bucks County, Pennsylvania, was pleased to find four London ministers attending the meeting also. Going to London Yearly Meeting in 1785, Patience Brayton (1733–1794), a minister from Swansey, Massachusetts, met six American traveling Quakers. The traveling ministers crisscrossed in their visits to meetings, and sustained each other. Friendships developed among American, Irish, and British ministers.[11]

Both men and women who traveled in the ministry were provided with traveling companions. Sometimes these were other ministers, sometimes not. Occasionally husbands accompanied their wives, but for the most part the women ministers traveled with other women. Close, supportive friendships were often forged between the women who endured physical hardships and faced ostracism together; they also experienced deep spiritual baptisms as they sought to uncover the will of God for their journey. Elizabeth

Shipley of London Grove Meeting and Esther White of Wilmington Monthly Meeting, who traveled to Great Britain together in 1743, were known for their lifelong devotion to one another.[12]

In the journals presented here, we find Elizabeth Hudson deeply attached to Jane Hoskins and suffering from jealousy when Jane becomes fond of another companion. Some friction existed off and on between the two women after this episode, culminating in Elizabeth Hudson's charge that Jane did not defend Elizabeth's reputation after they returned to Philadelphia. Ann Moore reports weeping bitter tears when she was forced to part with her companion, Ann Matthews, and feeling "stripped and very lonesome" without her. Later she was very upset when the woman she had chosen as her companion to travel to Great Britain decided against the trip.[13]

The women were further supported by the larger network of women ministers and by the women's meetings, which they attended as they traveled. While Quaker men and women generally met together for worship and separated only for business sessions, there was sometimes segregated worship during the latter. Several of the traveling women felt they were freer to preach before the women's group. Thus Patience Brayton writes of attending a meeting in Cork, Ireland: "I was desirous of doing no harm, and through fear sat the meeting silent; but after the men and women separated, it being their three-weeks meeting for discipline, I was largely engaged in testimony, and the Lord was pleased to water his heritage, to the comfort of my drooping spirit."[14]

Patience Brayton's feeling more comfortable with women reflects the continuing struggle of Quaker women against the sense of feeling unworthy as women to answer the call to ministry. Quaker men record in their journals that they often struggled against the call too, but women were further handicapped by believing that they belonged to the weaker sex and sometimes even by entertaining a prejudice against women in the ministry. These attitudes were so prevalent in that day that they frequently crept into the Society of Friends. Thus Jane Fenn (1693-1770), a young servant who migrated to Philadelphia in 1712, describes sitting in meeting in Pennsylvania one day and hearing an inner voice declare that she had been chosen for the ministry:

> Yet I must confess, this awful word of Divine command shocked me exceedingly, my soul and all within me trembled at the hearing of it; yea my outward tabernacle shook insomuch that many present observed the deep exercise I was under. I cried in spirit, "Lord I am weak and altogether incapable of such a task, I hope thou wilt spare me from such a mortification; besides I have spoken much against women appearing in that manner."[15]

Having finally given way in obedience to the commandment of the Holy Spirit and spoken in meeting several times, a woman Friend might expect to have her ministry recognized by her home meeting and to be appointed to its committee of ministers and elders. Thus on 8-31-1746 [October], we find the Philadelphia Monthly Meeting, to which Elizabeth Hudson belonged, minuting that "Ministers and Elders recommend admitting Sarah Morris, Ann Widdowfield and Elizabeth Hudson to sit in their meeting, they having for some time past appeared in a public testimony amongst us." The next step in her evolving role as a minister would be to obtain a certificate from her local meeting to travel to nearby meetings. Later she might feel a drawing from God to travel to visit Friends in other yearly meetings. In 1723 Susanna Morris obtained a certificate from the Quarterly Meeting of Ministers held Third Month, (May) 4th, 1723 to travel to visit Friends in the Southern Providences.[16]

In granting a woman a certificate, the monthly and quarterly meetings, through their Select Committees of ministers and elders, considered various factors: whether or not this was a true call from God, the soundness and consistency of the woman's preaching, her spiritual soundness or "conversation," the situation of her husband and children, her health, and the availability of a suitable traveling companion. By granting the minute, the meeting assumed responsibility for providing for her travel and for her family in her absence. In the case of overseas travel, her yearly meeting generally paid the expenses for the trip overseas. There were a few exceptions: Ann Moore, a minister of West River Yearly Meeting (later Baltimore Yearly Meeting) was supported by Philadelphia Yearly Meeting in her trip to England in 1760.[17]

Husbands were supposed to seek the agreement of wives, and wives, husbands before making trips in the ministry. If, however, the spouse did not agree and the other partner continued to feel under divine pressure to make the trip, the meeting would sometimes intervene on the would-be traveller's behalf. In 1699 Jane Biles told her husband, William, that she felt a concern to visit Great Britain, the land of her birth. William, however, felt that she was in too poor a state of health. Jane did not feel easy with his decision and so informed the General Meeting of Ministering Friends in the tenth month, (December) 1699. Again, two months later, she told the meeting that she still felt she should go, even though William could not agree. The couple were told to wait "for further assurance of mind of the Lord in it." Six months later the situation remained the same, and the meeting told Jane that she was at liberty to go, since the members were not satisfied with her husband's objections. The very next day William announced that he was now satisfied to "give up" Jane to her mission, and in fact thought of accom-

11

panying her. Thinking that he had come around too readily, the meeting was not prepared to give him a minute until another six months had passed. Jane decided to wait for him, and the two sailed together in the spring of 1701. Ironically, the nineteenth century scribe who recorded this trip wrote it as that of "William Biles and wife."[18]

For a younger, unmarried woman, sometimes the permission of her parents was requested by the meeting. In 1728 Phebe Willets of Cow's Neck, Long Island, at twenty-nine requested permission of Westbury Meeting to make a religious visit to Great Britain with Susanna Morris. Phebe's mother, Abigail Willets, objected to Phebe's leaving, and the meeting decided to wait a few months to see if Abigail would change her mind. Phebe, evidently, gave way to her mother's wishes for she did not go, and three years later she married Adam Mott and had several children, one of whom became the grandfather of James Mott, the husband of Lucretia Coffin Mott. Adam Mott died several years later, and, in 1741, Phebe married Tristram Dodge, a widower. In 1752 at the age of fifty-three she, at last, made the trip to Great Britain, sailing over and back with the venerable Susanna Morris.[19]

When Elizabeth Hudson acquainted her meeting with the fact that she was under a religious concern to visit Friends in Great Britain, the meeting appointed a committee to confer first with her parents and then with Elizabeth about the trip, and, finding her parents concurring, and Jane Fenn Hoskins, now a fifty-four year old, married traveling minister, willing to be her companion, issued a certificate for her to take abroad. Elizabeth's parents evidently agreed to provide her entire financial support on this trip.[20]

The certificate issued for Elizabeth Hudson expressly refers to the fact that she had Jane Hoskins as a traveling companion. Although many young unmarried women traveled in the ministry, there was extra care taken that they be suitably accompanied, especially toward the middle of the eighteenth century. Nevertheless, of the forty-seven women who traveled from the American colonies to Great Britain from 1700 to 1835, nine were single. Of these, four married after they were thirty, one was a widow, three remained single, and one died at age twenty-two.[21]

The granting of the certificate was regarded with reverence, and most ministers were extremely reluctant to go beyond what their certificate expressly outlined. Thus, in 1757, Ann Moore discovered that she felt under divine constraint to visit Albany, although her certificate stated that she was to go no further than Rahway, New Jersey. Only after much prayer and after meeting with the Rahway elders, did she feel it possible to proceed.[22]

It was understood that the traveling Quaker ministers keep some form of diary so that on their return to their home meeting they could account for their time and the money advanced to them. All the journals mention the homes where the minister stayed, the meetings which he or she "took," and the other ministers they encountered. In addition, many of the journals described the spiritual journey of the traveller; her periods of doubt, of inward baptisms and inward communion, her growth in faith, the dreams which she had "in the night season" and which were widely regarded as a form of Divine revelation, and the miracles that God wrought to save her when she was on His errand. These journals were passed down in Quaker families, frequently copied over by a devoted daughter or son, and edited freely in the process. Some of the ones regarded as more remarkable were published in the early nineteenth century, undergoing further editing, and were read in Quaker families along with the Bible as a part of family worship. Even today, quotations from these early Quaker journals are sometimes used in the books of discipline issued by various yearly meetings as a form of ad-

13

vice to their member meetings.[23]

Carol Edkins has compared early Quaker and Puritan spiritual biographies and noted that both followed formulas apparently designed to insure their acceptance into the community, but that there appeared to be slightly more room in the Quaker journals for individual expression. In the case of Quaker journals, there are two explanations for their formulaic quality. One is the degree of editing these journals went through before they were published. When I have compared journals in manuscript and in published form, I have inevitably found evidence of material that was deleted, apparently because it was regarded as controversial. For example, in Ann Moore's journal, reference to her being disappointed by a woman who had promised to travel with her is entirely omitted in the second copy of the manuscript and in its published form.[24]

The other explanation is the concept of subduing the self, "the creature," which was very prevalent among Quakers during the eighteenth century. By getting rid of all human desires and feelings within oneself, it was more possible to become an instrument of the will of the Holy Spirit. This emphasis, which has sometimes been called quietism, did not mean inactivity; Quaker ministers traveled widely during this period, and the Quakers entered upon some of their most important reforms, such as work with the Native Americans and for the abolition of slavery during this time. But it meant an extreme emphasis on keeping self in abeyance. John Woolman, the Quaker abolitionist, mentions his wife and child only once in his journal, not because he did not love them, but because to write of them would be to put self, the creature, forward. Similarly, Quaker mothers among the traveling ministers felt called on to surrender their concerns for their children to Christ and leave them entirely in His hands while they went on His errand. So sanctified has become

come the concept of motherhood that, even today, neither men nor women can understand a woman making this hard choice. Yet many of the nineteenth-century women ministers of other persuasions risked social ostracism because they sometimes found it necessary to leave their children in order to follow the Divine command. These women believed that they experienced the cross in leaving their families for these journeys but were confident that they were able to give their children a greater comfort than their mere presence in the home could offer, by sharing with them their adventures in faith.[25]

The necessity to avoid the mention of self is also responsible for some of the apparent circumlocution in the Quaker journals. Quakers of the period rarely said that they spoke in meeting. They said rather that "The Lord owned his servant," or "The Lord was pleased to manifest his ancient love amongst us," or "we had a sweet, comfortable time," or "the power of Truth was over all," or "Light breaking forth." Likewise, they spoke of being brought low, or in the dust, or in prison, when they felt unable to speak in meeting, especially when there were "itching ears" waiting to hear their message. Many ministers refused to speak unless they felt the power of the Holy Spirit urging them to their feet. As a result, they sometimes appointed meetings and then sat silent hour after hour, to the chagrin of those who had come long distances to hear them. While Quakers have always waited upon the movement of the Holy Spirit, the tendency to hold completely silent meetings rather than run the risk of "outrunning the Guide," was more prevalent in the eighteenth century.[26]

It is apparent in both Susanna Morris's and Ann Moore's journals that they were written for the edification of their children and whomever else might read them. Elizabeth Hudson is also clearly writing for a future audience. Many of the ministers in fact kept journals for the instruction of younger, untried ministers; the training up of new ministers being a sacred duty felt by all. This fact too leads to the development of the journal as a spiritual exercise, rather than a diary of secular events.

Unfortunately, fewer of the Quaker women's journals were published than those of their male counterparts, nor are they available today, except in rare book collections or a few scattered Quaker libraries. As a result, contemporary Quaker writers draw heavily on the male experience, or scramble for female quotes. To answer this felt need within the Society of Friends was one of my motives in deciding to seek publication for some Quaker women's journals. But I was also motivated by the expressed interest of non-Quaker young women in divinity schools to learn more about their earlier female counterparts.

The journals, however, do more than illustrate the role of Quaker women ministers in the eighteenth century. They are a rich source for understanding the culture of the American colonies in the eighteenth century; its language and customs, the interpretation placed on dreams, and the spiritual development of Quaker ministers. As such, they can take their place alongside many well-known and well-beloved male journals which have been published previously.

In deciding which journals to include, I reviewed as many as I could find written by the American women traveling ministers who went overseas in the eighteenth century. Aside from their foreign travels, there is no reason to think their experience differed from those of other Quaker traveling ministers in the colonial period. Each overseas minister was expected to spend some time in travel in the colonies before her trip abroad, and these aspects of the journals are valuable for the light they cast on the reception of women ministers in colonial America.

I was able to locate only eleven journals of women ministers who went overseas during the eighteenth century. (There are some seventeen journals by Quaker women who stayed in the American colonies. Some of these were ministers, others wrote from a secular viewpoint.) From those thirteen, I selected three which I was able to transcribe from manuscript form. The three journals have aspects in common; all list the homes and meetings visited, and all give some account of the woman's religious struggles. Each, however, has some aspect which makes it of further interest.

Susanna Morris (1682-1755) is the eldest of the group, and her journal has a pioneer ring, emphasizing how she endured great physical hardships with positive faith in God's protection. A humble woman, she was known for her simplicity and the evident warmth she showed in visiting Friends' families. The mother of thirteen children, she began her travels at forty, while she was still bearing children, and made the first of three trips to Europe when her youngest child was three. Her husband, Morris Morris, an elder in Abington Meeting, was fully supportive of her travels and, in her later years, traveled with her at times in her local ministry.

From a wealthy and prominent family in Philadelphia, which had the largest concentration of Quakers in the colonial period, Elizabeth Hudson (1722-1783) went through a lengthy conversion experience before taking up her ministry. This struggle is quite typical of others reported by early Quaker women ministers. Hers included a period of refusal to hear the voice of God, being angry at others who sought to counsel with her, and a final surrender first to preach, then to travel, and finally to go abroad. Elizabeth was single and twenty-five when she went overseas. While she made every effort to subdue her own will and to serve as a channel of the Holy Spirit, her journal reflects more of her personal experiences, joys, and irritations than do the others. Some of the spontaneity may simply result from the fact that this journal was never edited for posterity or publication. Certain passages reflect an original and creative mind at work in seeking symbolism for religious experience. Both deeply dedicated to doing the will of God, and independent, she sometimes clashed with the Friends in Great Britain when she insisted, against their wishes, on having public meetings to which the people of the town were invited, or, having called such meetings, did not speak because she did not feel so led by the Spirit. After her overseas adventures were over, she married in her early thirties and had several children.

Ann Moore (1720-1783), a poor Quaker from Maryland began her journeys at the age of forty-six, married to a ne'er-do-well and the mother of grown children. At the time of the French and Indian War she felt under divine obligation to preach to the British troops at Albany. Less educated than Elizabeth Hudson, Ann Moore was a valiant defender of women's right to preach, taking on both Presbyterian and Catholic priests in debates which inevitably started with Paul's injunction against women speaking in the churches. A warm, strong woman, she managed to live down the fact that her husband was disowned by Friends, perhaps for drinking, and that her stepson had joined the British army, and to triumph over her fear that people thought she had no right to preach when she could not control the behavior of her own family. She relied heavily on the guidance of the Holy Spirit to make her daily decisions.

Although very different in many respects, the three journals are alike in revealing that the women felt themselves to be under divine orders which they could disobey at their own peril. There is frequent reference in all three journals to the sweet peace which they are able to achieve by abandoning themselves entirely to divine obedience and serving as instruments of the Lord. For Susanna Morris and Ann Moore, this meant surrendering the "creaturely" concern they felt for their husbands and children, and giving them over to God's care.

In each of the journals, one senses the woman's growing confidence that she is fully capable of serving as a channel of the divine spirit, as she meets and overcomes obstacles within herself, as well as in her environment. There can be no question that answering the call to the ministry was a liberating experience for these eighteenth-century women, as it proved for their nineteenth-century counterparts, enabling them to break out of the traditional roles society had long prescribed for them. While they sought only to be obedient to God's bidding and to experience the sweet peace that was the reward of this obedience, their example had unexpected repercussions, causing other women to consider new options and perhaps leading to the move of Quaker women into the reform movements and the professions in the nineteenth century.

Lexicon Notes

Of the three journals I have chosen to edit, only one appears to be in the handwriting of the author. This is the journal of Elizabeth Hudson. In manuscript at the Quaker Collection, Haverford College, her journal has never before been published. However, it appears to have been recopied from an earlier original, when Hudson was elderly, and may have been edited by her or her husband. The Susanna Morris journal, at the Historical Society of Pennsylvania, is described as a manuscript copy and is written in a different hand than seen in Susanna Morris's own letters, also at the Historical Society. A manuscript copy of Ann Moore's journal is at the Friends Historical Library at Swarthmore, but it was evidently copied by her daughter, Rachel Price. A small section of the journal, that for 1775 is in Moore's original handwriting, and I have included this section. The rest of the original Moore journal is in the possession of Rosalie Douglas, the widow of a descendant, but is in too fragile of a condition to be copied or lent. Douglas and her husband have made a typewritten transcript, using modern spelling and punctuation, but containing errors in names, places, and Quaker expressions. Comparisons between the transcript and the manuscript at Swarthmore reveal that the latter was subjected to some editorial changes, but none of great significance. I have used the Price manuscript for this edition.

Susanna Morris's journal was written in three parts, and I have reproduced it just as it was. Elizabeth Hudson's journal was written with no divisions at all, and I have separated it into six parts for ease of reading. Ann Moore's journal was originally divided into six parts. I have followed these divisions except for breaking the long account of her second trip to Albany into two parts, II and III, and combining two short accounts of travels during the American Revolution into part IV.

Since I could not work from original manuscripts, except in one case, I decided to attempt to make the texts as accessible as possible to the modern reader without doing violence to the language of the day. Capitalization of common nouns has been eliminated, and eighteenth-century punctuation has been streamlined. Occasionally, very lengthy sentences have been broken up when it seemed vital to preserve meaning. British spellings have been retained throughout, because they are familiar to most readers of the English language. Other spellings have been modernized. The use of Friend, to designate a member of the Society of Friends, is sometimes capitalized in the original manuscripts, sometimes not. I have capitalized throughout.

Readers may wish to follow the travels of these women on maps. Because their spelling of place names, particularly in foreign countries, is phonetic, it is sometimes difficult to understand what they mean. Working with old maps of the period, I have followed these journeys and made minor corrections in the spelling where needed. When I have been unable to identify the place, I have retained the original, and presumably phonetic, spelling. Using modern maps, I have then placed in brackets the appropriate modern place names. In an effort to make the journals as useful as possible, I have also made an effort to find the towns and villages mentioned on a map of the period, and spell their names accordingly.

The names of many persons are mentioned in these journals. I have identified Quaker ministers, some elders, and those who accompanied the three women on their travels, but not the names of every homeowner where our travelers lodged.

In 1752 Great Britain and her colonies changed from the Julian to the Gregorian calendar, shifting the first month of the year from March to January. Dating before the shift was called Old Style. I have indicated, where appropriate, the corresponding new style month.

All these women knew the Bible very well, and wove words and phrases from it throughout their journals, without identifying the texts. To the best of my ability, I have given citations for texts which seem to be recognizable. However, Biblical language pervades all the journals, and readers will soon become familiar with the manner in which the journalists used its rolling cadences.

NOTES

1. Many Quakers today continue this tradition of having no designated ministers, but rather believe in the ministry of all believers. However, there are branches in Midwest and Far West of the United States which have professional pastors. These groups have also established pastoral outposts in Africa and Latin America.

2. George Fox, "The woman Learning in Silence; or, the Mysterie of the womans Subjection to her Husband, as also, the Daughter prophesying, wherein the Lord hath, and its fulfilling that he spake by the prophet Joel, I will pour out my Spirit unto all Flesh," *The Works of George Fox, Doctrinal Books*, vol. 1, edited by T. H. S. Wallace (State College, Pennsylvania: New Foundation Publications, George Fox Fund, 1990), 104.

   Margaret Fell, "Women's Speaking Justified; Proved and Allowed by the scriptures, all such as speak by the spirit and Power of the Lord Jesus," *A Sincere and Constant Love: An Introduction to the Work of Margaret Fell*, edited by Terry S. Wallace (Richmond, Indiana: Friends United Press, 1992).

3. William Penn, "Some Fruits of Solitude," in *The Select Works of William Penn* (London: William Phillips, 1825), 362.

4. *Journal of George Fox*, edited by John Nickalls, (London: London Yearly Meeting, 1975), 65.

5. Among other left-wing Puritan sects were Ranters, Seekers, Independents, Baptists, Diggers, Levellers. Please see Christopher Hill, *The World Turned Upside Down* (New York: Viking, 1972); George Nuttall, *The Holy Spirit in Puritan Faith and Experience* (Oxford: B. Blackwell, 1946); and Christine Trevett, *Women and Quakerism* (York: Sessions, 1991).

6. Research is scanty on the early Quaker women's meetings. Christine Trevett in *Women and Quakerism In the Seventeenth Century* (Sessions: New York, 1991), found the British women's meetings in the seventeenth century playing a subordinate role,

and Larry Ingle in his article "A Quaker Woman on Women's Role: Mary Penington to Friends, 1678," *Signs,* vol. 16: 3 concurs. Phyllis Mack, in *Visionary Women's Ecstatic Prophecy in Seventeenth-Century England* (University of California, 1992) has made the most thorough search of British women's minutes to date, and finds their power is various. Jack Marietta in *The Reformation of American Quakerism 1748-1783* (University of Pennsylvania, 1984) finds women in Bucks County taking more responsibility than expected.

My reading of American Quaker women minutes, mostly written in the first half of the eighteenth century, suggests that in some meetings women began to challenge male authority. More research is needed on the transatlantic Quaker community. Among the Quaker leaders of the nineteenth-century women's rights movement were: Lucretia Mott, Susan B. Anthony, Abby Kelley Foster, Angelina and Sarah Grimke, Sarah Pugh, to name a few. Later, Alice Paul, a Quaker from Moorestown, New Jersey, led a nonviolent struggle for women's suffrage and wrote the first Equal Rights Amendment which she named the Lucretia Mott amendment.

7. Jeannette Carter Gadt, "Women and Protestant Culture" (Ph.D. diss., University of California, 1974), 147; Johan Winsser, "Mary Dyer and the Monster story," *Quaker History* , vol. 79, no. 1: 20. See also Carol Karlsen, *The Devil in the Shape of a Woman,* (New York: Norton, 1987).

8. Jack Marietta, *The Reformation of American Quakerism,* 47-54; Epistle of advice to young Friends, Minutes, Philadelphia Yearly Meeting for Women, 1714. Microfilm, Quaker Collection, Haverford College (hereafter cited as QCHC).

9. Mary Peisley Neale, *The Lives of Samuel and Mary Neale,* (London: Charles Gilpin, 1845), 342.

10. "Ministering Friends Who Crossed the ocean for Truth's Sake," and "The Names of Ministering Friends from Europe who have Visited America," manuscript lists, Quaker Collection, Haverford College (hereaftrer cited as QCHC)

11. "An Account of Part of the Travels of Susanna Morris," Manuscript Copy, 40, Historical Society of Pennsylvania (hereafter cited as HSP).

12. "Memorial to Elizabeth Shipley and Memorial to Esther White," in *A Collection of Memorials* (Philadelphia Yearly Meeting, 1787), 371-376.

13. "An Abstract of the Travels with some other remarks of Eliz. Hudson, from 22 of lst month, 1732," 142. QCHC. "The Journal of Ann Moore," manuscript copy probably by her daughter, Rachel Price, Friends Historical Library (hereafter cited as FHL), Swarthmore College .

14. *A Short Account of the Life and Religious Labours of Patience Brayton* (New Bedford: A. Sheerman, 1801).

15. "Life of Jane Hoskens [sic]" in *Friends Library*, vol. 1 (Philadelphia, Rakestraw, 1837), 463.

16. Minutes, Philadelphia Monthly Meeting, 8-31-1746; Minutes Philadelphia Quarterly Meeting of Ministers, 3-4-1723. QCHC, Microfilm .

17. "Accounts Paid by Rachel Pemberton, Treasurer of the Yearly Meeting of Women Friends, 1757-1763" Pemberton Papers, vol. 16: 77, HSP. The accounts contain a list of sea stores bought by Mary Armitt for George Mafou and Ann Moore, the 20th of 12th month, 1760, amounting to 8 pounds, 8 shillings and two pence.

18. "Jane Biles" in *The Friend*, vol. 28, no. 12: 93.

19. Phebe Dodge (1699-1782), Westbury MM minutes 8-9-1728; 7-30-1754, , New York Yearly Meeting, Haviland Record Room. Thomas Cornell, *Adam and Anne Mott, Their Ancestors and Descendants* (Poughkeepsie, New York, 1890), 11-13, 215.

20. Minutes, Philadelphia Monthly Meeting. 11-29-1747, 12-26-1747. QCHC, Microfilm. Elizabeth frequently says in her journal that she needed no financial assistance.

21. "Ministering Friends of America who crossed the Ocean for Truth's Sake," unpublished manuscript, QCHC.

22. Ann Moore, *Journal*, Part IV, 302–303.

22. Howard Brinton, *Quaker Journals: Varieties of Religious Experience among Friends* (Wallingford, Pennsylvania: Pendle Hill, 1972), xi.

24. Carol Edkins, "Quest for Community" in *Women's Autobiography Essays in Criticism*, edited by Estelle Jelinik, (Bloomington: Indiana University Press, 1980), 41. Typescript of "The Journal of Ann Moore" trans. Rosalie E. Douglas, FHL; "The Journal of Ann Moore," a manuscript copy; FHL; "Ann Moore's Journal," in *Friends Miscellany*, vol. 4 (Philadelphia, 1833).

25. Howard Brinton, *Friends for Three Hundred Years* (New York: Harper & Brothers, 1952), 66, 181, 182. Philip Moulton, ed. *Journals and Major Essays of John Woolman* (Oxford: Oxford University Press, 1971).

26. Elizabeth Hudson, *Journal*, Part IV, 8.

PUBLISHED SOURCES

Bacon, Margaret Hope. *Mothers of Feminism: The Story of Quaker Women in America*. San Francisco: Harper & Row, 1986.
  "Quaker Women in Overseas Ministry," in *Quaker History*. vol. 77, no. 2 (Fall 1988): 105.

Barbour, Hugh. "Quaker Prophetesses and Mothers of Israel" in *The Influence of Quaker Women*, edited by Carol and John Stoneburner. Lewistown, New York: The Edwin Mellen Press, 1986.
  The Quakers in Puritan England. New Haven: Yale University Press, 1964.

Brinton, Howard. *Quaker Journals: Varieties of Religious Experiences Among Friends*. Wallingford, Pennsylvania: Pendle Hill Publications, 1972.

Cornell, Thomas. *Adam and Anne Mott, Their Ancestors and Descendants*. Poughkeepsie: New York, 1890.

Dunn, Mary Maples. "Women of Light" in *Women of America: a History*, edited by Carol Ruth Bekin and Mary Beth Norton. Boston: Houghton Mifflin, 1979.

Carol Edkins. "Quest for Community" in *Women's Autobiography: Essays in Criticism*, edited by Estelle Jelinik. Bloomington: Indiana University Press, 1980.

Fell, Margaret. "Women's Speaking Justified; Proved and Allowed by the scriptures, all such as speak by the spirit and Power of the Lord Jesus." In *A Sincere and Constant Love: an introduction to the work of Margaret Fell*, edited by Terry S. Wallace. Richmond, Indiana: Friends United Press, 1992.

Fox, George. *Journal of George Fox*, edited by John L. Nickalls. London: London Yearly Meeting, 1975.

The Woman learning in Silence: or the Mysterie of the womans Subjection to her Husband, as also, the Daughter prophesying, wherein the Lord hath, and is fulfilling that he spake by the Prophet Joel, I will pour out my Spirit onto all Flesh.

The Works of George Fox, Doctrinal Books vol. 1: 104. State College, Pennsylvania: New Foundation Publications, George Fox Fund, 1990.

Gadt, Jeannette Carter. "Women and Protestant Culture," Ph.D dis.. University of California, 1974.

Gwyn, Douglas. *Apocalypse of the Word; the Life and Message of George Fox*. Richmond, Indiana: Friends United Press, 1984.

Jones, Rufus. *The Quakers in the American Colonies*. London: Macmillan and Company, 1911.

Kunze, Bonnelyn Young. *Margaret Fell and the Rise of Quakerism*. London: Macmillan, 1994.

Manners, Emily, editor. *Elizabeth Hooten; First Quaker Woman Preacher*. London: Headley Brothers, 1914.

Mack, Phyllis. *Visionary Women: Ecstatic Prophecy in Seventeenth-Century England*. Berkeley: University of California Press, 1993.

Marietta, Jack. *Reformation of American Quakerism, 1748-1783*. Philadelphia: University of Pennsylvania Press, 1984.

Mosher, S. and E. Potts Brown. "Prophecy and Politics in Seventeenth-Century England" in *Witnesses for Change*. New Brunswick: Rutgers University Press, 1989.

Moulton, Philips P., editor, *Journals of Major Essays of John Woolman*. New York: Oxford University Press, 1971.

Nuttall, Geoffrey. *The Holy Spirit in Puritan Faith and Experience*. Oxford: B. Blackwell, 1946.

Penn, William. "Some Fruits of Solitude" in *The Select Works of William Penn*. New York: Praus Reprint Co., 1971.

Phillips, William. *A New Map of Great Britain and Ireland*. London, 1825.

Ross, Isabel. *Margaret Fell, Mother of Quakerism*. London: Longman's, 1949.

Taylor, Ernest E. "First Publishers of Truth," in *The Journal of the Friends Historical Society*. vol. 19, no. 3 (1922).

Trevett, Christine. *Women and Quakerism in the 17th Century*. York: Sessions, 1991.

Introduction

OTHER JOURNALS OF 18TH CENTURY TRAVELING QUAKER WOMEN MINISTERS

Ashbridge, Elizabeth. "Some account of the foreparts of the Life of Elizabeth Ashbridge, who died in Truth's service at the house of Robert Lackey, at Kilnock, in the County of Carlow in Ireland the 16th of 5th month, 1755." Quaker Collection, Haverford College (hereafter cited as QCHC), Haverford, Pennsylvania.

Brayton, Patience. *A Short Account of the Life and Religious Labours of Patience Brayton*. New Bedford, 1801.

Ellis, Margaret. "A Diary of Travels in the Ministry, 1739-1752." QCHC.

Hoskins, Jane Fenn. "The Life of That Faithful Servant of Christ, Jane Hoskens, A minister of the Gospel, Among the People Called Quakers." *Friends Library*. Philadelphia: Rakestraw,1850.

Hudson, Elizabeth. "An Abstract of the Travels with some other remarks of Eliza Hudson, from 22 1st month, [March] 1743." QCHC.

Jones, Rebecca. "Journal of Journey Home from England, 1788-1789." QCHC.

Moore, Ann. "Being a Narrative of Some Parts of her life, travels and religious labours." Friends Historical Library (hereafter cited as FHL) Swarthmore College, Swarthmore, Pennsylvania.
Morris, Deborah. "Diary, 1772-1773." FHL.

30

Swett, Mary. "Diary, 1797-1820" QCHC.

Speakman, Phebe Yarnall. "Account of a Voyage, 1796" in the Haddon, Estaugh, Hopkins Collection. QCHC.

Webb, Elizabeth. "A Short Memorial of the Dealings of God with me in the days of my youth," FHL.

Wright, Rebecca. "An Account of Rebecca Wright's Travels in Great Britain and Ireland. Also some interesting memoranda of her niece Ann Bishop." QCHC.

ADDITIONAL 18TH CENTURY QUAKER WOMEN'S JOURNALS

Allison, Martha Cooper. "Diary 1786-1799" QCHC.

Bringhurst, Hannah Potter. "Diary of her last months, 1782," QCHC.

Collins, Elizabeth. "Memoir of Elizabeth Collins," Philadelphia: Friend Books Store, 1859.

Collins, Esther Hunt. "Diary, 1787-1807, telling of meeting and personal affairs." QCHC.

Cook Margaret. *Journal.* FHL.

Cresson, Sarah. "Diary of Sarah Cresson, 1789-1829." HCQC.

Introduction

Dillwyn, Sarah. "Memorandum book of Sarah Dillwyn, giving an account of London Yearly Meeting in 1794." QCHC.

Drinker, Elizabeth. "The Diary of Elizabeth Drinker." Historical Society of Pennsylvania (hereafter cited as HSP), Philadelphia, Pennsylvania.

Fisher, Sarah Logan. "Diaries, 1776-1795." HSP.

Lightfoot, Mary. "Journal of a religious visit with Grace Fisher to Quaker meetings in the Concord Quarter, 1757." FHL.

Mifflin, Ann Emlen. "Commonplace Book and Religious Meditations." HSP.

Morris, Deborah. "Diary, 1772-1773" published in *The Friend*. vol. 67. FHL.

Morris, Margaret Hill. "Journal: 1751-1768 and 1776-1778." QCHC.

Shoemaker, Rebecca. "Diary, 1780–1786." HSP.

Warder, Ann Head. "Diary, 1786–1789." HSP.

Whitall, Anne Cooper. "Journal, 1976–1762." QCHC.

Wister, Sarah. "The Journal of Sarah Wister during the occupation of Philadelphia by the British Troops.

THE JOURNAL

of

SUSANNA MORRIS
1682 – 1755

SUSANNA MORRIS

1682-1755

The earliest of our three traveling ministers, Susanna Heath Morris, was born in England on the 27th of 8th month (October) 1682, the oldest daughter of Susanna and Robert Heath. Her parents were Quakers, and in 1701 they migrated to Pennsylvania and settled on land near the present site of Abington in Montgomery County, Pennsylvania, about ten miles north of Philadelphia. Here they joined Abington Meeting. The Heath family was a pious one; four of their five daughters eventually became ministers of the gospel.

At Abington Meeting Susanna shortly met Morris Morris, a Quaker who had been born in Wales in 1677. On the 27th of 7th month (September) 1703, they married each other in a Quaker ceremony at the meetinghouse in the presence of their families.

The bride was twenty-one, her husband, twenty-six. Their first child, a son, Evan, was born on the 25th of 4th month (June) the following year. Thereafter they had a child every two years or so for the next twenty-one years, a total of thirteen. David, the thirteenth child, was born after Susanna Morris's return from her first major trip in the ministry. Evan died young, and they lost several others, but managed to raise nine to maturity.

Following her first trip in the ministry, recorded in her journal, Susanna Morris visited meetings in New Jersey, then was confined to home by the birth of her thirteenth child,

David, when she was forty-three. In 1727 she traveled to Long Island, and in 1728 to New England. It was on the heels of this trip that she began to feel that she was called to visit Old England. Joseph Taylor,[1] a British Friend, was completing a religious visit to the meetings in the American colonies, and Susanna resolved to sail back to England with him, having first gained the approval of her monthly and quarterly meetings.[2] Unlike most of the traveling ministers, she was not given a female companion with whom to make the trip, but was expected to find one in Ireland. She was forty-six, and left behind children ranging in age from twenty-two to three. Although there are occasional glimpses in her journal of how much she missed her family, she says nothing about this parting, in true quietist style.

In her journal, she speaks of being shipwrecked off the coast of Ireland. Joseph Taylor, the British minister with whom she was traveling, gave an account of this shipwreck to John Griffith,[3] an American minister, describing how they had clung to the shrouds, and how Susanna Morris had rebuked him with a glance when he said that he thought they would all be drowned. Later she began to feel that the survivors would be safer if moved to the lower side of the boat, and although it appeared dangerous and illogical, she persuaded them all to move.

> Soon after they had fixed themselves, there came a great swell of the sea and threw the vessel quite flat on the other side, so that if they had not moved, they would all have been drowned.[4]

Following her first trip to Europe, which lasted three years, Susanna Morris traveled in the ministry to Long Island, and with her sister Hannah Hurford, also a minister, returned to Maryland, Virginia, and North Carolina. Susanna Morris had a special gift for visiting in Quaker families which she exercised during these travels. In 1741, the Morrises moved their membership to Richland Meeting in Bucks County. From this meeting she received a certificate in 1744 to make a second trip to England, at age sixty-one, accompanied this time by Elizabeth Morgan.[5]

They set sail on the 20th of seventh month (September), 1744, and returned on the 11th of eighth month (October), 1746. England was at war with both France and Spain, making travel hazardous, and in the North of England and Scotland, the return of the Scottish pretender had the people in an uproar. The two women, however, had no particular troubles until they were on their way home at which time they were twice chased by French privateers.

Although very glad to be home again, Susanna Morris felt she was still called to visit more meetings in England, and in 1752, at the age of seventy, she embarked once more, accompanied this time by Phebe Willets Mott Dodge, the minister from Long Island, and Mary Weston, a British minister, who had been traveling among Friends in America. In England she met Sophia Hume, a Quaker minister from Charleston, South Carolina, and the great granddaughter of Mary Fisher, who had been one of two pioneers to bring Quakerism to the Massachusetts Bay Colony in 1656.[6]

With the authority of her years and experience, Susanna Morris felt free on this trip to chide Friends for their mistaken ways and notions. Thus we find her warning Quakers in Exeter, England, against a wrong spirit and a "disbelief that the Lord required females to labor in the gospel and also a pleading for making provision for a defensive war." And in Bristol she preached against the "too frequent taking of tobacco in all shapes and the too frequent use of strong liquors. . . . likewise against that unsound speech: you to one person."[7] She was evidently ahead of her time with the testimony against tobacco, which she had also preached against

37

Susanna Morris

in New Jersey before setting sail, for she had written to Israel Pemberton, a prominent Philadelphia Quaker, carefully explaining that she had not preached against all use of tobacco, but only the too frequent use, and she hoped she had not "trespassed against the truth."[8]

Seventy was a great age to be traveling about in 1753. Susanna Morris attributed her ability to withstand it and not to become ill to the same divine intervention that had saved her from shipwreck. She wrote of having to climb "hills as steep as staircases," but being preserved from harm by the fact that when her horse threw her on the hills "he laid her down gently in soft mud."

Previously, Susanna Morris had written about herself as a woman, "one of the weaker sort of people," but now she became a spokeswoman for gender equality. In 1752, and again in 1753, she attended the London Yearly Meeting. Here the men assembled for regular sessions, but the women came together informally, a women's yearly meeting having been laid down in 1701. This state of affairs was upsetting to the American women Quakers, many of whom had had their own yearly meetings since the seventeenth century. The women's yearly meeting served as an important communication tool, permitting women to share information and exhortation with quarterly and monthly meetings, and to communicate, through epistles, between yearly meetings. The American women, who regularly addressed their British sisters, realized that their epistles were not reaching all women, but only those who had happened to come up to London with their husbands, brothers, fathers or sons.

In the 1753 session, Susanna Morris was exercised about the lack of a women's yearly meeting and spoke to this concern in the men's yearly meeting where she was accompanied by Sophia Hume, Mary Weston, Mary Peisley, and Catherine Payton.[9] Samuel Neale described the event:

I well remember the salutation of Susanna Morris, when they entered the meeting house; and she concluded with a short pathetic and living testimony, which had great reach over the meeting. The proposition, I had no doubt, was from the motion of Truth. After a considerable debate it was deferred, and recommendation sent down to the different Monthly Meetings to establish Women's Meetings where there were none, and thus the matter closed for this year.[10]

As a matter of fact, there the matter rested for thirty-one years until Rebecca Jones, along with three other American women, again accompanied their British sisters in a successful protest in 1784.

Following the London Yearly Meeting in June, Susanna continued attending meetings until August 21, when she and Phebe Dodge set sail for Philadelphia. Caught in a storm at sea off the American coast they lost their mast and rigging, and were kept from landing by contrary winds until the end of October.

For the next two years Susanna Morris continued to travel in the ministry in Bucks, Montgomery, and Chester counties as well as in New Jersey, and Delaware. Her beloved husband Morris accompanied her on many of these journeys, as well as one of her minister sisters, Mary Emlen. Finally the journeying became too much and she died on the 28th of March, 1755.

Susanna Morris wrote an account of her travels in the ministry during her later years, evidently working from earlier fragments of a journal. In several places she writes in the current tense, as in describing her daily religious exercises during her final voyage home. The journal, addressed to her children and others, is full of expressions of profound faith and gratitude.

A Map of the Meetings of Friends in England and Wales
exhibiting the boundaries of the respective Quarterly Meetings.

(Used with permission of the Friends Historical Library, Swarthmore College)

The Journal of Susanna Morris

Part I

An Account of Part of the Travels of Susanna Morris

I have had it in my mind for to let my children or any other honest inquirer know how I have fared some parts of my life chiefly on the ever blessed Truth's account for I think I can speak and that truly from my youth upward the Living God helped me to love him and all good people that were concerned to fear him and work righteousness, among other societies as well as our own, if I found it was really so according to their best understanding. And when I was about the twenty-ninth year of my age my understanding was opened so far that I came to know that the Lord my God did require a service of me in that great work of the ministry and indeed I thought it so great that it was very unlikely such a one as I should ever be fit for so great and good a work as that of ministering only from the fresh motions of Life always to the hearers for tis is only such that work for him. And O (saith my soul) that it may be so with all our ministry, time forever, for no other way that man can find will do any good, but his own time and his own power there is some good done in the Earth. Blessed be his holy name, and saith my soul that mankind would all come to praise the God of all their mercies continually whilst health is afforded to them. And now to my own travels, and good experiences of the Lord's help and many deliverances he has wrought for me herein are worthy of some note, yet I may not be able to set them forth as their worth is, but here and there a little as it is brought to my remembrance, I hope for the good of some weak ones. Yet willing and turning to do the will of God, I went not much abroad from my family until I had born all our thirteen children, but one and then I was drawn to visit friends in Carolina, Virginia, and Maryland with a good companion[11] but I think I can truly say that the Lord God's presence went along with us and favoured us among the people in gatherings where we met to wait on him and I do not remember that we were met with any opposers to what we had been given us to say to them in all those countries, but we met with some hardships otherways for in getting over the great Bay Chesapeake, we met with hard and boisterous winds and thereby drove us out to sea and had not the Lord favored us by an outstretched arm we had likely perished all of us that

were in that vessel, for it was an open boat, the master having left the hatches at home on the other side of bay. We set sail on the seventh day in order for to cross Chesapeake Bay to Nansemond River, but the winds grew so boisterous that we were drove out to the open ocean about ten leagues. And it pleased the Lord our God that we drove over a dreadful sandbar into an inlet called Currituck as we understood afterwards, for our master was so lost that he know not where he was. It was betwixt Carolina and Virginia. And now let me say that the Lord our God is a God of knowledge and by him the living are preserved and sometimes helped in a wonderful manner, and my dear children it is worthy of memory to observe to you how things fared with us in that so great a trial for we were like to be lost, the sea run over us and thereby the little provision we had were soaked in salt water and we and our horses were left destitute of food and to all appearances likely to perish, for we had lost our canoe and were surrounded by great waters and no inhabitants near us, but there was a grassy place near us and we thought it best to get the master's horse out and one of the men to ride thither at low water, that he might see whether or not it was an island. And the man went to it (and the horse ate some there) and then came back with tidings it was but an island, then we thought it best to get the poor creatures to the island, that if possible they might shift a while for themselves there, however the Lord might be pleased to do with us. Then the master got the other horses and took them about half way to the grass and there let them go, but instead of going to the grassy land they tacked contrary and I thought as foreign to land and no sign of grass there but white sand and some bushes, and when we saw their landing we were ready to think that the higher power knew best where to send our horses for so it was. And on the third day I was lying down on the deck in a still frame of mind and it there sprung into my mind to get up and look about me and I did so and as far as I could see there was coming two canoes and two men but they came not to us until evening and they informed our master what place we were in, but were not willing to put us on shore, but one of them said he would come tomorrow and when he took us on shore it was at the same place where our poor wounded horses landed without information or help of man. It was six miles to the first house to which we must go and the man that took us ashore was not willing to stay and go with us and the master was not able; all of our company got but little food from seventh day morning until the fourth day following in the afternoon, yet for all that I was so thankful that we were got on shore, that we, viz, Ann Roberts and I, was bent (if God willing) to set forth toward a poor widow's house as the man had informed us which lay near the sea six miles off but when we came with half a mile of the widow's house we were likely for to go out of way there being no path, the sea having flowed over where we should go when easterly winds and blew hard, but I thought that the Lord's mercy was greatly extended to us, his poor handmaids for the woman of the house came to the sea side to meet us and saluted us after this manner: good women, how come ye hither? Was it to do the will of God? And she, when we got to the cottage showed as kind as she could, and there we heard of our horses, after we had been there several days, for they were but about a quarter of a mile from the widow's house and that was many miles from any other; yet our horses had but one thing to hinder them from going therefore or an hundred miles away from us if (I thought) there had not been a hand of help at work it certainly would have been so for the place where they were was so haunted with mosquitoes.

Now some may say, how got you your saddles and clothes from the vessel? We got our horses and rode on them bareback the six miles again and yet got not our saddles but the master had sent by the man that was sent (as I may say from many miles to help us) to his neighborhood for people to get off the shallop, and when he came he would bring our things in his canoe. Therefore we had to ride the same way back again on the horses barebacked and that twelve miles at other times might have been a great hardship but surely the Lord makes hard things easy for those that are willing to serve him well.

And now my children let me tell you how we got safe to Friends in Carolina. I heard it was betwixt sixty and one hundred miles and no guide for us but the only one, and had he not supported our minds we might have fainted in our journey. But forever blessed be his most holy name and power, for our hearts were filled in thankfulness and cheerfulness to begin to set forward toward Carolina. We had a prosperous journey and got well there, and our poor wounded horses carried us amongst Friends, but mine died there. My companion's escaped only had a gathering on his belly by reason of the bruises that he got in the storm but she rode on him home again.

That journey happened to be when I was about forty years old. I have given a short account of the many trials the Lord helped us through and we got safe home to our husbands and families again, the Lord (I may say) was my exceeding great reward for I felt sweet peace in my bosom.

But when the Lord was pleased to send me from home to publish his gospel of peace among Friends at other meetings sometimes my peace was broken and for a time little left to my self as I thought and that seemed hard to bear, and then to wait for a willingness to do the will of God to the uttermost and the consent of husband and good Friends, I found the best for me that I might get in favour with God again for well doing. And so the blessed one did often send me in his service amongst his flock and family, sometimes to tell to others what the Lord, the God of the living, had done for my soul, and other times what the Lord did require at their hands and thus Dear Hearts the Lord dealt with me in the days of my childhood in the work of the ministry for mostly I went through a fight of affliction before I could be willing to give up to go abroad, but blessed be the name of

Isa. 1:12

the Lord, he so placed his fear in my heart that I durst not withstand his requirings, but often grumbled because of my own poverty and (as I often thought) unfitness. But I found the Lord was near his poor handmaid and filled the hungry with good things and furnished matter for his work's sakes and so surely now we may say, Trust ye children of the living God in the Lord for he is everlasting strength and ability enough to perform his mind and will and in doing thereof is the gain of sweet peace.

Now I safely forwards to speak of some other journeys of mine on the Truth's account. I have sometimes gone to a meeting nine or ten miles and home again at night, for that was pleasant to me when my service was over for the Lord that day, and I was sent to Friends meetings in the Jerseys and I spent six weeks at one time there, in those parts of Egg Harbor and Cape May and several other times I was sent to and fro in the East Jerseys amongst Friends there where I often thought we[12] had good service, blessed be the name of our Good Lord and Master, and the more because we were the weaker sort of his people and he had and has still a good regard to the humble and lowly although handmaids; therefore let none whom the Lord doth rightly require and put forth be rebellious but given up to his heavenly will and then they may find with my soul the great differences that is betwixt the fruits of true obedience and disobedience and let all that find that they are rightly called of God to that work be sure that they watch well over their own spirits, lest at any time they should stir themselves into that great work before the Lord really sent them forth for that would be the way to be indeed unproper servants and it may be do more hurt than good; but although I thus write I cannot charge myself with doing the like for I have suffered greatly from backwardness, but my desire is that I may write by the help of that good spirit that drafted me to that work in the beginning of my days.

And when I was about forty-three years of age, the Lord was pleased for to cast me into a grievous state of affliction, a trial indeed never by me to be forgotten. But we may say the will of God is to be done in earth as it is in heaven and how to make the children of men fit and willing he only knoweth the right way for to do it in us and for us, according to his own divine will and pleasure, for in the time of that unspeakable trial I was as one shut up in close prison,[13] waiting on him that is only able to give strength to make covenants with him and it was on this wise, that if my dear Lord would help me to strength, I would not disobey him but go in his errands whithersoever whensoever or in whatsoever he was pleased to require at my hands then would I give up to him again, for had at times a weighty concern of mind for several years to cross the great ocean in Truth's service where the Lord might be pleased to lead me, but I was so full of the Reasoner[14] that I believe I did displease my God and was so far in debt to him that he was pleased to put me in prison a long year and I never had in that time to open my mouth by way of testimony but after I had true strength given me to make those promises as abovesaid, my mouth was opened and my tongue was loosened and I was sent over the seas.

And soon after I got out to sea something of a weight fell on my mind, and I dreamed that our ship would be lost but there remained on my mind a solid weight for fear it should be so. But at times I thought I had been as some other dreams and yet I thought it safe to dwell humble and low before the Lord that I might be ready to learn of him what to do and what to leave undone for I believed that the humble he teaches of his way, and the meek he only can help in the time when he suffers his righteous judgments to be met with, as it is also said, when the Lord's judgments are in the earth his people learn righteousness and there may be great learnings in such great trials as that of shipwreck. And now to pass on, I again dreamed that same, and yet was weak as to being fixed in the belief of the Truth of it and thereby I dwelt in a fearful tossing of mind, until the Lord was pleased to favour me with his goodness, and in one of our meetings to make it known to me only (as I found afterwards) that we should surely suffer shipwreck and I firmly believed that it was the Lord that had told me what he had a mind to do with us. Then for a season I was in trouble and ready to say, had I gone through so much to fit me to go forth in his service and my Friend in his return home from his service on God's account, and yet now must we be swallowed up alive in the great sea. But O blessed forever be the name of our God, for I had soon a good answer returned into my bosom by our Preservation, and that if we would be faithful we should have our lives for a prey. And I hinted something of my mind to the captain who seemed to be somewhat startled at what I had said and lest he should be too much discouraged I had given me to tell him that I see him safe on shore. Our trial was two miles from Dungannon [Dungarvan] on the south-west coast of Ireland.

Now I may a little hint how the Lord dealt with me to help me in my weakness for I have thought that the Lord, knowing how weak I was, and yet willing to do his will he was pleased to give me a timely help to be the more fitted for the trial we had to go through. For sometime before it came to pass that the Lord was pleased to make the thing known unto me only and to no other, although there was there in the ship who I preferred before me, at which I was somewhat thoughtful, for when I hinted a little of what was made known to me in order to find out whether or no the Friend had any knowledge of that trial made known to him, but I found rather that my hint of it seemed to be (I thought) like idle tales to the Friend, Somewhat like Christ's Resurrection when only the tidings were brought to the disciples by the woman. So I forbear to go any further in the relation of it to him, and yet I was preserved so as not to stagger in my mind or disregard the manifestation made known to me from him that is true and as I endeavoured to dwell near him that is faithful and true, my habitation was pleasant. Unto the sudden outcry was proclaimed and nothing appearing but outward destruction of all our lives. Then for a time my outward tabernacle[15] greatly shook and trembled but blessed be the Great Lord of all our mercies the time of trembling was soon taken away and it was renewed to me what was made known to me on the great ocean when he was pleased to let me know what was like to befall us then. He the allwise God did also give me to believe that he would command the proud waves that they should not come at his servants to hurt them as it was said, touch not mine anointed, do my prophets no harm, and so it was my children, the great God did preserve us, I do believe for his own name sake. For although it was at the time called Christmas[16] and we had for two days little sustenance by food for our bodies and many times our heads were under the great waves which rolled over us, after the ship sunk by reason of the strokes she got on the dreadful rocks, afterwards she drove until she settled on a sand bank. In that distress I had no help of man or counselor but the Lord, and thereby thought it best for me to get to the upper side of the vessel, and my seat by the shrouds where I was favoured that I kept my hold, when the waves rolled over us. And we remained in that wet condition about nine hours, in cold time of frost and snow before any of us got relief and yet as I said before were not hurt, nor as I remember had so much as the headache or any surfeit of cold remaining in our bones by reason of that so great trial, and thus my dear children the Lord is pleased to favour his heritage, for so it was with us that though many (in the great trial) of the ship's company lost their lives, some perished with cold, others were drowned. And now by the way let me say that I write not this relation of my having the thing made known unto me only, because I would have anyone think the better of me, no that's not what I aim at! but that the poor in spirit or weak in their own eyes (if willing to serve the Lord) may take a little courage if possible by those things which I have related and to trust in the Lord and to be truly willing to serve him in all things that he doth require of them.

And now to pass on, we landed at a great manse house, a Roman Catholic who was with his wife very kind to us and she told us that their priest was concerned to pray to the Lord for our preservation and he after said to the hearers that they ought to be kind to us and do us no hurt no more than if their father the pope was there, for their sin should be the same. And now I may say that surely the Lord is worthy of the praise for that of turning the papist priest's heart so contrary to their own canon and it happened well for us for the great man with his own boat well manned brought us ashore to his own house. These sort of people were kind to us and they sent a letter to our Friends about twenty or thirty miles, which caused our Friends to come with necessaries suitable to supply our wants and horses to carry us with them home.

And after all those trials the God of all the living helped me well along in my service for him through many countries and in all those parts I was never laid up with sickness the remainder of that winter. I was some of the time with some other Friends in that good service (in the City of Cork) in visiting Friends in their families. My companion's name was Elizabeth Jacobs,[17] one from Waterford, a widow, and her house was the first amongst Friends that I came to after our shipwreck and she had already requested Friends for her certificate in order to visit Friends in old England, so I got a good companion to go with me and we went together and thought we had good service in many places where the Lord was pleased to cast our lots.

During our stay together we took ship at Dublin and had a good passage to Parks Gate and then to Chester. And we had several meetings amongst Friends, then we travelled toward London through Lancashire, Nottinghamshire, and Bedfordshire and had meetings in our way to London and were at the Yearly meeting there; which was (blessed be the Lord) a comfortable season to many for his people were favoured with his living presence amongst us during the time of that meeting, and after some stay in London we had fresh drawings in our minds to visit Friends in Holland and we took our journey from London to Colchester and had meetings among Friends in places as they lay in our way and and at Colchester we had several then we set forwards for Norwich and had also meeting in several towns and places betwixt the two cities. It was the time of their yearly meeting at Norwich and to the praise of our good God and Master it may be spoken; for I thought that we had good service amongst them, for his Truth gained ground in the hearts of his people which is matter of joy to my poor soul when it is so. From that city we went to a seaport town and had a good meeting (in that town) we were favoured with amongst them, although not many Friends. Yet in the main a good one. Then we embarked for Rotterdam and Holland, and had a good passage for which I have great cause to be thankful to the Lord, we had many precious meetings in that country and yet I may say, for my own experience, I then went through heavy burdens and I believe my good companion also, it being a place where the conversation amongst Friends is mostly by an interpreter, they being a people of an unknown tongue to us which was harder for us to find out or speak what was in our minds, but the God and Father of the spirits of all flesh so opened the way into the cases of those whose ways and doing so burden the Seed of God in us, yet for all it was so we got ease to ourselves before we left them. But now I may a little go back and pen down a memorandum of our first landing at Rotterdam. It was the 16th of the 5th month [July], 1729 and that night I may say the Lord who knows all things knew that I had to go through hardships. He was pleased to be good to me in that strange country for soon after I went a shore he so filled my heart with his goodness that in the night season my sleep departed from me, but blessed be his holy name I thought that which I did enjoy now to be better than any sleep for a time. My companion's name was Elizabeth Jacobs as aforesaid; we had a meeting with Friends there and then left them and went by water (in a draw boat) to Harlem and had a meeting with them there and then we lodged at the Friend's house that was our interpreter. His name was Peter Landon, and when we left that city we went by water to Amsterdam and had a meeting with Friends and others there to the comforting and encouraging us to go forward in the Lord's work. Then we had another meeting there which I thought did exceed the first, the honor of his great and blessed name, for there was in that meeting a young man from afar off (Germany) that was so enclosed in his mind by the goodness of the living God that he refused to take his food, saying to his landlady he had food enough the day before. We lodged at Eleanor Roulofs. We left that city and travelled by water to another called Horne [Hourn] and lodged at a Friend's house called Derick Misher, his wife and he were very kind to us for which my soul had great cause to be humble before God and through divine assistance, return him the praise, who alone is worthy for ever and evermore for all his favours every way to us, his poor handmaids as he seemed to be at times.

In our own sight, we had a good season with Friends and

others in their meeting house and the next day we set forward (in a sort of carriage called a stage coach or wagon) by land to a place in North Holland called Twisk, where there was two places that Friends met in by reason (I may venture to say) of the envy of the old adversary that so strives to break unity amongst people and instead of love, sows discord. So it happened among them, they were but one meeting and favoured with two ministers. One of them got one party and the other the rest of the meeting to each of their houses, and so kept for about ten years before we came there which caused us no small load of grief for some time. For at first our interpreter hid the case of them from us, but he was not able to keep the weight of their difference off us because the true lovers of God must suffer when his Truth suffers. After we left them and returned back to the city of Horne to our lodging there, came a solid man full of grief (as we were) and told us his trouble, and the more because of his children who are now growing up to man and woman's estates and he had a mind to have them to join with the right people called Quakers and those near him were as aforesaid but he was in the mind that we might be made instrumental for to get them to meet together again, for saith he, one of the ministers and his wife are gone to live at Amsterdam and so it was. We then left that place and took our journey for the Great City again where that Friend lived and I think I may say (and that truly) the God of peace helped us for we went straightway to the Friend and laid the case before him in a very close manner too tedious to mention to the full, and we strove with him for to get him in the mind to go again with us to that place where that separation was, together with his wife and a Friend or two to interpret. I write this account for the future so all of us may beware of letting in anything of that kind that would separate but rather as pillars of God's house suffer and with patience bear until his holy hand may turn things

53

that seemed to go across to our minds into order again. And now to the forgoing: when he prevailed with the Friend and his wife to go back, we also wrote to the Friends of that country how the case was in our minds and we desired (by a few lines) all of them to meet us in one of the places where they used to meet, that we might try if we could be instrumental to reconcile them together again, and accordingly (Blessed be the Lord) our labours proved better than at times we could expect and we had some more meetings with them mostly altogether, we had a good time with them and to all appearances left them in a good degree in peace and love with each other and seemed glad that we were sent amongst them. Then we left them and set in our journey toward Horne the second time and had one meeting more with Friends and then we set forward in a draw boat for Amsterdam again and forever blessed and praised be the Lord our God, for we again got a good parting meeting with Friends and many other people. Then we passed to Harlem and had another good meeting there.

6th month

I am concerned (to remark) before I pass on that on the 20th of the 6th month [August], I was in great heaviness of spirit in Amsterdam, in part for to see as I thought the great neglect in relation to true religion by all people in that so great a peopled place as that Lowland of Holland for there is in it I was informed, thirty walled cities, besides many country dwellings. Now to go forwards to hint a little here and there of my many provings, the Lord has hitherto helped me through for his name sake as a confirmation of his good pleasure. Then we went to Rotterdam and had two good meetings with them that time. And then we took ship for England

7th month

and had a good passage and arrived at Yarmouth the 13th of the 7th month [September], 1729. When I and my good companion came to England again the Lord (I thought) stirred us up for to separate ourselves for his work's sake and we did obey, although it was a cross to our natural will. To me it seemed hard at first for I thought I was too mean a creature to go without a public companion but as at many other times he that makes hard things easy, helped me still for his own precious name sake. Well now I may say that I fared better than might be expected in places amongst Friends to and from, until I came to Colchester the second time and there the Lord favoured me with a good Friend again, viz, Sarah Lay[18] who accompanied me for half a year through many countries and meetings where we came amongst Friends. And we went again to London, the second time, and all along I blessed the God of my life, we had good reception in most places. And from London we journeyed toward Bristol and visited Friends as we went, through many towns too tedious to mention, and from Bristol we travelled toward Wales where the Lord our good God gladdened our hearts many times among Friends there, for in many places there were not too high for Truth's testimony, although it was through the poorest sort of his people. And when I thought I had done my service for God in Wales we visited Chester and had two meetings and from thence to Morley and staid at a burial and had one meeting more, and then my peace was broken to go any further, but if I would have the company of my comfortable companion I found I must go back to Wales about 30 miles to a place called Donbe [Denbigh] where we got satisfactory meetings amongst those few Friends for they had not been long convinced of the way of Truth. And then I and two men Friends with me travelled back again, for Sarah Lay, my companion, was not well and did not go back to Wales with us. But let the Lord (saith my soul) for ever be obeyed for he would not let me go any further but I must go visit those few Friends in that remote corner far from any other meeting of Friends and it was very winterlike weather and as we went back we rode in no small danger on the sea sands for many miles together for when the tide's up it is all flooded over and the tide comes in very furiously to the land to what it does in America. After my return we visited the county of Chester and we went into Staffordshire visiting of Friends and some others that my concern led me to have a meeting with and it was to great satisfaction in general. And then we went into Lancashire on truth's account and into Yorkshire and had several meetings to good satisfaction thereaway and we had a good season with Friends at Kendal in their meeting house several times (and at our good Friend's house, John and Deborah Wilson[19] which was our home there). Then we went to Lancashire Yearly Meeting and lodged at John Dilworth's. From thence we travelled into Westmoreland visiting meetings as we went, then into the county of Durham and at Sunderland and lodged at Midford Flower with good expense, for it is worthy of some remark where the blessed truth is in dominion, and we had three meetings in that seaport.

And from then we embarked the second time for Holland. The master we went with was called a Friend but did not do Friendly by us for he went with us to Friesland and put us into a Dutch ship to go to Holland and we set out in obedience to God and had a fair wind and sailed sweetly for a while but at night the wind grew boisterous and the mariner young and unskillful so that we got fast on a sand bed and in much danger of losing our lives and no sleep could we get that night, but blessed be his most holy name that had been my preserver in the six troubles did not leave me in the seventh, for there was sent to us a boat well manned the next day and the vessel we were in held together so that we went to shore with it. But may we not think that it was a hardship for us to go to a place where none knew us, nor anyone to speak to in the vessel nor on the shore as we knew of, yet we were glad to have our lives spared to get once to shore again, and in silence resigned to the Lord's will to be done, and it so proved that one of the men had been a sailor that came with the boat and was kind to us, for he could make shift to speak to us when we got to shore. It was a city called Enques [Enkhuizen], the first on Holland shore and near a day's journey (for a stage wagon) before we got to our Friends, but the man that could speak to us, helped us for we told him our concern and I suppose he told the people for they were kind to us, for our money.

But by the way I thought our God was to be remembered for that with all his favours to me a poor creature as I am. Well, we go safe to the city called Horne [Hourn] where our Friends lived but none one could speak to us, but I being there the summer before with an interpreter, Friends knew me again (and their children) and well it was, so for I knew not the way to the Friend's house nor could speak Dutch but to make up that loss one of the Friend's children where I lodged the year before was a good way from home by the

Places Susanna Morris
visited in Holland

HOORN • • ENKHUIZEN

HAARLEM •   • AMSTERDAM

• ROTTERDAM

water side and I knew him and he me, and he went home immediately and so some of the Friends came to us and were glad to see us but then having no interpreter we must of necessity hasten to my former interpreter and so we gave Friends as it were but a slender visit in Holland and I came safe to England again in peace. My work there (through the Lord's favour) proved easier than I expected when I left England, for my God whom I desire to serve in all things accepted the will for the deed, after I had as Abraham given up myself to do his will freely—

And my children, all the children of men ought to be so resigned, and then hard things in many respects may become easy and when I came back to England the second time to Sunderland, and staid sometime with Friends there and to the praise of my good God, I was well received for his work's sake and had several meetings in that seaport town, then I travelled to Stockton with several good Friends in company, for my companion had now left me and went home to her husband, but Friends took care that I had as good companions as could be expected and sometimes I had a ministering Friend from one place to another with me. I lodged at Joseph Robertson's and his wife accompanied me sometimes (who was a minister.) From thence we travelled to Roseberry and had a good time with Friends there and lodged at Ann Forbank's. Thence to Whitby and had a meeting and lodged at the widow Linshill's, and from thence to Scarborough and had a good meeting there and lodged at Isaac Sollet's, a minister, and a good wife he had for a helpmate. Then I travelled to Barlington on the sea side, then I returned through Yorkshire and had many meetings with Friends as I passed through that country and so to Newcastle, and lodged at the widow Middleton's with good satisfaction. She was Robert Barclay's sister.[20] And from thence travelled through Northumberland and visited Friends in Truth for Truth's service there, and hence into Cumberland and at Pabsycrage [Pardshaw?] Meeting house at a quarterly meeting, I thought that the Lord greatly favoured us with his power for to smite against all sin, and we lodged at good old James Dickerson's, and at Cockermouth, where was a large gathering of much people at a burial where my God filled me with his good spirit, for to warn the people against all pride and drunkenness, which had no small effect on some there for I was told after that meeting, one man went home and burned his wig; for when pride was spoke of or rather smote at, the wigs were also put with other offenses, and truly my Friends to whomsoever these poor scrawls may happen to come to hand to read, I may tell them my mind about wigs, for I have been satisfied that the Lord our God is angry and not at all pleased at that calling of making those likenesses the work of men's hands which too many delight in, more than his handy works, for he is jealous of his worthy honor, and, saith my soul, that a word to the wise is sufficient for God's sake.

Well, now I set forward again and came to Whitehaven and staid to a meeting with Friends there, where my mind gave me to believe that I saw a woman in the meeting that I could freely go with to be my companion over sea to Ireland, for several had offered to accompany me, but I had not freedom to accept them, but thought still I must leave it till I came to the seaport and so it was. I had the same woman as companion though not a minister yet she was a sorrowful one who mourned for the abominations of the times and kept teaching of children, but she put by her school the week before I came thither, and knew not why until I came there and had no public companion to go with me to cross the sea. *8th month* And on the first of eighth month [October] I and the Friends embarked the second time for Ireland and that time six days arrived at Hollywood near Belfast; I travelled from thence to Newton, where we had two meetings, mostly with the people of the town; and the Lord our God favoured us largely with his good presence in the times of waiting on him, to his own praise do I desire to speak it at this time, for he alone is worthy, yea forever more amen, saith my soul. And so afterwards the Lord was so pleased to favour us with health for his work's sake, that we were not hindered, but travelled in a religious visit to and again through Ireland—Amongst our Friends and I had several meetings amongst other people in towns where the meetings were kept: but I may say the Lord owned us in these meetings with a measure of his divine power for to attend his work which he was pleased to call us to and I was accompanied with several good Friends which was an encouragement to me for to give up for to have meetings in such places amongst the Papists, but I being a stranger in these parts, the weight of the ministry fell much to my lot, and it so happened that I fell in with four quarterly meetings in those parts, which was for the west part of Ireland and I also fell in with four monthly meetings in that country and their half year's meeting in Dublin. And in that city a concern fell on me to visit Friends in their families and also at Edenberry. I may truly say blessed be the Lord for he greatly helped me in that good work for I think that the service of visiting a Godly sort is very beneficial to promote true Christianity, as the other worldly and profane visits beget ungodliness and corrupt ways. I staid that time about three weeks in Dublin to wait for a passage to England and in that time had very close work in both meetings for worship and in that of visiting many Friends' families, for it was chiefly to the widows and some others; and I have cause to think that it is the Lord's work and that he delighteth in it when it is done in his fear and to the innocency of his Truth. Then we left Dublin in good unity with Friends and sweet peace in my bosom and I embarked the second time for England. On the first day of the first month [March], 1731 and the second of

1st month

60

same we arrived at Whitehaven, having a pleasant passage. And then my mind began to go a little too fast home, for I was ready to say in my heart, O let me go home again if I must come back again but I can well think it was not good for me to think so, therefore let none that would do the best they can take example by me in that. So now I travelled through Cumberland then through Lancashire again and visited many meetings, and in Cheshire, Staffordshire, Worchestershire, and some parts of Hertford and Buckinghamshire and had at times good opportunities amongst Friends. And then I came to London for the third time and it was the fourth of third month [May]. And I may now say *3rd month* blessed be God for the favour of his eternal spirit that was my helper through all my various troubles and services for him who alone is eternally worthy to be feared forever and obeyed to all generations, so saith my soul, be it forever, Amen.

After I had several good meetings in London, I took a little journey into Essex. It being the third time, I made less stay to these parts, having about six meetings in Essex, then returned to London the fourth time and to their yearly meeting and to the Lord's praise it may be spoken for we were greatly favoured there with his good spirit, during all the time, and in five or six day's time I embarked with several Friends (one worthy of note John Richardson from Yorkshire who was drawn from home to visit Friends and others in Pennsylvania) [21] and fell down to Grave's End, and on the 27th of *4th month* the fourth month [June] they hoisted sails and set off from thence and in six weeks we came in sight of America and blessed be the Lord we had in the main a good passage, only having one storm—and I came again with sweet peace in my bosom to Philadelphia, being away in that visit for Truth's service three years, lacking two months. And now, saith my soul, the Lord our God is worthy of everlasting praise to all eternity that hath been pleased so to favour a poor worm to bring in safety to her outward home again.

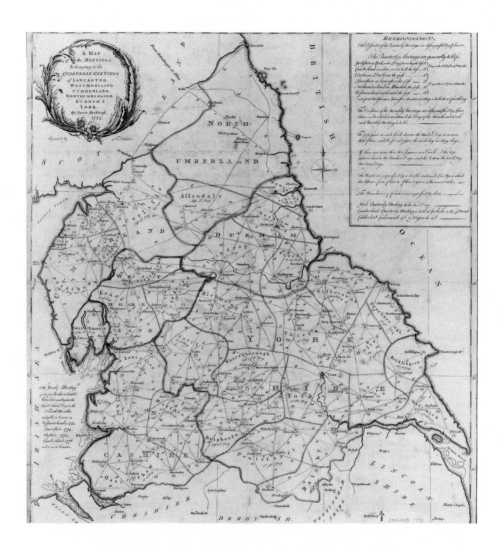

A MAP OF THE MEETINGS OF FRIENDS IN ENGLAND AND WALES
exhibiting the boundaries of the respective Quarterly Meetings

(Used with permission of the Friends Historical Library, Swarthmore College)

THE JOURNAL OF SUSANNA MORRIS

PART II

It pleased my good God and Heavenly Father to send me over the great ocean in the 62nd year of my age in the year 1744 and my companion was Elizabeth Morgan.[22] We embarked in the Philadelphia Galley bound for London North about Scotland but by reasons of contrary winds were safely put into Derry Harbor in the North of Ireland, having had ten weeks passage, wanting two days, where the people were kind to us for our money, and a comfortable meeting with such as were called Presbyterians about two miles from the city and from thence went with two orderly men, who for a hire, carried us with our clothes on horseback behind them to Coleraine where our good Master owned us with a good measure of his spirit to speak a little for his honour for he truly above all is to be honoured forever, and we visited Friends through most of the Northern parts of Ireland and many times when the Lord's living presence was met with my heart has been made gladder than in the increase of outward things I have been a sharer of. And then we got to Dublin where Friends received us kindly where we stayed some time, visiting some families and with them at their meeting houses; where the Lord was pleased to accompany us poor worms with a good share of his blessed spirit which was reviving to our dropping spirits blessed be his most holy name, & from thence we journeyed toward Waterford, a sea port, and visited Friends at places to and fro, thence in the same manner to Cork, then returned to Dublin again. In this my third visit to Ireland my chief concern was to encourage those that had a mind to please God and by the assistance of his blessed power to worship him in spirit and in truth.

And being at my worthy Friend, William Lightfoot,[23] the good part got hold of my mind and prevailed on me to write a little of my experience and of the Lord's dealings with me in this voyage and journey. The ever blessed one that so wrought upon me as to mortify the first nature and through his goodness I can truly say that my mind has been more and more concerned for the working down everything which would get above the good Seed. I think we are never safe unless we feel the plough of God's power and the hammer thereof so operating in us as to break us into tenderness, then it is that we know how to demean ourselves before him who can and does work such a change that for any of his ministers are truly made able to speak for the encouragement of the true travellers, and point out the way to the kingdom. Self with its willings and burnings must be mortified, otherwise the vessel will not be enough cleansed and if not, how can the work please the great minister of the sanctuary, whose life is our light and to do his will is our delight and greatest joy. Therefore let my soul bless and praise the living God who has been pleased to do for me a poor unworthy creature than ever I could either have asked of him or thought of. Although I have had many, yea, more than common deliverances both by shipwreck at sea and various trials at land in my pilgrimage thus far through time, yet I find it still safe for me and I believe all the children of my Father's house to think little of themselves, for all the good that any of us are capable of doing from the ability that the God and Father of all our mercies bestoweth on us for his own honour's sake only. Therefore saith my soul, let our mouths comparatively speaking lay in the dust and then in the Lord's time he will furnish with a sure evidence of that hope which will be an anchor, enabling to endure all things that the ever blessed one may see meet to try his servants with in this uncertain world and thereby shall we be enabled to look unto him for that recompense of reward, which only can make the hearts of his followers rejoice and sing for joy because their soul's comforter is yet to be met with and he that is a wonderful counselor and strength to their minds to hold on their way in seeking to know and do his will to the utmost whilst life and understanding is lengthened out to us according to the good purpose of God in making us, etc.

2nd month

On the 20th of the 2nd month [April] 1745, we took shipping from Dublin to Whitehaven and in our passage near the Isle of Man, we saw a vessel which appeared to be an enemy, sailing sometime one way, sometime another way, almost round us. At first I was a little shocked but when I turned my mind inward to the only counselor, I had to believe that the Lord would discourage them and I found a concern to pray for them that God might give them grace and influence them with his Holy Spirit to do justice and love mercy for his name's sake. Now my dear children and all that are well inclined, I may say of a truth I am glad the Almighty was pleased to beget in me the good spirit of pure love to those who appeared to be enemies, blessed be his great name forever. The Lord our God has in our day manifested his heavenly and divine will to the children of men, especially to such as truly seek him, giving them to understand that to do good for evil is conducive to his honour and to pray for our enemies is well pleasing to him, that hath created mankind to honour and serve him in his own way and according to his Divine Will in all things.

I have cause to bless the name of the Lord who hath brought me over this second time into Britain and may truly say at times am glad that I was made willing to do what I believe was my duty, for the honour of the living God and that he, the all wise one, thought me worthy to go on his errands. Sure I am that none could deem themselves more unfit for this service than I did and that strengthened by my being so far advanced in years yet when I reflect sometimes a fear attends lest I have been wanting in my duty in not doing it when I was younger, may not I say that our great and merciful Lord hath at times winked at some of our weaknesses; if there was but a willingness to do his will, and although at times we linger a little, hoping the will may be accepted yet I have at times been fearful of tempting or provoking the Lord thereby to anger and therefore have had to believe it was my duty to get into true silence and stillness, where I saw it to be my place to go on as I have with my companion Elizabeth Morgan through Ireland from whence we arrived at Whitehaven aforesaid.

From thence we set forwards toward London, the yearly meeting being near at hand, we passed through Cumberland, Westmoreland, Lancashire, Cheshire and Staffordshire, taking meetings amongst Friends as we went along to our mutual satisfaction. In many places I met with Friends who knew me better than I did them, and were glad to see me. With some of my Friends we were as one another's joy in the Lord our God who had so kindly wrought for our deliverance from perils both by sea and land, which makes my soul with the Lord's people bless and praise the living God. We passed through Warwickshire, taking meetings along till we got to London and thought the government of Christ was uppermost in meetings of Friends beyond my expectation, blessed be the Lord for his goodness manifested. In the great city of London he comforted the mourners and satisfied his poor with true bread which perished not. Nay may safely say, that were at the yearly meeting, the glory of the Lord is not yet departed from his spiritual Israel and, saith my soul, that all mankind the world over were but willing enough to have their minds stayed upon the Lord God of the living, that they might be made willing to part with all this world's glory for a sure portion of divine peace and holy quiet in their bosom, then would such know how to buy the truth themselves and a true care remain on the mind not to sell it.

After the national meeting was over we turned our faces northward and passed through many towns, shires and the fen country, labouring in our small measures as well as we could in the word of life, in the meetings of those whom men in times past called in scorn Quakers, but I have been afraid that some who were called so knew little of that holy fear which caused the godly in all ages at times to tremble at the feeling of the presence of the great God who is felt and witnessed by the true seekers of him in silence of all the runnings of restless flesh, and thereby understood how to wait for his appearance in their own hearts, and know his word there as a hammer to break them into tenderness; the offering of a broken heart and a contrite spirit is what the Lord accepts of in our days.

We came down to York to their quarterly meeting for that large country and at this season, viz, midsummer called yearly meeting. Here the Lord and Master favoured us with his good presence, which made my heart glad amongst his people. That meeting was attended by several ancient and worthy ministers, viz: John Richardson,[24] Joseph Storrs,[25] etc. From York we went on our way through the county of Durham and Newcastle upon Tyne, having a good reception in most places where we came. My heart was many times melted into tenderness considering what the Lord had done for me, in helping me to endure hardships and support under the most pinching exercises, therefore let him be had in everlasting remembrance to all future generations. Oh! that all mankind would love the Lord above all and follow his leadings and trust him with their all. And some Friends were pleased to speak favourably of our service, yet say I, let our mouths as it were lie in the dust and all the praise be ascribed to the God and Father of all our mercies that we and all his faithful servants and messengers may at last be sharers of that hope which is an anchor both sure and steadfast unto those who truly love the Lord above all other enjoyments here below.

From Newcastle we journeyed into Scotland where finding meetings small I let in reasonings and fear, thinking my gift was so little the people might imagine my service scarce worth my entertainment, and under these considerations would willingly have turned back into England again, but when I got to be truly still, found no peace in looking back and had to believe that I must visit those few there were and that to do the will of God was our duty in this life, and as I found my mind devoted thereto was favoured on the high way with the joys of God's salvation when no mortal eye beholds. And I may truly say we have no cause to complain for the Lord favoured us in our journeying through Scotland and though at times my poverty was great, yet blessed be his holy name he had never failed to give unto his riches in poverty and strength in time of weakness. But to hint a little further of our sorrowful travels through Scotland, for so it was with us at times for several reasons and had not the Lord, as well as his people, been kind unto us we might have fainted in our minds. But this I can truly say that to those little meetings where our lots were cast, the Lord always afforded me comfort and I believe my companion also although [the people of] the country, part of the time while we were there, some of them were afflicted with the account of the arrival of the pretender's son.[26] But blessed be the Lord God of our lives we met with no hurt and left our Friends in the places where we had been in much love, seemingly and I doubt not it was really so with most of them, and I am thankful that I was so subjected as to do the Lord's will in my small measure for sure I am that is the reasonable duty of all the Lord's people to be obedient to his requirings in all things even until death if they accept a crown of life, although it be in little things, for those who are not faithful in little things are not like to be favoured with great rewards of true peace in their own bosoms.

Now to proceed, we took our journey from Kelso in Scotland back to the country of Cumberland and had two heavenly meetings in the borders, so-called where is the dwelling place of one of our worthies called John Erwin.[27] Both he and his wife have been eminently servicable in the work of the ministry, but are now far advanced in years. And from thence we travelled to Carlisle City where was a considerable number of such as bore our name and some others I think at both morning and afternoon meetings. But the work seemed hard to us and truth suffered in the hearts of many of them and so we were made sharers with the suffering Seed in them, although some there said they had a good meeting that day. From thence we travelled into Westmoreland and so into Yorkshire and had some good sweet seasonable times with Friends in their meeting houses and sometimes in the evenings at Friends' houses, for which we have cause to speak well of the blessed name of our good God who has so eminently helped in time of great difficulties; whenever he alone was trusted in and relied upon; for there is no rock of salvation like unto the God of the living; he is the only true God that answers by fire, for all the right minded among the children of men, their works are, in the love of God, tried as by fiery trials that we poor worms may the more depend on the all wise giver of every good gift and may feel after fresh incomes of the renewing of love and life from him that can give and also take away at his pleasure that which we may chiefly delight in. And therefore oh! let the true Israelites long to be enabled to say, blessed and forever praised be the name and power of the Living God, forever more, world without end, Amen. For I am one that the Lord has brought through great and eminent dangers both by sea and land, some of which I could be glad to have wrote down; for the honour of God's sake, in a fuller and better manner than I can do: I would not have it done for my own, nor for the honour of any of mine but his alone who has created us for a purpose of his own, honour and glory. For I can but leave behind me a little testimony of the many favours which the Lord has favoured me with since I was fully resolved to obey the voice of the true shepherd. Let him lead whither he listeth, come life, come death: the sayings of Christ have been help-ful to my learning to trust in his arm of great power and give up to do his will, some of which are as follows: He that will save his life shall lose it, but he that will lose his life for my sake shall find it. There is no helper like unto the living God, and therefore his power and name is to be relied upon over and above all others. He alone can help all that truly trust in him for his assistance and give them to know an over-coming of the willings and runnings of first nature, and that is to some an hard thing to get the victory over, wherefore it may well be said that the worst enemies a man has are those of his own house.

Mark 8:35

From Yorkshire we travelled through Cheshire where the Lord helped my infirmities that I might be strengthened for his work's sake and Friends were well satisfied with my service amongst them. And in Wales I may say that the Lord favoured me with his living presence. At Shrewsbury I had an heavenly meeting for which let me praise the name and power of the most high for were it not for his mercies I should have failed long ago, therefore whatsoever reads this account let thy heart be the more fixed to seek to please the living God in all things, for there can be no better way for anyone to be found in. I am now at the age of sixty-three years and yet I found that I have need as much as ever to seek unto the Lord to be enabled to do his will.

People may easily say the words recorded in that prayer *Matt. 6:10* our blessed Lord taught his disciples, thy will be done in earth as it is done in heaven; but the right and only way to do it is for all mankind, both rich and poor, to seek the Lord, so as to find him a helper near, even in them to enable them to do his heavenly will, and I am well assured all that so do will be well rewarded for their pains. For dear hearts, believe me there is none that can serve a better master, for the Lord careth well for all the sheep of his pasture, every way, even soul and body. Those who hearken for his voice and will not by any means follow the wrong leader into his crooked and libertine ways but the Lord will reveal his loving kindness to the upright, for our God is unchangeable and his ways are unchangeable but the gate is straight and the way is narrow to the children of pride; neither will the twisting crooked enemy lead there, for he leads in the proud way, in it the flesh can get along with less care and crosses, with a sort of vain hope flattering themselves because there are so many in number and are no stricter than they, not considering rightly what it is that gives the only true evidence of the unfeigned hope of all the sanctified, which is the evidence of Christ within them. The true hope of everlasting glory doth give to all them that abide steadfast in the love of God through Jesus Christ our Lord, who suffered for the sins of man without the gates of Jerusalem and rose again and is ascended on high and has received gifts from God for men even for the rebellious to prepare the hearts of the children of men that are truly willing for to be thereby sanctified through faith on his blessed son our Lord and savior Jesus Christ unto whom belongs everlasting praises and to whom be it given forever.

And now I may say for his sake who hath called me to be obedient to the manifestation of his divine will both by sea and land, although he has been pleased to try me by and through some hardships having been thrice shipwrecked, in danger of the loss of my natural life. But two of the ships escaped being utterly lost, one of which was near North Carolina and the other on the coast of Holland. That which was quite lost was near Ireland. When shipwrecked on the coast of Holland, the Lord favoured us that the vessel endured all night many hard strokes on the sands, and in the morning when hanging out a flag of distress, being in sight of a city called Enthuza [Enkhuizen] the people came and fetched us thither, and I can say of a truth that the living Lord was a comforter to me and my dear companion Sarah Lay and that we were so in fellowship one with another that she held fast hold on me and said if she then must die she would go off with me, but blessed be the God of our lives, who again wrought wonders for my deliverance the third time, for the Lord much sweetened my many bitter cups not only formerly, but also in this journey and I have thought that none of the Lord's servants could well say that they had suffered enough, for the God of the living best knows when our sufferings are all gone through, but the best ye my children can do or for anyone else that truly are bent to follow the Lord through many trials is this: Let them shut their hearts up against the flesh, and steadily turn to the God of true hope, for he is ably to help through all hardships. Therefore, oh let all trust in him the Lord Jehovah, for in him is everlasting strength, blessed be his name forever and ever and to his praise may I yet say.

In our journey through Wales we met with a good reception amongst our Friends and also amongst other Christian like people who were loving to us and when we came to the city of Bristol, Friends there were no less kind to us poor instruments. And from Bristol we went to the city of Bath and had some service. And then towards London we travelled through several towns where we had good meetings with some good Friends which made my poor soul to rejoice the more in the God of our mercies, feeling that the glory was not departed from spiritual Israel. And now blessed be the Lord, for that I am yet favoured to lodge at the house of two worthy Friends in Reading in Berkshire, their name is Isaac and Sarah Pickerell.[28] And so we came to London, having meetings as they came in course and sometimes to good satisfaction. And in the city we had many good meetings and there was one thing worthy of remark: in consideration of the many approaching dangers that have so much threatened this nation yet the Lord has not forgot to be gracious to that great city of London, for he has sent many of his ministers to visit them, I believe, in order to help forward the work of humiliation and of reformation that the God of our lives may more and more delight to do them good, there being seven worthy ministers, male and female, from other parts of the kingdom and as one couple leaves the city another is sent. Wherefore my dear hearts, I am ready to say, surely the Love of God to mankind is great in so strengthening the minds of his people in these troublesome times. For although in the North of England where the troubles were very great, yet at the same time our Friends kept their meetings, yea one ministering Friend told me he crept through the strange army with their swords in their hands to get by them to meeting, and it is remarkable that there was not any other persuasions that kept any time of worship as is known of in any of those places where the enemy were. Wherefore have we not a renewed cause to hope that those afflicted ones who so pressed through all to keep their worship of almighty God and put their trust in the Lord Jehovah in whom is everlasting strength, will be well rewarded for sure I am that there is no other arm of power can work for our deliverance like our God, ever the God of the living.

Susanna Morris

Copy of a Letter Wrote to her Husband and Children

My dear husband and all our nine children from whom I am now far separated in body yet I found a more than common stirring in my mind and not knowing how long it may be ere I leave England am willing to put in writing what appears to be my duty towards you for your perusals at proper times etc.

It is appointed for all to die but when and which way the Lord our God only knows. Therefore it ought to be our chief concern so to walk in our day that we may know our peace to be made with God, before we go hence and be no more seen of men in this uncertain world. Oh that you may above all things choose the Holy fear of God in each of your hearts and then I know the Lord will greatly bless you with his own blessings of true wisdom and in that a good understanding will be added to that soul that truly waits on the Lord in faith and patience and then will your strength and comfort increase. This is the only way to be made wise to salvation. And dear hearts, ye may come to love the Lord Jesus that it may be with you as it is with me at certain times, to do the Lord's will may be more to you than your meat and drink. They will surely pass away but to obey the Lord in all things will greatly add to your everlasting happiness, bring true peace on earth and good will to men. All those who are of upright hearts to God's will, in all their commerce and converse amongst men will regard his honour. I can in sincerity say that the great preserver of men hath to his undertaking been pleased to keep me from murmuring or repining and although all the gold on the Indian shore could not have driven me over the dreadful brean, especially in these perilous times, yet believing the Lord our God required it of me, I dare not wish to have stayed at home. Oh, what is it the love of God in Christ Jesus our Lord cannot do for those that are of a willing mind, although they may be of the number that I have often thought myself of. For if consulting and thinking of my unworthiness and the smallness of my gift in the ministry would have excused me with true peace then had I never left my habitation. But blessed forever be our God, who in the midst of all my trials and troubles whenever I turned inward to the gift of his grace found peace was to be met with there. Certainly the flesh may without due care, (when trials and troubles come,) be in danger to go down to Egypt for help as King Saul did for want of a patient waiting for the prophet's coming which was not only the Lord's will but his duty. He lost the Kingdom. And saith my soul, let others do as they may, that you and I and all the well minded may so live in the fear of God that when we die it may be in his favour. And that it may be so with you, all dear children, let the fear of God be as much as possible before your eyes even the first in the morning before you entertain worldly thought and probably you may be favoured with a due regard to Truth all the day, whilst your hands may be employed in your lawful occasion. Oh! that these lines may be a means to provoke you or any of my fellow creatures so to live that God may always have the first fruits of your minds every morning and then I hope such will desire that God by his Blessed spirit may be with them till night, which when it approacheth let the thoughts of eternity be remembered—May the creature, like the good man Agur in his sorrow, crave neither poverty nor riches, only to desire to be fed with food convenient and I am of the mind where any are tried with riches in our days it proves hard for them to hunger enough after

Prov. 30:8

heavenly bread in its way and time and live in its primitive purity and plainness. Therefore saith my soul that all the children of men would lay these considerations closely to heart and seek to the fountain of pure wisdom to give a good understanding of his will that so in all things he before above and ever all may be sought after and enquired of that so all may know what they have to do for his honour and obey in all things. This is the way whereby a blessing will ensue and be the portion of such as are careful of his honour and obey his commands. These the Lord will bless with heavenly blessings and a sufficiency of the necessary temporals will be added accordingly as all men's cares may require. Our God is a God of knowledge and as Hannah said of old, by him actions are weighed and as he knows all things so it is best known to him who it is that cannot conduct themselves rightly with a large share of earthly treasure, and therefore may not we conclude that the all wise God in the riches of his heavenly mercies, doth not see meet for some of the most dear children to have a larger share of this world's goods and yet are enriched in faith and often enlivened with a hope to have the favours of heaven at last and be heirs of God's kingdom. Truly Dear Hearts when all things are rightly considered and truly weighed in stillness and calmness of mind without consulting flesh and blood, then and not till then will anyone find out the best way to please the living God in their day and age. The flesh will lead out of the ways of God, and rush greedily into the glories of this uncertain world, and the more some hath of it, the more danger they are in of forgetting the Lord. Therefore my dear ones, let it not be so with you, but trust the Lord with your all both in this world and that which is to come, and then I know that he who leads his people

I Sam. 2:3

into all truth will lead out of all untruths, all false ways, heights of pride of all sorts, for the proud heart cannot tread the courts of God whilst so they are afar off. And unless there be a turning to God with a sincere and penitent heart, and a humble walking before him be witnessed, there can be no entering his Kingdom. From a Friend to the Lord's ways in sincerity and plainness who would be glad all mankind may come to be Friends of Christ, known by the name of Susanna Morris, Manchester, 7th month, 1745.

7th month

From London the second time journeyed towards the yearly meeting to be held at Beal for the principality of Wales where my portion was to suffer for a time until he whose right it is came to rule in my soul over all and then the bitter became sweet and the creature bended to the will of the great creator to be as of herself nothing and then it is the best time to perform the will of our God and to speak what he pleaseth unto the people and I hope the Lord will bless our labours of love to the people in that as well as in the other parts of the kingdom where our lots were cast, blessed be the God of my life for that he was pleased so to help me a poor worm that in all my many troubles he the Lord my good God suffered me not to murmur or repine at the work and service which he called me to do for his honour's sake though at times in great fear lest the poor creature should fall short and not be enabled to hold out to the end or as some have done start aside like a broken bow which never carries home to the mark. But as in the Lord Jehovah there is everlasting strength and through his great goodness my soul was often renewed with the might of his own power which gave fresh resolutions and cause to hope that my chief care would be to serve the Lord in and according to the manifestations of his own blessed and heavenly will. Let others do as they may—For I think my dear ones that times nowadays are so perilous that there is no safe dwelling whilst in these poor houses of clay but as we are like-minded with Joshua, that man of God, who said, let others do as they will as for me and my house we will serve the Lord, and certainly the care of all such Christian like people is for God's honour more than their own and that all their families may serve the Lord truly and they are careful to example their families and to watch over them night and day that no undue liberties may at times be gone into nor connived at, having the cause of truth at heart. And, dear children, my desire that this concern may be your choice from one day to another that so the Lord may greatly delight in you and make you more and more servicable in his house in whatsoever he may require you to do for the Lord's will is to be done in earth as it's done in heaven. And therefore oh that I could be more instrumental to persuade all the children of men as well as my own so to seek the Lord earnestly for strength as they might always be truly willing to do the will of God in whatsoever is required of them and then those will not only be true lovers of him in their own soul's selves but likewise be enabled to be as lights in the world and be good helpers in all meetings for the service of truth and the church of God and learn of him day by day how to behave unto all men for God's sake, for it's our belief that all of them are and were made and created for no other end save for the purpose of his own glory—and oh that all could be as a wrestler and so strive until they knew an overcoming of the first nature that the second birth may be truly witnessed and thus, dear hearts, the good works will be going on in you if you could also come to the holy baptizer, Jesus Christ, and witness him at work in you to change the corrupt nature and make you what he would have you be, for it is only clean vessels that are truly fit for the great Lord and Master's use, such as are washed from the love of and lust after sin, neither

Josh. 24:15

Matt. 6:10

78

will he dwell with an unclean thing. Therefore let all consider well in time whether or no they are such as have truly laboured to be wholly separated from all sin if so then I know (blessed be the Lord our righteousness) that he will carry on his work in them according to his own divine will and heavenly pleasure as they abide steadfast in faith, not wavering, for those that waver are like unstable waters of the troubled sea that cast up mire and dirt, but all good works which are wrought by the divine helper in us and coupled with the fear of God will have acceptance with him.

And now to return to hint of my travels. I turned again to Leominister in Herefordshire where I had some both of sorrow and joy and that in the joy of God's salvation, for my soul was there set at liberty for a time and the Lord made way to speak to the states of some in that meeting and I hope that the work of true Christianity will go on in the Lord's time there. From thence I journeyed to a town called Ross to a quarterly meeting and was well favoured there with two meetings good and comfortable. Thence to Gloucester city, and here Friends carried kindly to us. Then we went to Tewksbury and had a meeting and then towards a town called Cheltenham, a very deep and dangerous road we had to travel through, but as the Lord's mercies are over all his works so I believed he was able to save us from hurt. And those considerations with his blessings made it more pleasant to me for I thought I had never rode such a way before but I have cause to say that the hardships were made up to my poor soul; for the best wine was met with in that the Lord favoured me with a share of that sweet peace which the world cannot give nor is it able to keep the enjoyment thereof from them that truly long to be the true servants of God, willing to serve him in his own way and time and I was greatly favoured with so much strength of body that it calls for humility and praise to God in as much as I have not been forced to lie by and not travel because of sickness although I got many hard coughs by taking cold in changing of lodgings in my going from place to place through Ireland, England, Scotland, and Wales in this my visit in Truth's service in those parts.

Now I may take account of my second return from London homewards to Pennsylvania—We got safe to Grave's End by water accompanied with several worthy good Friends from London who stayed with us until we had a time to wait upon God together (which was to some comfortable) on board the ship called the Mary. The owner of her was Daniel Flexny. It was on the llth day of 8th month [October] 1746 in the 64th

year of my age, and through mercy although on shipboard yet better in health than when I left London. On the 14th of same our ship's company thought we were in danger of being attacked by a French ship and strove to get their guns charged; but that ship turned from us and I think I may safely say that they were not suffered to hurt us, to the praise of God do I here make mention of it that after ages may always trust in the Lord. For a Truth there is nothing can be like unto that in all trials that are to be met with in the world. And as our sailing was north about Scotland, we were again surprised with another French ship as they again thought and truly the danger was not small that our ship was in, there having been published for print an account of 25 ships having been taken from those parts that we sailed through. Then may not some say, why went your captain that way? Because the wind stood for us this way but against us the other way, and winter so far advanced, so the captain went on without council of any man, but I hope and do know that some of us trusted in a far better arm than all the contrivance of men and all that the arm of flesh can do for them and truly now we have sailed mostly with a fair wind all the three weeks past, blessed be the great name of the God of all the living. And now by the beginning of the fifth week, and it being the first day of the week we are favoured with a good wind, for the week last past we hardly got forwards which was not the mariner's mind, but who knows the mind of our good God in all those things for I do believe that he careth for his servants and for my own part I can truly say that hitherto he hath greatly sweetened all my bitters to me although I think myself unworthy of the many favours all my life long, through my many and great trials: when I could truly resign the care and keeping of my all into his holy hands. And now we are come to another first day of the sixth week we are in and blessed be our great helper, for we yet enjoy good weather and a fair wind with

Susanna Morris

9th month

good health in the ship it being the 19th of 9th month [November] and, saith my soul, that the Lord would hasten his work if it be so his will in giving poor I a quick passage this time to my family and if not, his will be done and then give strength to be humbly thankful to him in an acceptable manner and preserve me the residue of my days always to be willing to come up in obedience to all his heavenly requirings. But I think I must set down what I have yet omitted, for the latter part of our passage we met with a great share of cross winds that kept us off the American shore and as I said before, the Lord knows best what is best for all his servants, for after we came ashore we understood that a French fleet of ships had been on those coasts, and although our passage was by reason of cross winds yet we may hope that the Lord had a good end in it and all was made up to those of us what had a sense of it for we had the most pleasant sailing that I thought could well be at that season, it being about the beginning of the tenth month [December]. And a few days after we arrived at Philadelphia it froze over the river Delaware, but forever blessed be the name of our God, I got safe and well home to my dear husband and children again.

10th month

And now for the encouragement of some honest hearted ones, I may leave it in writing that after I had been returned safe to my habitation again I thought I had as much need to watch and pray that I might neither go too fast nor be too backward in doing our great Master's will in all things, remembering that it is written that whatsoever we do all should be done to the honour and glory of God. And then during my stay in Pennsylvania I was often concerned to leave home to visit other meetings and sometimes in company with Friends to visit Friend's families in several quarters, in order for to encourage the growth of truth and righteousness amongst Friends. But now much from home in winter for my age could not well bear very cold seasons to travel in,

82

and so I may say blessed be the God of my life that has been so good to me and prevailed upon me to be willing to spend and be spent for God's cause and also helped my dear husband to give me up to the will of him who has called, by an high and holy calling to his service, in order for to have endeavors used to turn people from darkness to light and from the power of satan to the power of God and in true obedience to the divine will. My habitation was to me comfortable and I continued with my husband and family aforesaid near six years, except as (in that space of time) I found drawings in my mind to go to and fro in visiting meetings.

And now I think my great and good Lord and Master has engaged me to leave my habitation and visit Friends and others in some parts of Maryland and I began this journey the latter end of the ninth month [November] 1748 and the 66th year of my pilgrimage in this so uncertain world, hoping to be enabled to do my great Master's will therein, although it may be at certain times a cross to my own will and although it was so, I found it best to endeavor to be perfectly resigned that I might find ability given to do his will and so I set forth. My companion was Elizabeth Ashbridge.[29] We met each other at Wilmington in Newcastle county and from thence we travelled to George's Creek but had not meeting that time. Journeying thirty or forty miles we lodged at Joshua Vincent's but had not meeting, yet Friends' kindness to us was pleasant and satisfactory and we rode on the first day together about thirty miles and had one day's stay and then went thirty or forty miles a day until we came to Friends who belong to Choptank where we lodged at James Ratcliff's and the next day had a meeting with Friends and others at their meeting house where we were well favoured with the springing up and running forth of a living ministry to the refreshing of the hungry and thirsty after the righteousness of faith which is the gift of God to the seeking number among the children of men. And the next day the meeting was not inferior to the first, I thought, it was the comforting of our souls, blessed be the name of our God that so favoured for that early meeting ended well and the people in the house were orderly. Then we went on to the head of Sassafras River and had a meeting there and lodged at Joshua Vincent's again. From thence we set forwards to Little Creek Yearly Meeting where we were favoured two days and I hope it was to the honour of our good Master, and then we journeyed to Duck Creek meeting and lodged at the house of our worthy Friend William Hammans.[30] The Lord was pleased to favour us there. So to Newcastle where we had a meeting with Friends and others. From thence we came to Wilmington and lodged at William Shipley's[31] and thence to Kennett and some meetings more we enjoyed together in Chester County and then we parted in love and so blessed forever be the God of all peace, we got well home to our husbands and families again.

THE JOURNAL OF SUSANNA MORRIS
Part III

And yet again let me relate some more of my labours of love in the work of the gospel ministry, whereunto I was called (I may say safely) by a high and holy calling to be willing to do my heavenly Father's will therein and in whatsoever he the all wise might require of me who thinks at times am as a poor worm. And now to proceed to set down a little of my service: The next year of my age I was with my esteemed Friend Mary Evans[32] and some others in visiting Friends' families belonging to New Providence meeting and to good satisfaction seemingly to them and to us his servants, and, blessed forever be the name of him who liveth forever, we got safe home again. On the 19th of the sixth month [August] 1749 I with my worthy Friend Ann Foulke[33] engaged on a little journey among Friends beginning at Maiden Creek and had two good meetings there and thence to Tulpehocken and had a meeting at a Friend's house named John Elemans. It was amongst the new inhabitants. From thence to Oley and had two meetings and one more with a sick Friend and to good satisfaction as I thought. And we lodged at James Bowens and at Ellis Hugh's. Thence we went to the Forrest meeting and a good meeting we had there to satisfaction, and lodged at a Friend's house called John Scarlet. And from thence to Nantmeal, where I thought the Lord our God enlarged his sanctuary and the people seemed to be well satisfied and we lodged at Cadwallader John's[34] and the next day, blessed forever be the God of the living, for I thought at Uwchlan meeting we were favoured with the living presence of him who is worthy above all fading enjoyments to be always thought upon, for he it is who has in the book of his

85

remembrance all our actions, whether for or against his ever-lasting truth. So then assuredly great is the cause if mankind has to watch over all the motions of our own minds that in the great reckoning day it may go well with them when time here below will be to them no more. My sister Mary Emlen[35] was my helpmate and companion and to the praise of God (I may say) that has made me in some degree worthy to be one chosen of his servants in that good service to visit families after a Godly sort, for since I arrived from England I have been several times concerned in that of visiting in their families. And now again I am concerned to leave my home and go over the river Delaware with my sister Mary Emlen to visit Friends of Evesham meeting at each of their houses. And on the last of the month we got on our good service and at Haddonfield we were favoured with a good meeting where we met with our worthy Friend Josiah Forster. And we lodged at the widow Estaugh's[36] with kind reception. From thence we went with Friend Forster to his son William's where we made our home during the time of our religious visits to the families of that meeting. And I thought that Friends were so kind and so loving that we were as the children of one Father ought to be, having one Lord and one faith to trust in. The young man's wife had a good gift in the ministry and her husband a virtuous sober young man and they have nine daughters and one son. And blessed be the Lord, we had a good reception in most of the families and we had two meet-ings at Mount Holly, both of which seemed to be to good satisfaction, and at Evesham meeting house we met with John Churchman[37] and Joseph Brown and I think that we were one another's joy in the Lord. And had two good meetings at Haddonfield and our worthy Friend Forster accompanied us over the river two weeks after we went on our service on their side and one day more. And in Philadelphia I was favoured with two meetings, afternoon, and in the evening we had a large gathering by far more than in the afternoon, and the next week we met with them at the meeting of ministers and can truly say that I was glad I was there. And on the third day I was with the widow Dole at Frankfort. Little meeting yet to good satisfaction and on the fifth day following we were at Abington weekly meeting which was to me more comfortable than I did expect, blessed be the name of him to whom we must all give an account of our talents. And at the end of three weeks and one day I came safe home to my husband and family again accompanied by our son Joshua, I being in the 68th year of my age. And in the same year I was drawn to go into the woods up far in the forks of the Delaware, and accompanied with my good Friend Hugh Foulke[38] and his daughter, who I hope will submit to be made what the Lord willth her to be, for she seems to be a good steady woman and I was pleased with her company and with her father's also. And we had for that little journey four meetings to and fro amongst the woods. One was among some new settlers in the forks and one at Solomon Jennings'. And I was concerned to get a meeting at a worthy Dutch man's who with his wife, and brother-in-law and wife, were very loving to us and they with all the rest of the meeting seemed to be well satisfied with our religious visit and my reward was sweet peace in my bosom, which is what I hope ever to covet, more than anything that can be named here below, for nothing is to be compared with heavenly gifts from God, doing his will on Earth. And then I was again drawn to go in the same spring to visit Friends and some others up the forks of Schuylkill River beyond the Blue Mountains through the open plains and it blew so hard with snow from the Northwest that at last I began to fear that I should not be able to bear it. And in the 68th year of my pilgrimage, I may yet say that the Lord drawed me to visit the Jerseys and I set forth from home on the 31st of the 6th month [August], Phebe

6th month

87

Susanna Morris

Lancaster[39] was my pleasant companion. We crossed Delaware River in the upper parts of Bucks County near Durham,
and then travelled up as far as the Great Meadows and had
many good meetings with Friends and others to the satisfaction of many. Blessed be the name of our good God for he
over all is worthy to be sought unto for his good spirit helped
us well along. And we travelled without murmuring or repining at any hardships that did or might be met with in this
life in journeying. For blessed be the Lord forever, he is able
to make hard things easy to all his willing ones, who humbly
bow to him in resignation to have their hearts rightly fitted
for all his services that he the all wise being calleth into for
the glorifying of his ever blessed and the most holy name
that ever was named or ever can be to the end of time here
below. And we returned toward the Yearly Meeting to be
held at Philadelphia. In the 69th year of my age, I was at the
Yearly meeting at Shrewsbury with my good companion Mary
Evans and John Evans[40] and several other worthies besides,
and truly the Lord was pleased to favour us there. And I got
well home to my dear husband again. I also had another satisfactory journey with Friends in the Jerseys at several meetings. And we had to go from family to family of Friends,
labouring to encourage them in the way of holiness and good
work and true love to God. And I found a constraint on my
mind to speak very closely against the too frequent use of
strong drink or liquors and also against the too frequent and
needless use of tobacco in all its shapes and an evil also for I
know the Lord is greatly grieved because these things are so
much too much delighted in amongst mankind. And oh saith
my soul, that it were more denied for the sake of Zion's glory.
My good Friend Phebe Lancaster was my companion; and
we had joy and gladness in each other's company. When this
service was over we crossed the Delaware River, and through
mercy got we home. And blessed be the name of my great

master who was to me strength in weakness and a present help in many a trying hour for his own name's sake, yea he is over all worthy to be served and obeyed in all things.

I found drawings in my mind by the spirit of my great Master to cross the great ocean again, and visit old England in some parts where I had not been. In the seventieth year of my age, I gave up to the command of God for the crossing the great ocean and visiting Old England and the churches there the third time. And I left my home and came with my dear husband to Philadelphia Half Yearly Meeting which was held the 16th of 3rd month called March 1752 (according to the new style.) The meeting was large and to me a comfortable time and I doubt not to many others also. I stayed at Philadelphia until the 21st of the month and then embarked on board the ship, whereof Richard Boud was master. In the same ship came our Friend Mary Weston[41], on her return home from visiting North America, and a Friend from Long Island named Phebe Dodge[42] was under a concern of mind to visit the churches in old England. We had also the company of several men Friends who were going to London on their lawful occasion of trade. And through the Lord's mercy I and Phebe Dodge arrived safe at London on the 10th day of the 5th month, 1752, and came to the house of Mary Weston (who had left the ship in Margate Road.) And in the afternoon of the same day were at the meeting in Wapping. But I was during the time of the yearly meeting (which began a week after our arrival) very ill as to bodily health and my good shipmate, Mary Weston, having two maids that are Friends they were very helpful to me with the concurrence of their good master and mistress who are greatly helpful to many painful labourers as well as me.

My shipmate Phebe Dodge was drawn to visit the northern parts of England and my concern was to go westward, after I had been a little to the eastward and so we parted in

3rd month

5th month

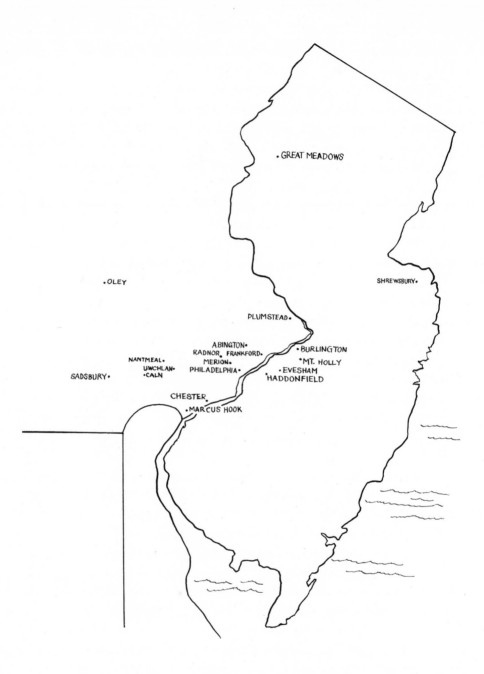

Places Susanna Morris visited in southeast Pennsylvania and New Jersey

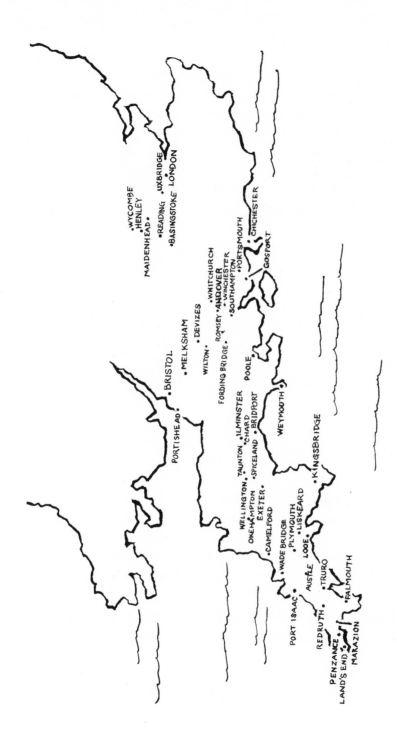

Places Susanna Morris visited in Southwest England

London though a cross to our wills for we had a desire to travel in company. During my stay in London I was at times at my kind Friend Henton Browns' house. His wife and daughters and all the family were very kind and loving towards me. And sometimes as occasion best suited I got to and lodged at other Friends' houses in different parts of London. And thanks be to the all wise disposer of all things, I found no other than brotherly and sisterly kindness through all Friend's families in that great place.

5th month

 I left London on or about the 27th day of the 5th month, 1752 with that worthy Friend Sophia Hume[43] for my companion, and set out on my journey towards the eastern parts of England, being attended by my loving kinsman Benjamin Bourne[44] and a hopeful young man named George Merchant. Sophia Hume was my companion through several counties. We lodged the first night at Chelmsford, 28 miles from London at the house of our Friend John Griffith. We were at several yearly meetings as at Colchester, at Ipswich, and at Woodbridge to good satisfaction and to the praise of him that calleth out of darkness into his marvellous light, and out of all the dark ways of man's contrivance. I have had great cause openly to declare against the lusts of the flesh and the pride of life and the making any provisions for the flesh to fulfill the lusts thereof, and I may say that the Lord was to my soul a rich rewarder, and made way in the hearts of his people that they were not offended at the freedom I came to use amongst them, and I was much pressed in spirit and a weighty concern fell upon me at Woodbridge to visit Friends in their respective families and we had a good company of several men Friends and I may say it was performed with good success. From thence we went towards the Yearly meeting at Norwich, where was a large concourse of many sorts of people, and the good presence of God was greatly manifested amongst us there as (blessed be God Almighty) it was also with us in other meetings where our lots were cast to and again betwixt those yearly meetings. We stayed sometime at and about Norwich, visiting Friends and the meeting thereaway, and then we came to London where Friends received us kindly to our mutual joy. For I may yet again say that the Lord in his infinite goodness made the weak strong for his blessed work's sake, for many times the flood gates of his mercies were opened to poor me. And we were favoured with abundance of his heavenly rain at certain times and may it not be desired that the God of all power might be trusted in over all to help the weak and feebleminded ones if rightly required for to go on his blessed errands wheresoever the Lord God of all the living doth lead them for his work and name's sake. And often after my return from the eastward parts of England to London, had some good service both in the city and the outparts, and at other meetings thereabout. Also I was at the burial of a worthy Friend at London named Mary Richabie, a Friend of Yorkshire[45], who had abode a considerable time there under a great concern of mind and had visited Friends in their families in a general manner throughout that great city and the suburbs thereof in a close manner to persuade to a more godly zeal at the heart. Yea, she neither spared poor nor the rich ones in the cause of God. And often she helped the poor out of what she had to subsist upon herself.

On the 2nd day of the 8th month, 1752 I set out from London on another journey towards the west of England; my cousin Benjamin Bourne attended me. One Theo Smith was to have gone out with us but was hindered, but he overtook us about 7 or 8 miles from London. We got to Uxbridge, 18 miles from London and at an evening meeting I had some service amongst Friends there. From thence I travelled the next day to High Wycombe, 15 miles further with several Friends beside my two guides before mentioned. And through mercy I found a good reception amongst Friends and some of

8th month

us were one another's joy in the Lord. At their meetings there I had a young minister join me as a companion named Ellen Parmare [Eleanor Passmore] and we travelled together to the Land's End and back again and when we returned there I parted from her, leaving her with her Friends.

We set out from Wycombe the 13th of the eighth month 1752 to Henly, (10 miles) being their market day had a meeting. In the evening on the 6th day the 14th went to Reading, 8 miles; on the seventh day, the 15th, went to Basingstoke in Hampshire, 18 miles. Stayed there on first day; had 3 meetings which began at 1, 3 and 7 o'clock. On second day the 17th went to Alton, lodged at Sam Warring's. On the 18th went to Frail, 4 miles, had a meeting beginning at 11 o'clock and went back that night to Samuel Warring's. Rachel Pinfold was there. On the fourth day, the 19th, had a meeting there, began at 11 o'clock. At some of these places there was but few Friends to meet together with us, but at other times we had full meetings with other people as well as Friends and when it was so I have found my heart much enlarged to them, desiring them to strive to acquaint themselves with God and then the assurance of peace will be their reward.

On 5th day the 20th went to Winchester, 17 miles, where although with a small company of Friends at an evening meeting, and next morning at another meeting, we fared better than could (by any appearance) be expected, but I may truly say that the Lord required them to get inward to a more close engagement of the heart and soul to know how the matter betwixt God and their own souls was, for all that we do ought to be done to the glory and honour of God. And after meeting there was over before the Friends were gone some entreaty was used for to leave off the vain customs that are too much amongst Friends' children. Then went to Southampton, 13 miles, on seventh day went to Portsmouth, 15 miles, and had a good reception there amongst Friends and many other people gathered with us at the meeting on first day. And some of them seemed glad of the opportunity and through the favours of the Almighty I was furnished with suitable matter for some poor mournful seekers amongst the Methodists, and I am in hopes that some will be yet gathered more and more unto God in spirit and have less and less reliance on the flesh. Then went to Gosport by water, 7 miles. On a second day the 24th went back to Portsmouth, and had a meeting in the evening and stayed there the next day. The 27th went to Barnt Green in Hamilton Parish and had a meeting, 10 miles from Gosport. Then to Havant, 6 miles from Barn [Barnt] Green. On 6th day went to Chichester in Sussex, 9 miles, had an evening meeting. On 7th day returned to Gosport. On first day morning the 30th had a little meeting at the widow Tower's, then went to Portsea [Portsmouth], had a meeting began at 2 o'clock, a large meeting it was, after which two young women came to us. At 5 went to meeting again and after meeting went over the water to Gosport. On second day had a little meeting in the evening; on third day, the 1st of ninth month, had a little meeting and then went to Southampton and was at their meeting; on the fourth day. After meeting went to Romsey, 8 miles, and had a meeting on the sixth day; on the seventh day went to Fording Bridge, 14 miles, where on first day the 17th we had three meetings, beginning at 10, 2 and 6 o'clock. On second day the 18th, went to Ringwood, 6 miles, and had an evening meeting. Third day the 19th, went to Poole in Dorsetshire, 13 miles. That evening William Pitts[46] of London came there. On the 4th day William Pitts stayed the meeting and went forwards on his journey. On the 5th day we stayed a meeting; on 6th and 7th day went to Island Purfleck [Purbeck]. On first day, the 24th, went to Corse Castle meeting at 11 o'clock. After meeting went with widow Hannah Pee at Corse Castle where we had a meeting in the family and second day went

9th month

to Weymouth, 20 miles, stayed their quarterly meeting, on the fourth day, the 27th, which was but small but had a large meeting. In the evening of the fifth day, the 28th went to Bridport, 16 miles, lodged at the house of the worthy ancient minister Samuel Bownas,[47] and had a meeting on 6th day at his house and on seventh day went to Exeter, 30 miles, stayed their meeting, on first day the first of the 10th month. Meeting began at 10 o'clock. There we met with Ann Mercy Bell,[48] of York and Phebe Cartwright and truly we were one another's joy in the Lord. Had also a meeting in the afternoon. On second day went to Newtown Bushel, 15 miles. Mercy Bell and some Friends went further but I and companion stayed a meeting there. On third day went to Kingsbridge, 20 miles, and on the road fell in company with Mercy Bell and other Friends. On fourth day had a meeting there at 2 o'clock and in the evening a meeting of ministers and elders. On fifth day a meeting at ten o'clock; after that was broke up the men and women met separately and in the evening a meeting which began at 6 and held till 9 o'clock. On sixth day we went to Hubberston, 11 miles, and had a meeting that evening in the house of James King where we lodged. On seventh day went to Plymouth, 14 miles. On first day, the 8th, was at their meeting at 10 o'clock and at 2; on fourth day came Mercy Bell and companion and on fifth day we went from there across the water at Saltash and came into Cornwall. Stayed a little at Landrake, 8 miles. Then went to Germans, 3 miles, had a meeting that evening; on 6th day came Mercy Bell and companion; on 7th day went to Liskeard, 8 miles. On first day the 15th went a mile or two out of the town to a meeting which began at 11 o'clock—and had a meeting in the town at 4. On second day went to Looe, 7 miles. Here also came Mercy Bell and companion. Had meeting at 5 o'clock. It being market day and there being a mountebank, Mercy Bell was concerned to go out of meeting and speak to the people, who gave attention to her. Then she came to meeting again, where both she and I had something given to deliver to the hearers and meeting ended to the praise of him who is the master of our assemblies. On third day went to Parr and lodged at a Friend's named George Fox. On fourth day went to Austle, 4 miles, cross the water. It was their monthly meeting but small. The woman's meeting was held at Samuel Hopwood's[49] house where we lodged and stayed their meeting on first day which was large. On second day the 23rd went to Penryn, 24 miles; on fourth day the 25th went to Falmouth, two miles; was at their meeting at 10 o'clock. Went back after meeting to Penryn and on fifth day went to Marazion, 16 miles, Samuel Hopwood with us. There was Mary Parkes. Had a little meeting that night. On the 6th day went to Penzance, 3 miles, where we had a meeting. On the first day, the 29th, went to Land's End, 12 miles, had a meeting that evening at Gray Chappel's; on second day went to Marazion. Samuel Hopwood and Mary Parkes bore us company. Had meeting at the meeting house; on third day went back to Penryn. There we met again with Mercy Bell and her companion and had a meeting that evening; on fourth day went to Falmouth Meeting at 11 o'clock. In the evening Mercy Bell and companion went back to Penryn. I and my companion lodged at Falmouth at the house of Jane Appley, a widow Friend. On sixth day the 3rd of 11th month we went back to Penryn. There was M. Parkes. On seventh day M. Parkes went with me to Redruth and had a meeting. On first day was at Countegood [Come-to-Good] in the parish of Kea, 3 miles from Truro. Then we went to Truro. On second day went to Woodbridge, 24 miles. Then went to a place called Saint Collum, 16 miles. Then to Wade Bridge, 8 miles. On the third day had a family meeting. On the fourth day went to Port Isaac, 8 miles had a meeting at 11 o'clock. Stayed on fifth day and had another meeting at 7 in the evening which

11th month

97

was very large. On sixth day went to Camelford, 8 miles, it was rainy. Dined there, then went to Eelescarry, 12 miles, it being so stormy there was several ships cast away. On seventh day it was calm and we went to Launceston and on first day the 19th had a meeting at 11 in the forenoon and another at 6 in the evening which was large, both held at John Parse's house where we lodged. On second day went from Launceston (which was the last town in Cornwall) to Oakhampton in Devonshire, 18 miles; on third day had a meeting at 10 o'clock in the meeting house. In the even at five had another at Peter Mackey's; on fourth day went to Exeter, 22 miles; on fifth day the 16th was at their meeting. And there my companion and I visited all down the south parts of the west of England from Portsmouth to Land's End, though a very hilly country and bad roads, I thought it was very hard for me to get up and down the hills, for some of them were more like to stairs in an house than any other thing, and so stony that my creature threw me off many times, but (forever blessed be my great Master and preserver) I was never much hurt and sometimes not hurt at all; for the creature bowed herself so low with me that it was like laying me down and the last time it was in the soft mud. In Cornwall we found many poor places very much stripped of sound-hearted Friends, but here it seemed as if there was a seeking number; that at times I hoped would in the Lord's time wholly resign to do the Lord's will and leave undone what his holy will and mind is should not be done.

And now we are got back again to the city of Exeter in Devonshire, where my first being there I was much grieved to find that a wrong spirit had got in amongst most of the elders and a disbelief that the Lord required the females to labour in the gospel and also a pleading for making provision for a defensive war. But notwithstanding, at my return hither I may say the Lord so filled with his goodness that I seemed to get the victory over all wrong spirits and hope I had some good service amongst them, for there is some sufferers for Christ's cause in that city.

On the 6th day and 17th of 11th month William Brown[50]   *11th month* came to Exeter. On the 7th day we went to Bradninch, eight miles from Exeter, and dined, then went to Collumpton, 13 miles. Stayed their meetings on first day, the 19th. In the evening went with several Friends to Culliford, had a meeting on second day, and on third day to Spice Land, 3 miles, and had a meeting at 11 o'clock. After meeting went to Uffcolm [Uffculme]. On fourth day went to Wellington, 7 miles, had a meeting about 6 o'clock. On fifth day morning a family meeting. Then went to Milverton, 4 miles, had a meeting that even at Thomas Pole's house where we lodged. On sixth day visited the families and on 7th day went to Battle Hay to Edward Pole's and had a family meeting; on first day the 26th went to Spice Land, 7 miles, had a meeting at 11 o'clock. After meeting went back with Edward Pole's. On second day went to Mount Silven, then to Minehad. On third day was at their meeting at ten o'clock, had also an evening meeting at 6 o'clock; on fourth day went to Taunton, 20 miles; on 6th day went to Cretuh, 3 miles, had a meeting at 6 in the even; on 7th day went back to Taunton, stayed their meeting, on first day the 3rd of 12th month. On 2nd day went to   *12th month* Illminister, 12 miles, lodged there at John Mallet's, had a meeting at 10 o'clock on third day. In the afternoon went to Chard, 9 miles, and stayed their meeting which began at 11 o'clock on fourth day, and on fifth day went to Mountacute, 12 miles, which was the last town in Somersetshire. On 6th day had a family meeting and on seventh day went to Compton in Devonshire, five miles, lodged at Jonah Thompson's; on first day the 10th went to Sherburn [Sherborne] meeting, began at 12 and 5 in the even. On 2nd day went to Ruddimore in Somersetshire, and had an evening meeting. On third day went to Glastonbury, 8 miles, weather stormy and wet, hail and rain. Their quarterly meeting began at 10 o'clock for worship which was pretty large and about one the men and women met separate. Had a meeting in the evening about 6 o'clock which was large. Stayed there on fifth day. Got cold by being very wet in my journey. On sixth day went to Exbridge [Axbridge] 14 miles, had an evening meeting at William Framton's where we lodged and stayed on seventh day; and on first day the 19th went to Lecourt meeting, 2 miles, began at eleven o'clock. After meeting went to Stock in the Parish of Churchill, had a family meeting at Richard Hipsley[51] where we lodged and stayed on second day and third day and on fourth day went to Clivenham [Clevedon] meeting, 4 miles, beginning at 11 o'clock. After meeting went to Nailsey [Nailsea], 3 miles, and on 5th day went to Portershead [Portishead], 3 miles, had a meeting on 6th day and in the evening visited some families and on 7th day the 23rd went to Bristol. On first day the 24th was at their meeting called the Friars morning and afternoon. The next first day was at Temple Street meeting morning and afternoon and had a meeting in the evening. On 2nd day, the 25th, being the day called Christmas had a meeting in the evening which was pretty large and stayed at Bristol till the 21st of the 1st month, 1753. During my stay there, I in company with some other Friends visited the most of Friend's families in Bristol—In this our visit we passed through many places in Devonshire and Cornwall, visiting Friends, and our worthy Friend Samuel Hopwood accompanied us to the Land's End and several other places where we had other people with us and but few Friends. Yet notwithstanding it was so, I thought that the Lord of God did many times open with his holy hand and fill with blessings for us all.

At Taunton in Somersetshire I lodged at Elizabeth Gifford's, a widow and a Friend-like woman indeed, and her son was our guide to several places where I thought Truth was too much oppressed; but at the town Taunton we found many Friends and had two blessed seasons with Friends and others at their meeting house. And we journeyed to and fro as before related in the west of England till we came to Bristol where a concern came upon my mind and rested upon me to visit Friends of that city in their respective families and the Lord assisted me therein. And I laid it before some Friends, hoping that some of them would assist in that so needful an occasion; and to the praise of the Heavenly Father the service seemed better received than could have been expected, for they never had the like visit before in that city.

In some places a constraint came upon me to cry out against the too frequent taking of tobacco in all shapes and the too frequent use of strong liquors, and my dear fellow labourers, let me say of a truth I am fully of the mind that these things are a great obstruction to that glorious work that is to be wrought with fear and trembling, and I think that I have the mind of truth therein and sure I am that I was constrained so to testify to many in this my journey to and again; yea, in public meetings and likewise against that unsound speech: you to one or a single person.

Leaving Bristol the 21th of 1st month, 1753, went to Bath, 14 miles, was at their meeting on first day beginning at 10, 2, and 6 o'clock. Our Friend Richard Hipsley was there. On 2nd day visited some families, and on third day went to Bradford, six miles in Wiltshire. Was at their meeting on 4th day. Began at 11 o'clock and another at 6 o'clock. On the 5th day stayed there and visited some families, on sixth day detained by wet weather; on seventh day went to Melksham, 5 miles. There came to see us Daniel Badger on first day the 28th. Stayed their meeting; began at 11 o'clock and had an evening meeting at 6, and stayed their meeting on third day. On fourth day went to Devizes, near eight miles, had a meet-

1st month

ing there that evening; on 5th day and the first of the 2nd month went to Lavington, 5 miles, and had an evening meeting where the people were somewhat rude; on 6th day went to Westbury under the Plaine, 10 miles, it was their monthly meeting but small. In the evening had a meeting which was held in the chambers of Susanna Frivers who was ill, which was as large as the room could hold. On seventh day went to Wilton, 20 miles, had a family meeting at Oliver Hayhurst's where we lodged. And on the 1st day of the 4th month went to Salisbury, 3 miles, was at their meeting at 10 o'clock which was pretty large, and again in the afternoon. There was a Friend named John Boyes in prison for not paying tithes. On second day went back to Wilton; on third day went to Shaftsbury, 16 miles, had a meeting there and returned to Wilton on 5th day and stayed there on 6th day and had an evening meeting on seventh day. Went again to Salisbury and was at their meeting on 1st day forenoon and afternoon. On 2nd day the 12th went to Andover in Hampshire, 16 miles; on 4th day went to Whitchurch, had a meeting in the even; on 5th day went to Newbury in Berkshire, had a meeting at a Friend's house, and on 7th day at another Friend's house. On first day was at their meeting morning and afternoon. On 2nd day went to Baghurst meeting at 2 o'clock and in the even had a family meeting at the widow Marshall's, and on 3rd day one at Daniel White's. Stayed there on the 4th day and on the 5th day went to Reading. Was at their meeting on 6th day and also on first day forenoon and afternoon, and an evening meeting at 6 o'clock. On the 2nd went to Maidenhead, had a meeting there on 3rd day at 11 o'clock and another in the evening. On 4th day went to Henly in Oxfordshire, had a meeting at 11 o'clock and another at 6 in the evening; on 5th day the 1st of the 3rd month, went to Marlow, about six miles, had a meeting in the town hall which was large, though no Friend dwelling in this town, but I was

3rd month

largely opened to the people who seemed very sober and orderly and I thought it was a favour from heaven to those people. After dinner went to Wycombe, 5 miles, and on 6th day had an evening meeting. Here I left my companion being the same place where she joined with me.

From Wycombe I journeyed toward London (having some meetings in my way) where my Friends were glad to see me safe returned and I was also glad to see them for we were made glad in the Lord our God together at times both in the meeting and Friend's houses. The Lord crowned our sittings with the Holy Wing of his good presence to the breaking of our hearts into tenderness. But it was where Friends were a little still in body and mind, not occupied in needless things. One such blessed opportunity was at Daniel and Mary Weston's house to the praise of God may it be ascribed for He overall is worthy for ever and ever.

I may say that I am an unprofitable servant, having done but my duty to gain my own soul's peace. Then I journeyed to Reading and lodged at an ancient Friend's. He and his wife were kind to me and the Lord our God favoured us there with his good presence at several meetings in that town. And from then went to Jordans and had a good meeting with few Friends there. And from thence to Uxbridge where was several Friends of London, viz: R. Partridge[52] and George Whitehead,[53] Mary Weston and a hopeful son of Thomas Whitehead, a minister of London. And the Lord's blessing was made known unto us in that meeting. Then I returned with Mary Weston in her chaise to her home. She and I visited some meetings in and about London, until I think I may say the Lord was pleased to visit me with sickness. And it was about a month before I could get strength to go on my service again. But in my weakness I found the good will of him that was in the bush when the bush burned and was not consumed. I had in my illness good cause to say that his re-

Exod. 3:2

gard was to his people in that city in order for their further-ance in the knowledge of the truth. And in that good exer-cise of visiting in their families and their quarter belonging to Devonshire house meeting I think we were at about two hundred of them in the month before the yearly meeting at London and seemingly had a good reception and after the service of the large and good opportunity to Great London was well over I was again concerned to let Friends know that a concern fell on my mind to visit Friends yet further amongst them in London and I hope as far as we could get the work done, it was to general satisfaction to Friends and us that accompanied one another in the service for at times we were both men and women in the service and of a truth I may well say that the Lord does own the service from family to family by favouring with his good spirit therein.[54] On the 21st of

6th month

6th month, 1753, the 6th day of the week I with my com-panion Phebe Dodge of Long Island set forward from Lon-don to Gravels End in a coach along with our landlady Sarah Brown and also Mercy Bell from York and several other Friends from London, and after dinner we had a little time of waiting upon the Lord for strength to perform our undertak-

9th month

ings to cross the ocean. And now it being the 17th day of the 9th month, 1753 I have often times had a mind to set some-thing down daily and now I think it is yet revived how I had fared and I think the Lord was good to me in my silent retire-ment for his presence and upon the great rowling ocean which was a dreadful place to my weak nature, for I have found it so many a time. I now am in the seventy-first year of my pil-grimage and in a moderate state of health. Thanks be to the God of my life, for I can say that the Lord our gracious God has added to my days numerous more than could well be ex-pected and the last night my heart was much comforted with the joys of his salvation in my setting up in my bed to wait for his arising, and blessed be his Holy name and that for ever more and this day also I have found him to be a rich rewarder to my soul. And now another day is almost spent. I am in the mind that my time here will be spent mostly in fear of one sort or another, but blessed be the name of our great benefactor for he over all can make hard things easy in his own blessed time, and therefore have hope as anchor that if we have trouble at night, joy may be met with in the morning. Wherefore to his care and keeping do I commit my all for it is the Lord that careth for us. And this day I may say that the Lord has answered my desire last night and today, which was that we might have a fair wind and a moderate one, which engaged me for to be thankful to the giver of all good to us every way, and hitherto we had a prosperous voyage and in three weeks got almost halfway across the great ocean it is supposed from sounding on the English shore. And this being the 5th day of this week and yet favoured with a good wind, praises be given to the great preserver of men. We met with an East India ship and they sent their boat and men on board us with silk and muslin goods for our people to buy of them, which hindered us some hours good sailing, but I had not freedom to buy so much as one handkerchief and am not sorry for it. And now the rest of this week: My heart is yet helped but yet find a weak part in the creature, fitter for pity than praise, if not blame at times. And also find help from one that is mighty even to help to the uttermost all that truly seek for help oftener than the morning light, sometimes by sigh or groaning that in words are not uttered.

And now this being the seventh day of this week it seems to be to me a time of heaviness and poverty of spirit. And now the first day of another week and the Lord has favoured with a good wind although the last night had shifts of wind. Yet now fair for us to get to our desired port of Philadelphia. Blessed be his most holy name and that forever more, and he also favoured us with two meetings this day, and I am in some hopes that they may in some good degree tend to God's own honour, for all the ship's crew met with us; some in the fore-noon and the rest in the afternoon, and all seemed quiet and sober. But the second day there arose a fierce gale or storm of wind and rain inasmuch that we were for a time in danger to be overwhelmed in the deeps. But blessed be the Lord our God, for I thought his own arm would be our salvation and blessed be his holy name, for the last night my bitters were sweetened to me although in the night season, and what sleep I got was comfortable to me. And now the third day of the second week since I began to pen down some little matters daily, and as to this day, I think the living God is yet our friend, for although we have but a slack wind yet we go on our way toward home.

And in that may I not well say, He is our friend and oh! that all our ship's company were willing to be the friend of God and his Christ and that they might be what he would have them to be for as said our Great Lord "you are my friends if you do whatsoever I bid you" and it is our duty diligently for to seek to know and then are we not in duty bound for to obey him over all oppositions forever. And now we are in the afternoon of the fourth day of this week, and it is yet a favourable time because as yet we have a moderate wind, but much hard rain, being about 200 miles from New Foundland, but our captain fears a hard gale, for the moon is to change this night. But I am in hopes that the Lord will favour us in that also. And now it is the afternoon of the sixth day of this week and I may truly say that our Lord and good master is near us and our present help in this so needful a season or I know not what would have become of us, for my part I often times am so poor and low in my spirits that if the Lord's good-ness did not bear me up I should faint on the great ocean, for agoing a sea voyage was always to me a cross thing to my nature. Now it being the 7th day of the week, blessed be the

John 15:14

106

name and power of the great keeper of his children for we were yet again favoured with a good wind to help us on our way homeward, and thanks be given to the most high that hath hitherto helped that we most of us enjoy a middling good state of health which is a mercy greatly worthy of thankfulness to God that is merciful to all that seek him in his own time and are perfectly willing to do the Lord's will.

And now this being the last day of the 9th month and first day of the week, I yet see that the Lord has helped my soul with several favours: as fair wind, although a hard gale which hindered our captain from partaking with us of a comfortable meeting held in the great cabin and every first day since we came from London if I remember right. For those favours ought we not to be very thankful to him with whom we have all of us to do, and for all the deeds done in our day and time here below must be accountable. And now it is the second day of the week and a good wind we are favoured with, but yet today at times my heart is tinctured with heaviness, the reason thereof I do not yet know, but I hope in the holy arm of God's salvation for of a truth, for his is everlasting strength. Yesterday it was so stormy and I so sick that I set nothing down, but may say my good master helped me to a comfortable night's rest. This being the third day of the week we are favoured with pleasant but not so fair a gale as we think would be best for us. Yet who can say that we are certain for may we not say and that safely that our great owner knows the best what is best for all his creatures. Therefore oh! that we may be enough willing for to trust in the Lord our God and that forever.

And now for this day, I have not much to say for we had a poor wind and so much bustle in the ship that was a cross to some with me that we could not get a convenient time for to sit a while together for to wait on the Lord for to renew our strength, as blessed be his great name for two or three of

9th month

us are comforted in such opportunities, although not a vocal word spoken with any of us. And now the sixth day and the Great I am, has favoured us with a good wind, agreeable to what was much desired yesterday, which gives fresh and good cause for to say of a truth, that the God of the living is always worthy to be sought unto, for he is a God hearing prayer and answering those whom he hath opened their hearts as he did Lydia's in the days of old, and truly my heart is comforted in consideration of his manifold favours to my poor soul, many times almost ready to be overwhelmed with troublesome thoughts. Somewhat like sorrowful David when Saul was suffered for to seek his life when he said one day or another I shall fall by the hand of Saul. On seventh day we had hard rain and rugged winds—and now on first day I think we might well say that were sorely tried with grievous hurricane of winds and at 6 o'clock in the morning they thought best to cut down one of the masts and did it, yet the mate said he did not expect that the ship could hold long or words to that purpose, but forever blessed be our great redeemer, for we only lost most of the sails and some other utensils that belonged to the ship, though several of her workmen had a narrow escape for their lives. But oh! let me say now again that I believe that the great God was not willing that we should be overthrown but his own outstretched arm helped against the raging sea and the old enemy, and for the same all of us ought in great humiliation never to forget such a wonderful deliverance. And now on the second day we got little wind, and a good sun for us to dry our wet beds and clothes and all the ship's crew were hard at work to get up other sails and now 3rd day we are yet favoured with a good wind and hope that we may get well to reach of our habitations in the Lord's time. My choice companion Phebe Dodge to Long Island and I to Bucks County where my dear husband, and family lives, I hope. This being the 4th day of the

Exod. 13:14

1 Sam. 27:1

108

week we have a slow wind and being too much westerly we got but little on our way, and since the storm I may make a remark that as our lives was so mercifully saved we were instrumental in saving the life of a land bird that lighted on the vessel, it being so wearied and almost spent that the men catched it in their hands, a thing one might think impossible for a little creature to fly so far as we supposed it did.

Now 6th Day, we yet are like people walking forward and backward before a King's gates but may not get in until he please to cause them to be opened and then I hope we shall get well in. And now it is the 6th day of the week and we are much the same, to and again. Yet for all that we have had good fair weather and a good wind for ships to get out to sea and out of Delaware Bay. And this day our people had a suitable time to raise up something for a small mast instead of that which was cut down in the storm; which I think is a favour from the most high God for we could not get so well on without it. And now on the seventh day we are yet struggling to get along. The wind being somewhat fairer but unsettled and not long one way. And now the afternoon of the first day as aforesaid the seventh week since we left London. And I may say with some others in the cabin says that our living good God helped us with some refreshment of soul in a silent meeting together, but I having been in the mind that the Lord had some service for me in the afternoon in the steerage amongst the common sail in order for to encourage them for to forsake all evil, and the Lord would have mercy on them. And I hope at least that it may be of help to some of them.

We spoke with a vessel bound from New York to the Island of St. Christophers. She had set sail about three days ago. And now it being 2nd day we may truly say that our patience is yet largely tried with cross winds. Yet forever blessed be the name and power of our good God who over all is worthy to be trusted and waited upon. For I am in good hopes that in his own time I shall get safe to my dear husband and family again. And the 3rd day of this week and I can say that in the night season the Lord my helper sweetened my bitters for it seemed to be my lot as it was with the Israelites of old: they were to eat the passover with bitter herbs. And O that the true born of my dear heavenly Father may be made so to be experiencers with David: The Lord's rod and staff had comforted him. And truly I have now partaken the same, and am also made this day to say that the Lord is God of the living in this our age as those that has trodden the paths of just, as with that kingly prophet.

Exod. 12:8

Ps. 23:4

We are also favoured this afternoon with a favourable wind, blessed be our God. And now the fourth day the wind is better for us than some days past, which ought for to help us to seek to our great Giver for thankful hearts to him for that favour with many more which is received too slightly in our age. And now to be short: we got a moderate fair wind until we passed by several ships at anchor in the river. And soon after we passed by them, shifts the good wind and turns for them. Then we had shift and got well to Philadelphia and landed the latter end of the 10th month. Now still blessed be the great Owner of all mankind.

10th month

My mind was stayed to have a meeting at Darby with my husband and some other Friends of Philadelphia and we were thankful to him with whom we have to do. We had a good meeting and we with my sister Mary Emlem came back again to their town and from hence we got safe home to our week day meeting and I thought that I had great cause to be humble and thankful to the God of my life that has brought me over the dreadful ocean several times. But I am at times afraid least I am not enough so, but I am in hopes that those thoughts proceed from a godly jealousy over ourselves least we should come short in our duty toward the Great I am, that is only able for to keep his creatures humble when they return from such great undertakings for him and may safely say that the Lord's will, not that any flesh, should glory in his presence but in him.

That winter I went not from my home until the spring general meeting held at Philadelphia and in the main I thought the Lord favoured our meetings with his living presence which is a merciful favour, and comforted some of our sorrows for many abominations of this age. And after the time of that meeting was over, my husband, Elizabeth Morgan, and I went over Schuylkill to Radnor and had a meeting there with Friends. And at the widow Harrison's in the evening had a retiring season to the gladdening some of their hearts. She was a widow in affliction and she seemed to be worthy of a visit after a Godly sort. And thence went to Merion Meeting and for my part I thought there we fared well in the Lord our God together, forever blessed be his holy name.

And now I think I may safely say I was drawn by the cords of divine love for to pay a visit to all the monthly meetings in Bucks County. And there is four follows one after another in the same week. And had in the journey some more meetings. And through the Lord's goodness mostly to good satisfaction. And my good Friend, Phebe Thomas,[55] was my companion in that little journey.

And after some stay at home with my husband and family I found drawings in my mind for to visit Friends in the Jerseys and my good companion, Phebe Thomas, with me and we, with my dear husband, set out together first to Plumstead, about 15 miles, where we had a heavenly meeting with Friends. And from thence we journeyed to Burlington in order for to stay the time of the yearly meeting which was not so large as it might have been had not sickness been so much in many families. But blessed be the God the living, we had a comfortable season with several worthy Friends which I did not expect for to see there, namely William Hammans, Samuel Nottingham,[56] John Bowne from Long Island and his wife, but our English Friends not there. And after the time of that meeting was over we set forward from meeting to meeting all down the river, beginning at Holly town [Mt. Holly], and the last at Cohansie [Greenwich], and I hope that I may say that both Friends and we were both satisfied with our visits amongst them. For sometimes we had good times in Friends' families. Then crossed the river to Marcus Hook, and that day and first day had a meeting at Chester, and then hastened home. Then having had for some time drawings in both our minds for to visit Friends in Chester county, we laid it before Friends at our minister's meeting and in order for to perform our duty we set forward the 9th of the 11th month and the 70th year of my age and had the first [meeting] at Peter Reverdon's and we lodged at John Jacob's, and had a full house of various young people, and I hope it was to satisfaction. And from thence we went to Moses Coates's and he with several good Friends accompanied us to the Valley meeting, and there I thought we fared well, and thence we went back to Friend Coates's and had a comfortable meeting with a few Friends and some others. Then to Valley meeting again and I thought that my companion there was so divinely opened to testimony that her service was preferable to mine. And then we went to Uwchlan and there we also fared well in the Lord our God together. And from thence to Nantmeal where we got good satisfaction, and from thence to John Jacobs' and had a solid sitting there for his wife was afflicted with a pain in one side and so lame (though young) that she could not well get to meeting. And the next day, it being the seventh day, travelled thence to East Caln. The first day, our guide Moses Coates left us and his son Thomas kindly accompa-

11th month

nied us to Sadsbury. From thence to Isaac Woodrow's and was glad that we were there for they lived a considerable way from meeting and had a large family of children who with their parents were loving to us. From thence we went to Marlborough week day meeting and they had no knowledge of us beforehand and notwithstanding it was so, there was, with those who came with us, a large company which I was glad to see for the Lord's sake. And we heard also that sickness was in several families, all which helped me to hope that the Lord was amongst them, and they knew it.

And we went with John Herford and his wife where was 9 children and an old father near 90 years and one servant, and my mind was warmed to have a family retirement and it was to me and I hope to the rest of us a gladdening season. And from thence went to New Garden meeting where I think the good old ways of life has been this day opened in the meeting, blessed be the Lord our God, for his divine favours are so numerous and I think no tongue of man is able to set forth his bountifulness so fully as in itself is until our holy Key opens the way for God's honour.

THE JOURNAL OF SUSANNA MORRIS

Notes - Introduction

1. Joseph Taylor, a British minister, visited the American colonies in 1727. "Dictionary of Quaker Biography," (hereafter cited as DQB), at the Quaker Collection, Haverford College.

2. *Minutes*, Abington Monthly Meeting, 7-30-1728; *Minutes*, Bucks Quarterly Meeting of Ministers and Elders, 9-2-1728, microfilm. Quaker Collection, Haverford College, (hereafter cited as QCHC).

3. John Griffith (1713-1776) was born in Radnorshire and in 1726 emigrated to Pennsylvania, where he lived for a time with the Morrises and became a traveling minister. DQB.

4. "John Griffith's Account of Susanna Morris" in *Friends Miscellany* (Philadelphia, 1831) vol. 1: 155.

5. Elizabeth Morgan (1698-1778), a traveling minister, was a member of Gwynedd Meeting, Bucks County, Pennsylvania, and mother of five children. "Ministering Friends of America who crossed the Ocean for Truth's Sake," 4, QCHC.

6. For Phebe Willets Mott Dodge, please see Introduction, note 19. Mary Pace Weston (1712–1766) was the daughter of Joseph and Ann Pace of England. At age twenty-nine she married Daniel Weston. She traveled widely in the ministry, including a trip to the American colonies in 1750. Sophia Hume (1702-1774), of Charleston, S. C., granddaughter of Mary Fisher, was brought up as an Anglican, but became a convinced Friend in 1740, and a public Friend in 1747. She wrote *An Exhortation to the Inhabitants of the Province of South Carolina* which was published in 1748, and *A Caution to such as Observe Days and Times* in 1763. DQB.

7. Susanna Morris's *Journal,* Part III, 8. QCHC. Original manuscript is at the Historical Society of Pennsylvania, (hereafter cited as HSP).

8. Susanna Morris to Israel Pemberton, 1-25-52. Pemberton Papers, vol. 6: 158, HSP.

9. Mary Peisley (1717-1757), of Mt. Mellick Meeting, Ireland, traveled in the ministry in England prior to her trip to the American colonies. On her return she married the traveling minister, Samuel Neale (1729-1792). Three days after the wedding, she died. Catherine Payton (1726-1794) was a traveling British minister. Before her trip to the American colonies she traveled widely in the British Isles. In 1772 she married a widower, William Phillips. Her *Memoirs* as Catherine Phillips were published.

10. "Susanna Morris," *The Friend*, vol. 31, no. 27 (3-13-1858): 212

Notes - Part I

11. Her companion was Ann Roberts (1678-1750), a minister of Gwynedd Meeting, Bucks County, Pennsylvania, who traveled in the ministry to England in 1733 with Mary Pennell and returned two years later. "Ministering Friends," 3, QCHC.

12. Her companion was again Ann Roberts.

13. Likening oneself to a prisoner was a frequent Quaker expression at this time. The implication was that only the Holy Spirit could set one free.

14. The Reasoner was Satan, who presented rationalizations for not doing the Lord's will.

15. "Outward tabernacle" meant the flesh which the spirit inhabited.

16. Friends did not believe in celebrating Christmas, saying that every day should be equally observed as the Lord's day.

17. Elizabeth Jacob (1675-1740), neé Head, was a widely traveled minister. Susanna Morris calls her Jacobs, but this is not correct. DQB.

18. Sarah Lay (1677-1735) was born in Kent, England, and traveled widely in the ministry. She married Benjamin Lay, the abolitionist, and with him emigrated to Pennsylvania in 1731. She died at Abington in 1735. DQB.

19. John Wilson (1692-1752) of Kendal was four times clerk of London Yearly Meeting. His wife was Deborah Wilson, also a traveling minister.

20. Robert Barclay (1648-1690), the author of *Barclay's Apology*, the first and most important theological justification for Friends, was a well-beloved figure in the Religious Society of Friends, and all members of his family were respected. We find Elizabeth Hudson visiting his grandson. William Braithewaite, *The Beginnings of Quakerism*, edited by Henry J. Cadbury (Cambridge University Press, 1970), 226.

21. John Richardson (1667-1753) became a traveling minister in 1686. He traveled to the American colonies in 1701 and again in 1731, when he sailed with Susanna Morris. DQB.

Notes - Part II

22. For Elizabeth Morgan, please see Susanna Morris's *Journal*, Introduction, note 5.

23. William Lightfoot (1732-1797) of Pikeland, Chester County, a member of Uwchlan Monthly Meeting, drew up marriage certificates as well as birth and burial records. In 1762 he traveled with John Woolman as far as Fort Allen on his Indian journey. DQB.

24. For John Richardson, please see Susanna Morris's *Journal*, Part I, note 21.

25. Joseph Storrs (1670-1751) became a minister in 1700 and in 1702 married a fellow minister, Katherine Frost. DQB.

26. Charles Edward, son of James, was called the Young Pretender, or "Bonnie Prince Charlie" and was proclaimed king on arrival in Edinburgh in 1745.

27. Susanna Morris may have meant John Irwen. Both he and his wife were ministers. Daniel Stanton mentions them in his journal in 1749. *Friends Library* vol. 12: 157.

28. Isaac Pickerell (1678?—1756), a Quaker minister, was born in Reading but moved to London in 1723. DQB.

29. Elizabeth Sampson Sullivan Ashbridge (1713-1756) was born in Cheshire, England. She ran away and married very young. After her husband died she lived in Dublin, then emigrated to the American colonies as an indentured servant. Here she married again a man called Sullivan who took to drink and became a soldier. Elizabeth meanwhile was converted to Quakerism and became a distinguished traveling woman minister. After her husband's death she married Aaron Ashbridge in 1746, and in 1753 she died while on a religious visit to Ireland. *Some Account of the early part of the life of Elizabeth Ashbridge* (Liverpool, 1806).

30. William Hammans (1683-1755) was born in England but moved to the American colonies, settling first in Chester and then in Maryland at Duck Creek. He was a powerful minister. John Smith, "The Lives of the Ministers of the Gospels among the People called Quakers," unpublished MMS, 1770, vol. 2: 105.

31. William Shipley was the husband of Elizabeth Shipley, a traveling Quaker minister who visited Great Britain in 1742. "Ministering Friends," 4, QCHC.

Notes - Part III

32. Mary Nicholls Evans (1695-1769), a traveling minister, married Owen Evans of Gwynedd Meeting. She visited most of the colonies and Tortola. DQB.

33. Ann Foulke (1693-1773) was born in Wales. She moved in 1698 to Gwynedd, Pennsylvania, where her parents became Quakers. In 1713 she married Hugh Foulke (1685-1760). In 1727 she became a traveling minister and in 1730 moved to Richland, Pennsylvania. DQB.

34. John Cadwalader, Jr. (Susanna Morris called him Cadwallader John) was recognized as a minister in 1728. John Woolman stayed with him on his way back from Waylusing. DQB. Phillips P. Moulton, editor, *Journal and Major Essays of John Woolman* (New York: Oxford University Press, 1971), 136.

35. Mary Heath, the daughter of Robert and Susanna Heath, was born in Great Britain and came to Bucks County, Pennsylvania, where she married George Emlen and became a traveling minister. Mentioned in the "Life of Daniel Stanton," *Friends Library*, vol. 9: 148.

36. Elizabeth Haddon Estaugh (1680-1762) came to New Jersey in 1701 as proprietor of lands originally owned by her father. She married John Estaugh, a traveling minister, in 1702. She developed a talent for healing and was known for her lotions. The present town of Haddonfield is named for her. *Notable American Women, 1607–1950*, editors, Edward T. James, Janet Wilson James, and Paul S. Boyer (Cambridge: Belknap Press, 1950), 584–585.

37. John Churchman (1705-1775) of Nottingham, Pennsylvania, a traveling minister, visited England, Scotland, Wales, Ireland and Holland in 1750. "Ministering Friends," 4. QCHC.

38. Hugh Foulke (1685-1760) of Gwynedd became a traveling minister in 1720 and moved to Richland in 1730. His wife, also a minister, was Ann Foulke. DQB.

39. Phebe Wardell was born in Wales and came to the American colonies with her parents. In 1725 she married Thomas Lancaster of Wrightstown Meeting. Both were ministers. After his death in 1752 she married Samuel Thomas of Richland

meeting. Clarence Roberts, *Early Friends Families of Upper Bucks*, (Philadelphia: Webster, 1925), 367.

40. John Evans (1689-1756) of Gwynedd Meeting became a minister in 1720, and visited most of the northern colonies. DQB.

41. For Mary Weston, please see Susanna Morris's *Journal*, Introduction, note 6.

42. For Phebe Dodge, please see Susanna Morris's *Journal*, Introduction, note 6.

43. For Sophia Hume, please see Susanna Morris's *Journal*, Introduction, note 6.

44. Benjamin Bourne (1684-1757) was clerk of London Yearly Meeting at the time. DQB.

45. Mary Richabie or Rickaby was a traveling minister of Yorkshire who visited Ireland in 1742. Thomas Wight and John Rutty, *History of the Rise and Progress of the People called Quakers in Ireland*, Dublin, 1751, 362.

46. William Pitts (1709?-1760) became a minister in 1738. A former distiller, he gave up this business to preach. DQB.

47. Samuel Bownas (1676-1753) became a minister in 1696 and went to America in 1702 where he was imprisoned in New England. In 1726 he made a second visit and in 1741 became the clerk of London Yearly Meeting. DQB. He wrote a book of advice to young persons entering the ministry. *A Description of the Qualifications Necessary to a Gospel Minister* (London, 1750; Pendle Hill Publications, 1989.)

48. Ann Mercy (1707–1776) of York, a teacher, married Nathaniel Bell in 1731, became a recognized minister in 1746, and traveled in the ministry in 1747, 1752, and 1758. In 1753 she visited London, spent some time calling people to repentance, and signed a petition for a London Women's Yearly Meeting. *Piety Promoted* II, (London, 1812), 454-455.

49. Samuel Hopwood (1674-1760) became a minister in 1699. In 1741 he visited the American colonies for five years. DQB.

50. William Brown (?-1780), member of meeting in Nottingham, Pennsylvania, traveled to England in 1750 as a minister. DQB.

51. Richard Hipsley (1708-1767) of Stock became a minister in 1743 and visited Ireland in 1747. DQB.

52. Richard Partridge (1682?-1759) was born in New England, moved to England in 1703, and settled in London. He was a minister who spoke rarely but well. DQB.

53. George Whitehead, born in 1729, was the son of Thomas Whitehead, a minister and bookkeeper. DQB.

54. Susanna Morris does not mention that at this yearly meeting she spoke of her concern that the London Yearly Meeting establish a separate yearly meeting for women, according to Samuel Neale. Please see Susanna Morris's *Journal*, Introduction, note 10.

55. Formerly, Phebe Lancaster. Please see note 39 above.

56. Samuel Nottingham (1716-1787), a traveling minister, visited Long Island in 1747. He lived for some time on Tortola, and he and his wife freed their slaves. DQB.

THE JOURNAL

of

ELIZABETH HUDSON

1722 – 1783

ELIZABETH HUDSON
1722-1783

Of our three women ministers, Elizabeth Hudson (known universally as Eliza) was the wealthiest and best educated. The third daughter of William Hudson and Jane Evans, she was born on the 20th of 12th month (February 1722), into a family that lived in some comfort in the city of Philadelphia. Her grandfather, William Hudson, had been mayor of that city. Her father, also William, was a wealthy tanner who had large estates. Her mother, Jane, came from a well-known Quaker family. The Hudsons were among the sort of prominent families in early Philadelphia described by Frederick Tolles in *Meeting House and Counting House*.[1] They lived well and insisted on having everything "the best, but plain" as suited Quakers.

The Hudsons had a large family of eleven children, of whom six daughters and one son survived. Of the daughters, three married and three remained unmarried. This was not an unusual pattern; Quakers did not put as much pressure as other sects upon women to marry due to their respect for women, and their willingness for women to play other roles than that of wife and mother. The fact that her parents agreed to Eliza's desire at twenty-five to travel overseas in the ministry, and to support her financially on this trip, suggests their attitude toward women.

The Hudson daughters were probably educated initially at a dame school where they learned to read, write and cipher. Higher education for girls was limited until 1754, when Anthony Benezet established a school specifically for their education, but daughters in the Quaker upper classes were often tutored at home. As Eliza Hudson writes in her journal, she often visited the home of Isaac Norris II at Fair Hill, and developed a "lust for books" in his great library. Her spelling, punctuation, and use of language is far superior to those of most of her contemporaries. It is interesting to note also that although she endeavored to keep low and humble, she seems to have had more self-confidence than did the other women here studied. Her correspondence reveals her to be on familiar terms with the Quaker Grandees of her time, and in her journal we discover she noted when persons of high rank attended her meetings.[2]

Nevertheless, Elizabeth Hudson shared with other ministers a deep concern to be guided completely by the Holy Spirit. She describes several experiences in which she announced a meeting, and then could not speak, because she was not so guided. Her sponsors found this embarrassing, but to Elizabeth it was a necessary part of waiting on the Lord. She is scrupulously honest in describing situations in which she felt she did not sufficiently await guidance, and paid a heavy price as a result.

Elizabeth Hudson's journal appears to have been written, or at least copied, in old age, working from notes taken as she traveled. It has a freshness and spontaneity that other such journals sometimes lack. Why this excellent journal was not published in whole or in part is something of a mystery. As readers of the journal will discover, there had been some tension between Eliza Hudson and Jane Hoskins during their travels, and apparently Jane Hoskins did not come to Elizabeth Hudson's aid when she was attacked on returning home, perhaps for being too independent while traveling. Elizabeth does not elucidate, although later in her journal she speaks of some in the yearly meeting who opposed her. We can only guess that she became somewhat controversial, and that may be the reason why the journal has sat unappreciated for so many years.

In Jane Hoskins' published journal, she makes no mention of having a companion on her 1747 journey to England which she describes as painful. She writes, however, of how well good companions in ministry work together, and how disappointing it can be when it happens otherwise, and ends with a prayer for those who have departed from the right path.

After her return, Eliza Hudson traveled to Pennsylvania and Delaware meetings, and became engaged to Anthony Morris, a Quaker minister and wealthy brewer sixteen years her senior who had recently lost his wife. In May of 1752 they were married, and Eliza became a stepmother to a large family, and the mistress of a city home and two country estates. She continued to travel in the ministry until her first child, William, was born in March of 1758 at the Morris's country home, "Peckham," in Southwick. Then she fell into a deep depression which did not lift until 1760, when the Morrises moved to a second and more retired country home, "Solitude," also in Southwick. Here her second son, Luke, was born in April of 1760. A third son, born in late 1761, died in infancy. Eliza Hudson's journal ends abruptly, at the bottom of a page, in the middle of a description of a scene in which her oldest son had accidentally discharged a pistol at a little girl, but both had miraculously survived. Obviously the following page has been lost.

From letters and minutes we know that she continued to be active in the Philadelphia Quaker community until close to her death at the age of sixty-one in 1783.

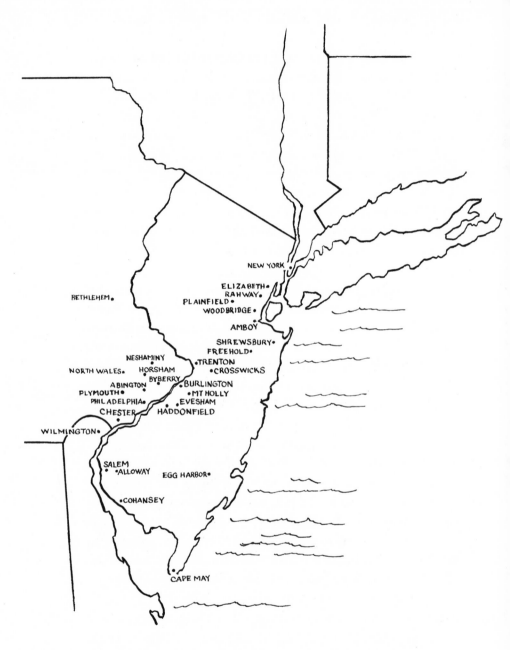

PLACES ELIZABETH HUDSON VISITED IN PENNSYLVANIA AND NEW JERSEY

THE JOURNAL OF ELIZABETH HUDSON

PART I

***An Abstract of the Travels and some other remarks of
Eliza Hudson, from 22nd of 1st month [March] 1742.***

On which day it pleased the Lord to open my mouth the
first time in publick which was in prayer in Philadelphia at
the Bank Meeting House, a day I trust never to be forgot by
me, being a day of fresh visitation to my poor soul as I had
long lain under the weight and exercise of the ministry, it
having from the fifteenth year of my age till that time in
which I in deep humility gave up, appeared as an incumbent
duty upon me. And frequently in that time found my mind
warmly influenced thereto, but for divers years the Cross of
Christ which fain must, in giving up thereto, become more
subject to, prevented my giving up in Obedience to the said
requiring, though divers times had to see my acceptance with
God depended thereon, and that if I withstood him in the
way of his leading he would withdraw those sweet influences
of his divine love which in the early part of my life he had
been graciously pleased to favour me with, to the tending
and melting of my heart, making me so far in love with him,
as that I was willing to forsake those of my companions who
I had greatly delighted in and those amusements which the
youth falsely call innocent became a burden and an offense
to me for, was now convinced of the preciousness of time
that was never lengthened out to us to be wasted in vanity or
was our beings given us in this world to serve or gratify a vain
mind, but for a far more noble end, to wit to serve the Lord.

127

This sense it pleased God to awaken in me even in my infancy before I knew how to serve him or indeed where to seek him for as yet though the Lord called I knew not that it was he, but devoted most of my time to the reading of the scriptures and Friends' books, the reading whereof often melted me into tears of joy, especially when I met with passages that suited my then seeking state, and was greatly affected when was directed to an inward silent waiting on God and that if ever I came to the saving knowledge of him it must be by the revelation of his word in the secret of my heart, which appeared to me to be in a state of pollution though I had never been guilty of those sins the world calls gross yet found that the indulging of my self in childish folly had kept me in a state of forgetfulness of God which was an offense he would not wink at and as a further incitement it was given me to see that the power of preservation was in the Lord only and that if I was preserved from those things which by falling to the practice of would incur God's eternal displeasure, it must proceed from him. Wherefore great exercise of mind came upon me with earnest cries to the Lord that he might be pleased to bring me into an acquaintance with that which would give me victory over sin and establish me in his favour, restoring onto my soul the joys of his salvation. Thus it pleased the Lord to hold me for some time in a wrestling frame of spirit without suffering me to prevail until his day dawned up on my soul and his day star arose in my heart which by taking heed unto it I became more and more acquainted with the law of the Lord which I delighted to meditate on both day and night for it was exceeding pleasant to me to follow the dictates of it. And whilst I kept near a blessing attended for I witnessed a growing in grace and the saving knowledge of God which was a day of great joy, a day when was oft had to the banqueting house where the banner was love, which is indeed a festival time, a time when the dainties of the Lord's house is brought forth with wine well refined, in which day many of the Lord's servants were sent with glad tidings of great joy, when could say with the Psalmist, I love to tread thy courts for all the ways of the Lord was the ways of pleasantness and his paths peace, under which blessed situation of mind I continued for several years until the aforesaid requiring which I was unwilling to give up to for sundry reasons, but what bore principle weight with me was my unfitness for such an awful undertaking and fear of my being mistaken respecting my being called thereto and the ill consequence attending such mistakes was continually before my eye with many other discouraging considerations which induced me to put off every appearance of it in my mind and by one means or other diverted it from properly taking hold of me, to prevent which I made books my study and more then heretofore shunned retirement till at length I by so doing rendered myself unworthy for the visits of my wonderful counselor who by this time began to withdraw his instruction from me and leave me to the imaginations of my own heart that are said to be continually evil, and for the space of six months, was almost insensible of good either in or out of meetings and indeed could scarcely ask for deliverance, such was my then weak state, even to such a great degree weak that thought could rest contented under that stupid condition during my stay in this life if I might be admitted to a state of quiet in the next, for to submit to that duty was become intolerable to think of. For all who appeared in that way became contemptuous in my eye and it was with great difficulty I sat under their testimonies. All preaching seemed foolishness to me and an interruption to my way of thinking so that dreaded a Friend's getting up in a meeting and sometimes when they did I've sat and condemn their impertinence as judging it such for any one man to teach another, especially people of superior understandings. Thus was I lost as a

Ps. 84:10

tempestuous sea doth lose a vessel without an anchor, and many were the disturbed commotions of my mind both from causes within and without, for many troubles arose in this time of great probation whereby my foundation in religion was shaken as also divers of my friendships with those particulars who had before made large profession, so that I found myself very much left both by God and man, yet could not all this while give up to the call though on conditions of being restored to my former tranquility of mind, yet was oft under great anguish of soul that when it was night I wished for day and when day wished for the night—wishing for a habitation remote from men, begrudged the inhabiters of the cliffs their places of abode as judging them in a happier situation, sometimes anxiously sought death but it fled from me and became not my refuge, so in this dissolute condition I passed several tedious months till it pleased kind providence to send several of his ministers amongst us, to wit E. P., S. H., J. H.[3] who were good instruments in the hands of the Lord towards rousing of me from out of that horrible (state) I had fell into through disobedience. What had the first agreeable impression on me was an appearance of S. H. [Samuel Hopwood] on the subject of a shepherd and his sheep, repeating those divers accidents sheep are subjected to, as several beasts of prey with their aptness to stray from the fold and that they sometimes get amongst briars by which means they often got tore both flesh and wool off their backs, and how the Shepherd conducted in such cases, out of which the observations he drew suitable instruction that made such lasting impressions on my mind as could not easily be erased out, and left me somewhat better reconciled to preaching, and by degrees prejudice was removed and there appeared again a beauty in the ministry under which was now once more baptized and being under the effects of the humbling power of Truth, came to love waiting with the Lord that he would be pleased to revisit my soul and give me strength so to do would give up to any of his requiring, when he that was never slow to hear heard and knew the sincerity of my heart.

So in his wonted goodness answered my petition and in a few months that concern now revived and in great awfulness I gave up as above mentioned and found great peace in so during such as is not easily described of which may justly say with the Queen of the South that the one half was not told me of the rich reward of obedience, in which undertaking may say with the apostle of Christ that a Dispensation of the Gospel was committed to me and woe was unto to me if I preached it not. So that in the dread and fear of the Lord did sometimes appear and was oft favoured in them days with great enlargement of heart towards the Lord and my fellow creatures and the drawing cards of his love soon drew me to visit some of our adjacent meetings in the Jerseys so took the opportunity to go with our dear worthy friends, C. W. and E. S.[4] who were on a visit from England and was at Haddonfield, Adamses, Evesham, and Mount Holly, where parted with said friends and returned home having met with considerable satisfaction in this little tour.

1744 In this year in the first month [March] I went to a meeting at Germantown in order to meet our Friend E. Stephens[5] who found some drawings on her mind to visit several adjacent meetings, and having no companion was desirous of my company, and I being at liberty went with her to Horsham, Plymouth, Byberry, Abington, and then returned to my old friend Norris'[6] at Fair Hill in whose family had contracted an intimate and agreeable acquaintance, particularly with my most valuable sincere friend Elizabeth Norris who was affectionately tender to me during my religious exercise in which she was made an useful instrument in the hand of the Lord, being of a sympathetick spirit. In those days of sorrow set great store by her friendship as indeed do

1st month

Elizabeth Hudson

even to this day, for our hearts became truly united to each other I believe not inferior to that degree of friendship which subsisted betwixt Jonathan and David, which strength of love induced me to leave my father's house and spend most of my time with her at their country seat, which was a situation that suited my inclination to retirement and had also the opportunity of their library in which was a good collection of books that at times I entertained myself with having some lust of books and indeed in time found had too high a relish for them, they being very engrossing both of our time and thoughts, and I finding this to be the effect of my studies, found it best to deny myself of them which was no easy task.

So in this agreeable solitude I spent most of this year attending meetings as they came in course.

1745 This year on the 19th day of the seventh month [September] having had some drawings on my mind for some time before, I set out with our Friend Elizabeth Sullivan [later Ashbridge] in order to visit the Jerseys and that night reached Jacob Lippincott where we lodged and on the 20th had a meeting at Pilesgrove which proved a solid good meeting though it pleased the Lord for some time to try me very sorely and give me to see my one weakness, which sight and sense deeply humbled me and engaged me to come up more fully in the discharge of my duty to him.

21st. Went to Salem and lodged with the widow Halls and next day being First Day we were at their meeting which proved as the former—

24th. Went and had a meeting at the head of Alloway Creek which was large and to edification E. S. [Elizabeth Sullivan] had an open time.

25th. Was at the lower meeting in which it pleased our Lord to favour with his presence. Lodged that night at I. Daniel's, next day went to Cohansey and had a large meeting and Eliza was highly favored to the satisfaction of most

7th month

132

that heard her. That night lodged at I. Brick's and set out the next day for the Capes [Cape May] in company with divers kind Friends, who rendered our otherwise long and tedious journey very pleasant. Reached it that night and lodged at our worthy ancient Friend Millicent Townsend's[7] and the next day being Seventh Day and not proper to have a meeting we spent that day pretty much in viewing the works of nature, particularly the sea which appeared very awful to me and afforded me some profitable amusement. Returned that night to our quarters and the next day had a large good meeting, and the next day set out for the other meeting at the Capes which proved a dark, gloomy time to us, things being but low as to truth. Went that evening over the bay to Egg Harbor. Lodged at S. Summer's, and the next day had a meeting not much to our satisfaction. Went that night as far as Robert Smith's and the next day had a meeting to small satisfaction, yet thought there was good stirrings amongst some that were not Friends. Set out after meeting and travelled on horse-back over the meadows being seven miles over and very boggy unpleasant riding and we struggled for time brought us within the night which happened not to favour us with her glittering orbs for we could not see each other's horses so our journey was rendered difficult as well as unpleasant. Several of our horses got mired yet by the good providence of God, whose eye is over his people for their preservation, was ours that we received no hurt, for which mercy my mind was filled with thankfulness. Lodged that night at Job Ridgeway's, and the next had a meeting at Little Egg Harbor, where we found it hard work to travel with the seed of God which in divers places lies buried under the rubbish of the surfeiting cares of this life which being visible objects to our senses, first attract our observation of them, then by the aid of our fruitful fancy we conceive some beauty in them, then which is very natural, desires are begot after the possession of that which most strikes our fancy as an amiable object, when for the most part by our setting too high a value thereon we pursue it with such vigor and industry as that ten to one but that the principle part of our time is engrossed in the pursuit of it, and if by chance it answer our expectations, which let me say seldom does, our affections by degrees are entirely centered therein and the whole man falls a sacrifice to that darling delight and every member in the body becomes subservient thereto, and we ourselves according to the doctrine of Christ become servants to our lusts, for his servants we are unto whom we yield our members, servants to obey, and by means an indifference towards the things of God is fallen into if not an entire forsaking of him, the fountain of living water, which if we come but to drink deep draughts of, our thirst after the things of this life will be assuaged.

Lodged the night at Jervis Farrow's. Next day rode fifty miles to the widow Newbold, where we lodged that night and the next day set out and reached Trenton. Lodged at William Morris's. Next day being first day my companion attended both their meetings, but as to myself was greatly indisposed and staid at my lodgings and received great tenderness from our good landlady with the rest of the family, and what they administered had such good effect, the next day I ventured to set out on our journey, though attended with some difficulty. Reached J. Williams' at Bethlehem where we staid several days to rest ourselves and horses, finding there was great occasion, having travelled hard from the time we set out. Had in that time one meeting but not to my satisfaction. And on the tenth of said month set out in company with several Friends who were so kind as to accompany us for Black River in hopes of reaching it that night but were disappointed by reason of our missing our way it being somewhat intricate, and no entertainment but what we purchased by great entreaty, there being no publick houses on this road and our number too large for a private one, so that it was difficult to get lodging but the night coming on was forced to sue hard to be taken in at the first house which we thought capable of entertaining us with our horses who were with this fatiguing day's journey very weary. After some time of waiting at the door of one who was a justice of the peace for an answer to our request, they admitted us in where we found the man of the house in a very low way, with whom we sat and fell into some serious discourse that seemed far from being disagreeable to him or his family several of whom were present, through the course of which Betty [Elizabeth Sullivan] had an opportunity of discovering those people had been her intimate acquaintance at the time of her residing on Staten Island before her convincement, which when she discovered herself to them surprised them exceedingly, to see such a change in her dress and deportment, which naturally induced them to inquire into the cause and manner of her change, which she readily informed them concerning in such an effecting manner as engaged their serious attention and perhaps had its service for the people was very kind during our stay with them and were loath to take any pay from us for the trouble we gave the family. In the morning we set out on our journey and got to a Friend's house six miles distant to breakfast and that afternoon rode ten miles to another Friend's house in order to have a meeting there the next day, which being first day it suited well for the people that were not Friends to attend it and by which means we had a large meeting in a barn. Many appeared in the forepart of the meeting very light and airy but it pleased the Lord to favour us with the arisings of his heart melting power which soon melted some of the most vain into tears and a solemn silence spread itself over the whole assembly and to me it was a baptizing time not to be forgot. Returned back that evening to the place from whence we came and had a night's meeting held in the Friend's house but it was much too small to contain the number of people who came so that many stood out of doors. This meeting was mostly of Presbyterians and proved to edification in the end, but the beginning was very distressing for I think in the course of my experience I never sat under a heavier cloud of death and darkness which we groaned under for some considerable time. But the Divine arm which has ever been near the faithful labourer, knowing the singleness of our views in appointing said meeting, was then stretched out and conveyed strength with power in which my companion got up and was highly favoured insomuch that the mouths of gainsayers were stopped, for we understood after the meeting that such were there with an intent to have opposed us, if could meet with any handle against us, for they, understanding we were women, judged it no difficult task to confute us. The persons thus designing were the priest with some others he counted most fit for his purpose. But let his reasons be what they might, he thought proper, contrary to his intention, to sneak off after meeting with the crowd without any remarks on the preaching, leaving his companions in the lurch who were not so wise as he but staid and urged beyond all bounds of modesty an argument which Betty waved, it being late and she much fatigued with the service of the meeting which perhaps they might take as an argument of her incapacity, which emboldened them to insist on it which they did to a degree of rudeness, but I believe they withal that heard what passed were convinced that they did not gain much credit by it. 13th. Set out for Plainfield, reached it that night and next day had a meeting where had hard work and thought there was quite too much depending on the externals of religion and as much too little of a lively exercise after the life and power of it. Here we met with Samuel Large who accompanied us to Shrewsbury. Went that night to John Shotwell's,[8] and the next day had a meeting at

Rahway. Same evening one at Elizabeth Town, but neither to my satisfaction. The 17th was at their monthly meeting at Woodbridge, much after the same sense. 18th. Set out for Shrewsbury, crossed the Amboy ferry which was so extreme rough that it was not only rendered unpleasant but dangerous as all thought, and for my part thought myself nearer the confines of eternity than either before or since, and set our deliverance down to no other account than the interposition of an all wise providence which has often been manifest to be over us for good. Was filled with joy and and thankfulness when favoured to set our feet once more on the shore and the people at the inn was glad to see us land safe which they told us was more than they expected. Staid to refresh ourselves then set out in order to get as far on our journey that night as that we might reach Shrewsbury meeting next day, but night with rain came on and none of our company versed in the way, we lost ourselves in the woods and our guide so bewildered that it was late at night before we could find any house at all to put our heads in and the first that we were directed to by a faint glimmering light was such a poor hut as could not afford us either lodging or food of any sort, and what made it more melancholy was a poor creature being there confined in chains, having lost his senses, so that our stay here was short, just whilst we dried our clothes, then set out to seek lodgings where we might get admittance. And after several repulses was by a kind Baptist woman taken in and kindly though poorly entertained. The next morning we offered our kind landlady pay for the trouble we gave her but that she absolutely refused, saying that all the pay she desired was that when any of our Friends came that way we would direct them to her house, and was anxious we should have a meeting there, telling us that their minister had left them for some time, and they had none to preach the word to them, which our not consenting to brought us to the stool of repentance, and for aught I know we fared the worse, for though next day we reached the meeting, it was by no means satisfactory. Filled up this week visiting families in and about there, had one publick meeting at Squan where we met K. B. and P. D.[9] but this proved one of the barren spots where there's little to be done or little to be got. We lodged there one night and then returned to the yearly meeting held at Shrewsbury which began the day we came there, when we had the pleasure to meet with divers of our good Friends from in and near Philadelphia, much to my comfort and satisfaction. Attended all the meetings as they came in course, which proved trying ones to me. I did not appear in any of them. Then returned homewards, parting with my companion at Burlington in much love in which had travelled during our little tour of about seven weeks which on the whole was to my satisfaction.

1746 Staid this year mostly at home save visiting neighboring meetings as Wilmington, Chester, Haddonfield, Burlington and divers other places.

1747 Set out on a journey for Long Island in company with our Friend J. Hoskins.[10] Our first meeting was at Plymouth the 4th of 3rd month [May]. Had a lively good meeting which was a satisfactory evidence to my being right in the undertaking which had weighed well and gave up in the cross. So lodged at I. Pugh's and the next day had a meeting in his house which was large and truth favoured to our mutual refreshment. The state of many was spoke to. Next day had one in another Friend's house but not to any agreeable purpose. Went that night to J. Evans,[11] my relation and intimate friend who I love and honour in the truth, one remarkable for his steady sincerity in his friendships, clear discerning, and sound judgment, as also an able minister of the gospel. 7th. Had two meetings at North Wales in which my companion had good service. The next day had a meeting in the family with Betty Ellis who was indisposed, divers Friends

3rd month

being there it proved to our mutual comfort and joy for we were made truly to rejoice in the Lord and one in another. Having at this precious opportunity sweet fellowship together which so united our hearts that the bonds of our union may be said to be strong and such as length of time or distance of space I hope can never weaken.

9th. Had a hard meeting at Horsham. 10th to Byberry, same sort. 11th at Neshaminy an humbling meeting to me but Jane seemed favoured. Lodged at A. H. Had an evening meeting in his family which proved to our satisfaction. 12th. Went to the Falls meeting in which our heavenly father was pleased to favour us with his life giving presence, breaking of that divine bread amongst us which nourishes up unto Eternal Life. Next day set out for Trenton and on first day attended two meetings and through the merciful condescension of our great master was much favoured in both. 14th. Left my companion and went to Crosswick Quarterly Meeting where met with our Friends J. Griffith and D.F.[12] who returned with me to Trenton in order to join us in company as far as Flushing upon Long Island where the yearly meeting is held. 15th. Set out on our journey and went with H. K. to Amboy while Jane proceeded as far on her way as Woodbridge, where in the morning I met her and we proceeded on our journey. Reached J. Bowne's same night where we lodged during the course of the yearly meeting which was large and satisfactory upon the whole.

Here we met with S. Nottingham[13] from old England who had landed some time before at New York to which place we went after the meeting was over. I went by land and my companion by water and on the 21st of said month had a precious meeting in which had a word of comfort for the mourners in Zion, and to tell my belief that things would revive and their numbers increase. Staid till the 23rd, then set out for Rahway. The next day Jane went to their meeting at Woodbridge but

I was detained at S. Smith's, indisposed until evening, when attended their meeting at Rahway, attended by my good Friend M. Bowne[14] who with her daughter had accompanied us from York. 29th went to Plainfield where we had a pretty good meeting. Next day went to Stoney Brook where had a hard cloudy time of it.

1st of 4th month [June]. Had a meeting at Crosswicks where found it hard work to minister to the Seed of God which is held in heavy bondage, but had peace in the discharge of our duty. 2nd. A meeting at Freehold where had a meeting not easily to be forgot. There was in the fore part of the meeting a great power of Death and Darkness, but it pleased God to arise for our help and enabled us to discharge our duties and filled our breast with peace such as the world cannot give or take away. 4th. Had a meeting at Upper Springfield which proved comfortable unto us all. 5th. Had one at Lower Springfield and a precious time it was. Went home with our worthy Friend A. Farington in whose house the God of peace rested. Had good satisfaction in his family. 6th. Had a meeting at Mount Holly in which was as nearly tried as ever I was in all my life. And in a singular way found a concern from the weight of the pressure of the word to stand up, having a good matter opened to me, but it was when on my feet all hid from me and in an awful silence England was presented as an incumbent duty laid on me to visit in company with J. Hoskins, who had it likewise on her mind but had never in all our journey proposed my going with her, or had I ever mentioned my having any thoughts of such an undertaking, though the thing had often been presented to me for good part of two years and at times saw clearly must some time give up to that hard duty, yet pled my youth and inexperience and was in hopes might have been excused from it, but he who speaks the word and all must obey, and who knows how to fit and qualify even babes for his service and

needs not the wisdom and strength of his creatures to carry
on his work by or with. And whilst I stood speechless it was
in this manner presented: wilt thou go on my errand. I will
be with thee through all the trials incident thereto and at
this time will I stretch out my arms, be mouth and wisdom to
thee. If not I'll withdraw my Holy Spirit from thee, rent the
crown from thee and confer it on another more worthy. Here
life and death seemed set before me with the choice thereof,
and the dreadful consequence of my disobedience herein filled
me with horror and amazement when in the utmost agony of
soul I made covenant with the Lord that if he would be pleased
to be with me in the way he'd have me to walk I would follow his leadings. When in an instant all anxious care was
removed, and the matter I stood up with opened again and
strength given to deliver the same beyond what I had ever
known. After the meeting great exercise of soul fell upon
me. I had promised and could not go back yet how to perform knew not. Which distress was seen by my companion
and after insisting sometime on knowing what was the cause
of my sorrow which I had not freedom to acquaint her with,
she asked me if it was not from an apprehension of it being
my duty to go as her company to England which could not
deny. So then she told me how it had been with her respecting me, and added it would give her the greatest pleasure, to
have me go with her and hoped I should find it my place, but
that all those things must be left to the disposal of Almighty
God.

From hence we went to Burlington and was at their First
Day meeting, but the weight of the journey increasing could
do little but pour out my soul to the Lord in secret crying for
strength to give up freely. From hence we returned towards
Philadelphia, lodging by the way at Fair Hill. Went home
the next day, staid some time, then went to Fair Hill to spend
the winter, pretty much for the advantage of being retired,

giving opportunity for the concern to ripen. Sometimes my distress was so great, Death was most eligible, and was what I sought refuge in. At other times my soul so abounded in that Divine love that wishes health and salvation to all men that life itself was not dear to me but for their sakes could give up all, and all I had to give up appeared but a feeble sacrifice unworthy of the acceptance of him who had in his command that cattle of a thousand hills. Thus was I led on through this furnace of sore afflictions and in some sort was fitted for the undertaking, yet when the time came that I must lay it before Friends it seemed too hard a task for me. So from time to time I put it off till the Reasoner and the accuser of the Brethren got in and almost made shipwreck of faith, so that my exercise of soul became too great for my natural strength, for it so preyed on my spirits as to bring on a most violent fever which for all appearance brought me near the brink of the grave, and had it been the Lord's will to put a period to my days, I believe I had then gone to that fixed rest where the wicked cease from troubling and an end of all those painful vicissitudes we are subjected to whilst here is arrived but it did not so seem to him good, and in his own time raised me up again so that I must assent to the might of his power to bring down to the grave and raise up again, almost kill then make alive, by and in which his power is magnified and exalted above all. After being confined three months mostly to my bed, I was by degrees restored to some degree of health so that could get out to meetings. Some of the first was down to Chester when our Friends T. Gawthorp, J. G., P.D.[15] took shipping for England, with whom had a satisfactory meeting at parting. Staid a day or two then went home to Fair Hill where I staid till the 11th month [January] when found it my place to acquaint Friends of my concern to visit Friends in Europe, first doing it in the morning meeting where met with no objection so proceeded according to order,

142

laying it before Friends of the monthly meeting who after deliberate consideration gave me such a certificate as served my purpose.

So that with the concurrence of my intended companion, J. Hoskins, looked out for a vessel that I might be easy in taking my passage in, which proved to be the Pembrook, Captain Arthur Burris, Commander, Norris & Griffiths, owners. (It was also satisfactory to my companion going in such ship.) And set on board the 26th of 11th month [January], reached Chester that night, and the next day about noon set sail with a fair wind under the enjoyment of divine peace. 28th. Got out of our capes and the wind kept fair for the space of ten days which took us one third of our passage, but then had contrary winds for some days, met with nothing remarkable in our voyage save several providential escapes from the enemies, it being the time of the Spanish and French war. We were chased twice, the latter about two weeks after we left our capes and singularly preserved. For some time our company apprehended no danger but as they said, supposed her an honest fellow going to the West, they bearing that course and the reverse to ours. But I found my mind very uneasy about her and expressing my thoughts to my companion found we were of one mind respecting our fears of her being an enemy which in some sort confirmed me in the belief of it and I endeavoured to retire in my mind into that word which is the refuge of the righteous and through divine favour found access to it which proved a strong tower preserving me from all anxious fears save of him who is to be feared and approached with reverence. Had sat but a little time in silence when was called by my companion to come and view the vessel when found she was nearer us than when I went off the deck. Upon which we spake to our captain who with his glass examined her more closely and perceived her bearing down with all her sails out upon us having held

us in play until she had got to the windward of us. This
discovery greatly alarmed the ship's company who held it im-
practicable for us either to make sufficient resistance or run
from her as she had such
great advantage of us. I

just staid to hear
their opinions and
retired in great
calmness, staying
some time before I
went up again, and
when I did to my
very great surprise
beheld a thick fog
like smoke betwixt
us and the other
ship which at first
sight appeared as if
it had been on fire,
and varied very
little from its first appearance during my observation of it.
Our first sight of it was just as the sun set and night came on.
So we lost sight of it entirely. We both went to sleep as at
other times under no dreadful apprehension but resigned to
the will of providence, yet were truly thankful to the Lord
for his goodness to us, the sense whereof not only rested in
our minds but greatly humbled them. And a comfortable
voyage we had, dwelling in the sweet communion which is
the life of the saints and people of God, and although I went
on board under a weak state of health and was severely hindered with sea sickness which held me considerable part of
our voyage, yet I never once repined there at but patiently
submitted all the various dispensations of all wise providence,
and therein enjoy great satisfaction. That day five weeks we

went on board we landed in Dublin to the great joy of our
Friends who had strongly suspected that we had been taken,
and indeed great was our pleasure to see so many of our dear
Friends who came to see us and congratulate us on our safe
arrival. And a most hearty welcome was received from our
dear worthy Samuel Judd at whose house we lodged during
our stay in the city, who with his family used me with great
tenderness as well as Christian sympathy which is ever acceptable to strangers, especially those who are engaged in
that service we were engaged in which admits of many close
exercising deep seasons. And I may say in behalf of Friends
in that nation they are remarkable courteous to strangers,
compassionate to those in affliction and ready to communicate and do good to them that stand in need. And although
I stood not in need of being administered unto as a person
necessitous, as to outward things, yet in other respects hold
myself greatly obliged to them for the very great tenderness
toward me in that time of infancy in which I visited that
nation, in which state found many nursing fathers and mothers, though this nation can't boast of an equal number of
worthies with a neighboring one, yet the disparity as to numbers is in some sort made up by the sincerity of those few,
who love without dissimulation those that visit them and for
the work's sake. I don't know that in all the time I was amongst
them I ever heard an ill natured remark of me or an endeavour
to lessen our service, but ever a readiness to forward us therein
which has endeared them to me in such sort as their memory
is precious and with the Holy Apostle may say, I make men-   *Eph. 1:16*
tion of them in my prayers to Almighty God.

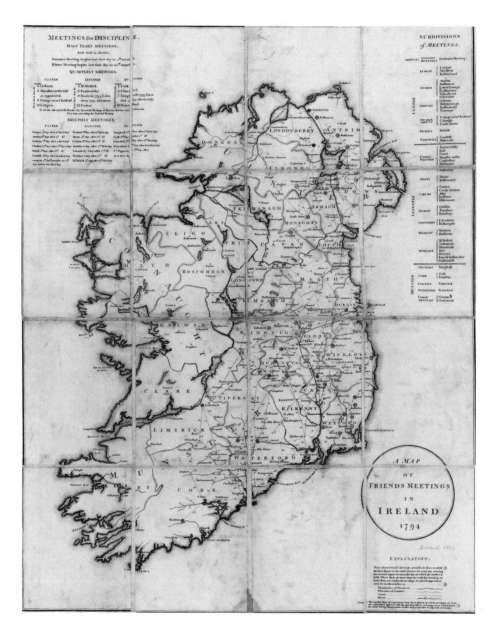

A Map of Friends Meetings in Ireland, 1794

(Used with permission of Friends Historical Library, Swarthmore College)

THE JOURNAL OF ELIZABETH HUDSON

PART II

It was the first of the third month [May] that we landed and first day of the week. Next day being their two weeks meeting we went to it and both of us had something to say that was not disagreeable I believe to Friends. Next day went to their weekday meeting at Meath Street. Solid meeting. Next day visited our worthy Friend John Barclay's family. Had an agreeable sitting there. I had something to say particular to the young people which seemed to have an agreeable place with them and during our stay in that city they behaved very loving to us. The next day our kind landlord took us in a coach to Furry Park, a beautiful seat of Joseph Fade,[16] who was then ill with the gout in his stomach which in a few days proved his death. He was very sensible and took a Friendly notice of us and an agreeable visit it was to us. 6th of said month went to their weekday meeting held at Sycamore Alley. 9th at the Meath Street where was held the womans' meeting which was large and satisfactory, there being a solid power spread over that awful assembly. 10th. Had a meeting for the youth. 11th was the ministers' meeting preceding the yearly meeting. 12th. Attended the burial of Joseph Fade the corpse being carried to Sycamore Alley attended by a vast great number of gentry and others, the most crowded meeting I ever was in the service of the meeting. If any there was fell to my share for no one spoke save myself and I think upon the whole had no cause to boast, for though I stood up in the power of life and what was said was by that influence, yet the whole seemed marred and my peace destroyed by my abrupt conclusion which was occasioned from

147

the seizure of a cowardly fear which caused me to sit down in the midst of good matter. And though it remained with the pressure, had no resolution to get up again, though I had great encouragement I had a very low time after this for several days. My much loved M. Peisley[17] concluded in prayer, she being come to attend the service of the national meeting when begun our agreeable acquaintance as also with my dear well beloved Friend Abigail Watson,[18] formerly Bowles, who had in the early part of her life visited our continent. She was one of those nursing mothers I hinted at before. My companion and I with her attended all the meetings which were held for the service of this said meeting as they came in course most of which were large, lively good meetings, divers living testimonies being therein borne to the general stirring up of the most pure mind. It was as a heart cementing time to many of us and the bands of our Holy union were strengthened and so that we seemed one another's joy in the Lord, each preferring the other to themselves so that a becoming deference was observed throughout the meetings and time for the life of truth to rise in dominion which is too often in these large gatherings obstructed by the appearances of those forward spirits whose delight and life consists in words, especially their own, but there was little of this sort of appearances during the course of these our great good meetings, wherein it must be acknowledged that divine presence was enjoyed to our mutual joy.

We had several comfortable seasons in the family where we lodged, with those of our Friends who came to visit us. We staid in the city and visited divers Friends' family, with the meetings both first and weekdays as they came in the course till the 31st of 3rd month [May], then set out attended by divers of our good Friends from Dublin towards the North. Reached Drogheda that day and had a large meeting of the people of the town which my companion had the service of, save in prayer in which I had close work, feeling dark spirits. Next day we parted from our dear Friends in a great deal of love who returned home except two who accompanied as far as Lurgan. Reached Jonesborough the same day and lodged at an inn and the next day reached Newry by dinner time so staid and refreshed ourselves at an inn which happened to be situated opposite the market and it being their market day a very numerous concourse of people there was which I stood some time beholding and made some serious observation upon, each one assiduously pursuing that branch of business that belonged to them. I found my soul filled with concern for their immortal parts with such a degree of gospel love which wishes health and salvation to all men, which led me to breathe to God for them, even to wrestle in spirit with great fervor. I thought I felt for some time the weight of their sins and did not know but that I must go out into the street, which filled me with awful dread, but after weighing the concern and no particular message offering found freedom to waive so doing.

Got to Lurgan that night and lodged at our worthy Friend John Turner's[19] who with his spouse was very kind to us. 5th. Had two meetings to pretty good satisfaction. 6th. Went and had a meeting at Moyallen which was solid and my worthy companion had the service with J. Turner who appeared very lively. Next day went and had a meeting at Ballyhagen. It proved a good meeting, there was a word of comfort to the sorrowful in heart. I witnessed a fresh supply of that Divine Strength which qualifies for service. Next day had a meeting at Red Ford near Charlemont which was an hard one. 9th. Rode to Morgan Wilson's and next day had a meeting neither large nor satisfactory, only that there is peace in doing our duty. 11th. Rode to Coleraine. 12th had two very good meetings, the latter for the towns people who came many of them in light and airy spirits and for some time were an interruption to us in our exercise. But there came that over the meeting which brought them under subjection.

That night to Ballinacree and next day we had an extraordinary meeting. The very Gospel Treasure seemed opened to us for which blessed visitation of Divine goodness my soul magnified that Eternal power which created and supporteth all things by whom his handmaids are noticed, that we have at times to say with the mother of our Lord to wit, for he that is mighty hath done to me great things, and holy is his name. Not withstanding this truth is here and here away at a low ebb. That night we rode to Grange and next day had an exercising meeting after which went to Antrim. Next day had a meeting in which it was given me to see the danger of the God of this world blinding our eyes so also the necessity of the administration of eye salve. 16th to Lisburn where we on the 17th had a comfortable meeting. I was sensible here of the help of Friends' spirits in a singular manner which nearly united them to us and we to them which induced us to make some stay at our worthy Friend Hancocks. 19th. Went to Ballinderry where divers Friends from Lurgan and parts adjacent met us and it pleased our gracious master to favour our souls in an eminent manner. I think without tincture of vanity I may say the gospel was preached in the demonstration of the spirit and the power. The whole body seemed mutually refreshed. The subject that offered that meeting was, to thy tent oh Jacob, thy dwelling oh Israel, from which portion of the scripture I had a great deal to say by way of comparison between the circumstance of that people and us as a people. Was led to mention particularly the end of our first visitation and cull out of the world fashions, customs and spirit of it, the design of the almighty herein being to make us a peculiar people and royal priesthood that a people he might have to exult his holy name amongst, showing wherein our strength lay and what steps must be taken to

Luke 1:49

Num. 24:5

150

answer the great end of our call, also wherein some had fallen short with the causes of their feebleness, how they might be restored, etc. 20th. Had a meeting at Hillsborough where was present the Countess Dowager of Kildare, Lady Hillsborough, her daughter, with all their attendance who behaved very orderly as became the occasion. During the time of our appearance, the countess especially, who by a look that bespoke her displeasure reprimanded her daughter for her smiling at her lap dog. Next day had another meeting at Lisburn, not finding ourselves clear, had an open time and have hopes it was of service, and returned that night to Lurgan and on the 26th had a meeting very proving to me. There was some home doctrine delivered touching the proper qualification for ministry. 28th. There was a burial which was attended, my companion had the service chiefly of that meeting.

Not finding ourselves clear, went again to Ballyhagen on the 2nd of the 5th month [July] had a meeting with Friends not to be complained of, as also one with the people of the neighborhood in which there wanted not words; it was held in the widow Richardson's malt house, and rode to Castleshane and had a poor meeting with what few Friends are there. I am sorely exercised in spirit to see Truth's cause suffer for want of faithful truehearted soldiers to espouse its cause. Oh that there were such raised up amongst this people here and here away, great is the travail of my soul for this people throughout the nation and many are my deep baptisms on their account. 8th. Went to Cootehill in order to attend their province meeting which began the 9th and proved a solid, refreshing meeting. I think the very power of the gospel was revealed amongst us and our spirits subjected thereby to the exalting and refreshment of the precious seed of God in ourselves. Oh that the savour of the dew of Heaven may rest long upon our branches—10th being first day and our minds being drawn out towards the people of the town,

5th month

publick notice was given and very large meetings we had to satisfaction, there was open service both fore and afternoon. 11th. Rode to Oldcastle. 13th had a poor meeting. 14th went towards the Moate. This day at eight o'clock began the greatest eclipse of the sun I ever see. Got to Mullingar. Lodged at an inn. Next day reached Moate and were kindly received by our Friends. Lodged at James Clibburn's, whose wife was J. Barclay's daughter whom we had seen at Dublin. 19th. Went to Athlone, had a large meeting in a dancing room, Friend J. Hoskins had the service. The people in general behaved soberly. That night went back to Moate. Stayed their weekday meeting which was to our satisfaction. 21st went to Birr and next day had a meeting. 23rd went to Jonathan Barnes and on the 24th had large open satisfactory meeting, the gospel I think was preached in the life and power of it. The subject enlarged upon was what the true baptism with its blessed effects which it ever has on those baptized thereby by which only we are made children of God, heirs of the Kingdom of Heaven, members of Christ's Church, etc. We were mutually refreshed by this opportunity. 26th. Was favoured in the family with the renewed touches of divine love, had a time in prayer. Set out soon after for Roscrea and had a very large good meeting. We were both favoured and I was truly thankful as it was a meeting of those that were not of our society who behaved well throughout the whole sitting. Next day went to Nenah, had a large meeting in the Town Hall of the town's people mostly, who having had notice of our coming were gathered about the house in great numbers inasmuch that the people feared the house which was old and supported by pillars would give way. Therefore, unknown to us, two companies of soldiers who were stationed in the town, and had designed attending the meeting, guarded the house and would not let the mob go in or anybody till we were ready, when they made a lane from the opposite house where we dined quite up the steps into the room where we was to meet. And two of their principal officers lent us their hands to help us up the steps which indeed was not altogether unnecessary for my knees were ready to smite each other, I never was more awfully affected in my life or found a greater weight come upon me, upon such an occasion which made me cry to the Lord with great earnestness and forever reverenced be his holy power, he in an extraordinary manner favored our souls and filled with good matter, it was a season to be commemorated by many, I believe, by me it is.

Next day set out for Limerick, got there that night. The 30th was their weekday meeting which we attended. Stayed also to their first day meeting which we attended in the morning and my companion had good service, but it was to me a suffering time. Afternoon I was indisposed so that could not well go out, but I believe my companion was favoured.

And next day which was the 2nd of 6th month [August] set out for Cashel but did not reach it so that was obliged to put up short of it at a place called Golden Bridge. 3rd. Had a meeting at Cashel, where had hard service, after which went to Clonmell next day had a meeting and that night to Kilconner to our Friend Joseph Fennell's whose spouse we had seen at Dublin. 5th. Had a meeting and finding ourselves somewhat fatigued staid to rest ourselves and horses till the 8th when had another meeting being first day. 9th. Set out for Cork, lodged by the way at Jonas Devonshire's country house and reached it the next day. The 12th being their weekday meeting went to it and the 14th was first day I attended all three meetings but my companion was indisposed so that she inclined to stay their weekday meeting and they all proved satisfactory to me and our Friends were agreeable that made our stay very agreeable to me. My companion finding some drawings in her mind to visit Bandon and Kinsale, acquainted Friends of it who consented to accompanying us thither. 16th.

6th month

153

Had a very good meeting at Bandon but not being clear, appointed another to be held in the same place the next day evening but one, for had given notice of our being at Kinsale the next day where divers Friends from Cork beside those who accompanied us gave us the meeting. The meeting was large and satisfactory and mostly towns people there being no Friends at this place. Lodged there that night and set out next morning for Bandon. Had strong drawings on both our minds as we rode through a village to have a meeting with the people, which we communicated to each other, and the Friends with us who fell in with it and though the time was short so that we could but give an hour's notice there was a large house filled with people, many of whom had not been at a meeting before, as none had ever been held there before. It proved an open good meeting and what Friends were there expressed their satisfaction. Had but just time to reach the meeting in season which was larger than before and for aught I know, excelled it in goodness. To me the best wine came at the last. The meeting here at Bandon was held in their town hall. We lodged at inns for the time we left Cork till our return; there being no Friends to entertain us, got back to Cork on the 19th where staid till first day, went to all the meetings where I fared well as also their week day meeting and was in this our stay nearly united to the faithful, though there was a controversy to be held with the unfaithful and unstable amongst them for such there were who were driven about with every wind of doctrine whom my soul had a testimony against and could not join with, no not so as to break bread with them, remembering that saying eat not with him that hath an evil eye, these spirits brought great exercise upon me wherever I met with them. 24th. Set out with divers Friends for Youghal. 25th had a hard silent meeting. My companion having drawings on her mind, inclined to another with the people of the town, which was large though to my

John 2:10

Prov. 23:6

154

apprehension to no great purpose, great I know were my sufferings in both, for when truth did not favour I could not rejoice but found peace in keeping low and retired in spirit. Stayed till the 29th when set out for Waterford but could not reach it that night and were obliged to put up at an ordinary inn at a place called Killmacthomas where met with but poor entertainment and little rest, all the best of their but mean apartments at best being taken up with other guests in being the time of the assizes held at Waterford, the counsellors and others were repairing there in great crowds. I believe there were upwards of fifty lodged in a small house many of whom were people low in life and very disturbing inmates. Next day reached the above said place early in the morning and on the 2nd of the 7th month [September] had a meeting as also one on the 4th. Had pretty good satisfaction in sitting with them though no extraordinary service. 5th to Ross next day had a meeting, after which we went to William Goff and next day had a meeting at the Forrest Meeting House in which had hard things to deliver, yet not without the divine consolating love of our Heavenly Father, tempered therewith. From thence to Silver Springs where lodged that night and next day went to Wexford where had an open meeting with the people of the town, after which went to Joseph Williams. Next day had a solid meeting with divers Friends in his house. 10th went to Coladine next day; had a meeting to pretty good account. Here my companion fell ill but soon recovered after a few days rest so that I was obliged to leave her to attend a meeting that was appointed for us at John Smithson's which was large and exercising. Returned that night to my companion who I found better, and the next day reached Kilcock, lodged at Robin Lackey's, next day went to Kilconner to our worthy Friends John Watson's whose wife had visited America when Bowles, whom I had seen at Dublin, and contracted an intimacy with which proved to

7th month

my advantage, she being one of the few nursing mothers that our Israel is favoured with. She was then on a religious visit to England and though far advanced in years and feeble in body yet fervent in spirit, zealous for the cause of truth which she was qualified to maintain boldly. I esteemed her one of our first rank female warriors. Her doctrinal appearance manifested a superior authority over the weakness of her declining nature which when out of meeting frequently prevailed and tendered her unfit for any service but that her master early called her to and which she seemed to prefer to natural life which was freely given up and devoted to the noble cause. I never had the pleasure of seeing her again, for she left England a few days before we set out for it, but was divers times favoured with instructing, consolatory letters from her, some of which are living testimonies of her sincere regard for me as well as good will to the cause I was engaged in, and had oft to wade through deep baptisms in which state she truly sympathized.

From thence to a province meeting held at Carlow which began the 17th and held two days. I think they were very satisfactory good meetings. Here we met with our dear Friend Mary Peisley whom had seen in Dublin and contracted a near friendship with. She was then going on for the city in order to take her passage for England on a religious visit. 20th. Was at a large meeting at Castle Dermot where were divers of the Friends belonging to Newton and Bally-Racket. 21st. Had a small good meeting at Ballitore. 22nd. Had a meeting at Athy in the town hall where was our good Friend James Gough[20] from Mt. Mellick who was so kind to meet us in order to conduct us thither, he had the principal service that day. 23rd. Had at meeting at Bally-Carrol after which went to Mt. Mellick and on the 26th had two meeting in which Friend Hoskins had extraordinary service but for my part was silent and very low. 27th. Had a meeting at Ballinakill which proved to mutual satisfaction of both preachers and hearers, as for me my spirits were greatly refreshed.

From thence to Mt. Rath, had a meeting with Friends only very poor low time with us, yet not left without the evidence of life. 29th. Had a meeting at Burris in a Friend's malthouse, my companion had the principal service for through my backwardness I sat under the burden of the world so long that the proper time slipped in which should have stood up which was of hurt to both my self and the meeting and I believe made hard work for my companion for where there is not a keeping our ranks each in our own line of duty, it flings the whole out of joint and a meeting seldom if ever recovers when thus the gospel property is invaded. I have oft compared the ministry to a fountain or spring of water and ministers to pipes through which the water is conveyed to divers parts of a city, some greater, some lesser according to the distance the stream is to be conveyed or the body of water is to convey, and very frequently we see one pipe so fixed as to be in some sort dependent on an other and if any impediment happens to either it frustrates the grand design of conveyance, and no pipe so small or minute but there is some service or part to act and its not acting that part may possibly so disconcert the whole as to incommode a great part if not the whole city.

Some observations of this sort has been teaching to me under these considerations, to wit that the superior or inferior, as some may esteem, are equally dependent upon the same fountain, and were in themselves as dead inanimate matter until this divine fountain of Eternal Life circulated or flowed in and through them, which was never rendered more pure or delicate by the excellence or beauty of the pipe, it being completely so in its own nature, and if suffered a free course will not only sanctify it, but beautify it. And if the case will admit of superiority it consists in this entirely of being most pure, free from all impurity of our frail natures, which depends upon our subjection to this Holy Current of living ministry, suffering it to ebb and flow according to its natural course, neither endeavouring in our own wills or wisdom to raise it beyond its limited bounds or raising or tuning the voice to make others believe it higher tide with us than it really is, for by so doing we only muddy the water and offend our sensible hearers, rendering that which simply dropped would have administered life, a messenger of death. And one appearance of this sort may defile the pipe, esteeming ourselves; such more then, slightly considered may appear to us, for it's no less than suppressing the pure and giving way to the impure spring which will render us, with its self, odious to the living.

That night to Mt Rath. 30th to Mt. Mellick and had an evening meeting with Friends very large and satisfactory. 31st. Went to Dundrum and the 1st of 8th month [October] had two meeting with Friends only and on the 4th had one with the town's people. My companion had all the service. After which meeting rode to Hillock and next day reached Dublin where we met with an affectionate welcome from our worthy landlord and divers others of our dear friends whom my soul loves in the Lord and they are there engraved as epistles of lasting impression.

Here we staid and attended meetings as they came in course until the 16th in which time had many precious opportunities both in their publick and private meetings in Friends' families, then set out for Wicklow, attended by divers Friends from Dublin and on the 17th had good meetings, one with Friends and the other with the town's people. Next day back to the city. 23rd. I went accompanied by several of our kind Friends to Balliboys next day had an open time with the few Friends that are there, next day back to my companion. Stayed with her at Dublin until the 27th when set out

8th month

for province meeting to be held at Mt. Mellick, it not suiting
my companion, a Friend I had a friendship for took me in her
chaise and was an agreeable companion. Got part of the way
that day and lodged at an Inn. Got up before day and reached
the morning meeting. Here I met with Sarah Artis and Mary
Kirby[21] from England who had visited the nation and was on
their return home by way of Dublin. All the meetings were
satisfactory both for business and worship.

31st. Had a meeting at Rathangan which though small
was a solid, comfortable meeting. 2nd of 9th month [No-
vember] had a meeting at Timahoe in which was particularly
exercised. Next day reached Dublin, found my companion
well and with open arms to receive me, staid till the national
meeting and attended the service of it, which fell pretty much
to my companion there, after which prepared for our voyage
to England. And on the 18th of 9th month [November] went
on board a vessel, Captain Pritchard master, bound for Bristol,
but met with contrary winds and after being two days at sea
was driven back off the Hill Slothe a few miles from Dublin.
It then being the seventh day of the week I could not help
looking back towards our Friends we had left with strong
desires of once more seeing them. I proposed taking boat to
go back, but was opposed which discouraged me for a time
until the cords of Divine Love drew so strongly I broke out
into a flood of tears which moved both Captain and companion, that late as it was they set out with me and we got
safe ashore. Found our landlord's family up and several of our
Friends there expecting our return. Our joy seemed mutual.
Next day I found I was not clear so went to their meeting at
Meath Street and found close particular service on a subject
that had in some other meeting offered itself but judging I
was not qualified to handle it as it ought to be, waived it
until it became a burden too heavy. I delivered it in fear and
trembling and believe was favoured by the divine influence

9th month

Ps. 14: 1

to make the necessary distinctions on a difficult subject which was thus introduced. The fool has said in his heart there is no God which was the result of every atheist. Was led to speak many home things to them who held such pernicious principles whom I had to believe the Lord would awaken to a sense of his powerful existence. After meeting a Friend told me he did not wonder I was driven back, to deliver such necessary doctrine. As soon as had done and sat down, meeting broke up and at the door I met a messenger to let me know the wind was fair and we must hasten on board. I found my mind much relieved and was quite easy to go. That afternoon we set sail with a fine gale which increased to a storm, which brought on snow and steady rain. It was very cold and the tops of the mountains appeared white. It was a very tempestuous night indeed, and next day as we sailed up the Bristol channel we saw several vessels that had been overset in the storm we rode it out in. In the beholding whereof my mind was awfully affected and could not do less than pour out my soul in humble thankfulness to the Lord, by whose beneficient goodness alone it was that we had been preserved from the like danger which indeed threatened us. I think in 36 hours we hauled up to the wharf at Bristol, went ashore, and put up with our kind Friend Richard Champion.[22] Here we staid and took the necessary rest after our short but hazardous voyage, staying from the 22nd of 9th month [November] until the 17th of 10th [December] taking the meetings as they came in course, divers of which was satisfactory, but indisposition prevented my companion from attending all of them. Here we had the pleasure of meeting with our dear and honourable Friend Benjamin Kidd[23] whose company and service at meetings in my companion's absence was very acceptable to me, though at that time not so intimately acquainted as some time after.

From hence we went to Bath and had a meeting on the

10th month

20th where I had no bad meeting though silent, the service falling to my companion's lot. 20th. Took coach for London where we arrived the 23rd. Were met some miles of the city by E. Bland and I. Pemberton,[24] our Friend and countryman, who we were pleased to see.

Lodged at Thomas Ilyams and attended meetings as they came in course until the lst of 12th month [February] then went to Bromley, had an evening meeting and returned to London where we staid and attended meetings as they came in course first and week day, pretty constant. Took a turn out to Tottenham to their first day meeting, where it was judged forty Friends from London came, but if to hear they were disappointed for neither of us had any thing to say—Returned to London to their fourth day meeting held at Grace Church Street. 3rd of 1st month [March] set out in a coach for Hertford Quarterly Meeting, reached it by meeting time which we attended to our great comfort for the blessing of the everlasting Hills was showered down upon us which mutually rejoiced us as in the house of prayer. After the service of said meetings returned to London. 14th of said month set out for Bristol yearly meeting, lodged the first night at Clapton, next day our Friends Daniel Weston and Joseph Row[25] met us in order to accompany us to Maidenhead where had the first meeting in which my companion had an extraordinary time which I rejoiced in as I had earnestly prayed for her being favoured at that time as I perceived for what end I did not know, a man writing down what was delivered—but hearing no more of it hope there was no cause for caviling at what he heard.

17th. Got to Reading Yearly meeting, where we were again met with our Friend B. K. [Benjamin Kidd] which held 3 days where I believe there was solemn service. 19th had an evening meeting at Newbury, pretty satisfactory. Next day to Chippenham. 21st reached Bristol and on the 23rd their

12th month

1st month

161

yearly meeting began which held till the 27th when was the parting at which were several eminent Friends to wit, S. Bownas, [Samuel Bownas][26] Isaac Sharpless,[27] I. Thompson[28] and sundry others. The service of the whole was carried on in a reputable order, stayed their first day meetings which were not the worst.

1st of 2nd month [April]. Set out for London, reached it the 7th, went in company with our Friend Charles Norris[29] who we met at Bristol, my particular acquaintance when at home. Staid their yearly meeting which was large and attended by divers Friends of the ministry of the first rank, B. Kidd, S. Bownas, Edmund Peckover[30] and our most esteemed M. Peisley who had visited the North and was now on her travels taking this meeting in her way. 23rd. Set out for the North, intending to take the meetings as they fell out in our way thither. Reached Stocks that night. The 24th. Had a meeting at Billericay after which went to Chelmsford. 25th had a meeting. 26th to Keldon and had a meeting after which rode to Colchester. 28th. The yearly meeting began, held till the 31st which meetings was well attended, both by Friends and a superior power. From this meeting we had the company of Friends to Ipswich where had a meeting and that night to Woodbridge accompanied by our Friend Jonathon Peckover who had brought his chaise for us. The 4th of 4th month [June] came on their yearly meeting at which were sundry of our worthies in the ministry to wit S. Bownas who had kept us company with John Wilson[31] and his wife of Kendal from Colchester. This meeting throughout the whole proved large, good meetings, I may say the ancient of days was with us and opened unto his dependent ministers the Gospel Treasury from whence was handed good matter, both of things new and old.

From this place set on the 7th and had a meeting at Leiston pretty satisfactory. 9th. Had one at Beccles which in my opinion was a hard uncomfortable meeting yet my companion preached well. I attempted but it came off badly, could make nothing out to any good purpose. 10th. Set out for Norwich. Stayed their first day meetings, my companion had the service of them all. For my part had a very suffering season of which in some measure want of experience brought upon me, for when meeting did not turn out so well as I could desire I was too impatient and restless under such disappointments, and oft was tempted to murmur and repine in spirit, that I was thus left and beset with difficulties, which time and experience taught me was no acceptable disposition to him who holds times and seasons in his mighty hand, and dispense of them according to his own good pleasure causing the glory of his presence to shine upon us when the whole soul is enlivened by it and becomes fruitful, and again hides his face as though his wrath was kindled against us—when the whole purpose of the divine will is only to learn us a becoming subjection such as was the Holy Apostle's when he says to this purpose that he knew how to suffer want as *Phil. 4:12* well as to abound and could bear abasement, boasting so much in no state, as that of the Cross of Christ, which his experience in the Christian faith convinced him was the power of God to salvation. Therefore was his glory in it, and indeed, as I grew in religion I found I must bear greater suffering, than they which compared with them were but light afflictions, these being but the beginnings of sorrows with me, and believed that if what was to have befell me had been revealed I could not have supported under their prospect, but such is his wisdom and mercy to us, who are such weak creatures that reflection upon past and apprehension of future sorrows are more than human nature can prudently support under, that the future is hid from us and the past ought to have no disagreeable impression upon our minds as no ill can accrue from afflictions or the causes of them when the cause is removed. Therefore a rational mind truly subject to the divine inspiration is taught to understand that only the present is ours, having nothing to do with past or future, in any other sense than this, that in whatsoever we have acted or done contrary to that Holy Impulse which the apostle called the grace of God must be repented of, forgiveness sought for and an amendment for time to come, laboured for, and those snares that have heretofore proved fatal carefully shunned, and a watchful eye kept, lest any new ones prove more powerful than the former, and of more dreadful consequence—Had also the company of our well beloved Friend Edmund Peckover who was my real Friend and made from the first of my acquaintance or knowledge of him a useful instrument in the hand of God to me. 12th to Tottenham and had a small satisfactory meeting on the 12th, after which Edmund accompanied to his own house at Wells where we were agreeably entertained and had a pretty good meeting. 15th set out for Linn. 16th. Had a meeting in which Edmund had an extraordinary time in prayer, in the course of which he desired the Lord might again bless the earth with the sun beams that she might yield her increases for the support of the human bodies, there having been such heavy rains it was not only dangerous travelling in those fen countries but greatly feared that the grain would have been damaged and the sheep suffer, as is oft the case that not only many are drowned but such wet seasons bring a toll amongst them, and what I remark this for is; it soon appeared and a fine spell ensued and I oft had with pleasure to behold the promising harvest as I travelled the country northward and saw much of it safely gathered into storehouses. I was brought very low in spirit, often led into deep baptisms, insomuch that I cried to heaven that he might lighten them or dissolve the tabernacle which at times trembled under the weight of them. Things looked but gloomy as to religion in many places so that my appeal was to the Lord, who is there that will stand up for thy great name, etc.

18th being the first day was at two meetings, next day it was fine and clear weather so we set out and crossed the wash which is an arm of the sea, that when the tide is in admits of large vessels coming up but when down the sands are so dry that people ride over them, yet not without difficulty and sometimes danger by reason of quicksands. We were told of divers who had lost their lives and by some persuaded to go another way, but that not suiting our purpose as meetings were laid out for us, ventured over and by the good providence of God got safe over. Rode 20 miles to Spalding, a town in Lincolnshire. 20th. Had a meeting in which hard things delivered, after which went in company with divers Friends toward the quarterly meeting to be held at Lincoln to begin the next day. 21st. Reached Hereford that night very much fatigued what with hard service in meeting and a tedious ride after, though both were somewhat mitigated by our Friends' great kindness and care over us, which they were not wanting in though our lodging was at an Inn the entertainment was very good and comfortable which so far refreshed us that we arose the next morning early with cheerfulness to pursue our journey and got in good time to the meeting being then 18 miles off it, though my spirits soon flagged and great exercise came upon me insomuch that I cried to the Lord who was my only refuge in all my straits, that he might if it were his will lighten the load or weight I found my soul oppressed with or take my natural life, which if it were an acceptable sacrifice to him, could freely resign it to him, for it was given me to see that there was times of great suffering for me to be subjected to not only for my own refinement, and enlargement into the mysteries of the suffering of Christ, which resulted in his death upon the cross and what all his disciples must lust of, but for the church's

Elizabeth Hudson

sake which there was no possibility of speaking to the state of, unless baptized by that Holy power of light and love by which the worlds commenced their beings, and are still upheld, which when we are under the weight of can speak as the oracle of God, and not only witness those sacred truths confined in mystery from the wise and learned of this world, unfolded to us but are in some sort enabled to unfold them to others. Under this heavy load I with the rest of our Friends went to meeting, bowed indeed in spirit inasmuch that I could have prostrated my self with my mouth in the dust

Lam. 3:29

166

as some of the servants of the Lord had done in time past, could it have answered any good purpose. But ever blessed be the name of him who was heretofore gracious to his dependent servants, is still gracious, and was in this time of great trial pleased to manifest his power and love, by appearing in spirit in his wanted glory. I never had the beauty of religion or an Holy life more clearly opened to me or the love of God so fully illustrated and made to partake of which in a more large degree extended not only to his obedient children but the rebellious and that not to them present barely but as wide as his creation did the canopy or banner of God's love seem to spread itself, so that when my mouth was opened could say of a Truth and from right understanding that he was love and that universally towards his creation.

Next day had another with the people of the town to which great numbers came and behaved with uncommon attention and sobriety. This meeting also turned out to our satisfaction. That night rode to Gainsborough, that next day had a large but exercising meeting. The people behaved very unbecoming such an occasion. 23rd. Rode to Warnfroth [Warmsworth?] in Yorkshire on the 25th. Being the first day and a general meeting we attended it in which my companion had good service. 27th. Set out for the city of York where was to be held the quarterly meeting. Lodged at Fenny-Bridge at an inn and next day dined at Tadcaster where we met our Friend John Haslam[32] and divers other Friends. 28th. It began and held for two days in which meetings Truth favoured through the course of our exercise. And as we had travelled hard to reach this meeting judged it proper to stay to rest ourselves and horses and attended their meetings as they came in course.

4th of the 5th month [July]. Set out for Leeds. Stopped at Tadcaster to see a poor Friend buried, had service at the grave. Got to Leeds that night and next day had a meeting. 6th. I

5th month

went to a meeting at Gildersome accompanied by William Longmire[33] and wife. My companion staid at Leeds. Returned that night to her again. 7th. Went to their weekday meeting which was a comfortable one and also two on first day in which Truth favoured. 10th. We had a meeting at Rawdon in which my companion had an open time much to the satisfaction of Friends. Lodged at our dear Friend William Hind's who with his family are such as cheerfully entertain their Friends having heart and house always open to them. 12th. I left my companion and went to a meeting at Bradford accompanied by my Friends above mentioned which after some travail of soul turned out well. Returned the same night to my companion and staid until the 13th when we went to Highley and had a meeting in which my companion had the service. 14th went to Lotherdale and had a poor hard meeting. 15th went to Skipton, lodged at David Hall's. 16th had a meeting in which my companion had acceptable service but I was silent save in prayer. 17th had a meeting at Airton which proved an open good meeting and as I sat amongst them had livingly revived in my mind that the Lord would bless his seed in that place and if those few Friends kept faithful he would add to their number. May the Lord grant it may be so.

19th. Had a meeting at Settle wherein that good hand appeared which upholds all who singly put their trust in him and though he is at times pleased to prove with poverty yet he again visits with the smiles of his countenance and at those times when we appear in our own eyes all weakness he enables to discharge our duty beyond what we have reason to expect. 20th. Went to Bentham and on the 21st had an extraordinary meeting which was as a cordial to my poor soul which had had a time of fast. Here we met with our Friend J. Griffith[34] from America and sundry other Friends from Kendal with whom we rejoiced in spirit in a fresh sense of Divine love. 22nd. Went to Kendal, lodged at our worthy Friends', John Wilson who was a nursing father to me, and a man of quick discerning and sound judgement, sincere and steady in his friendships, seemed always to rejoice when Truth favoured, let who would be employed in its cause, and though there was but few better qualified than he, yet as few clearer of self concern or a spirit that seeks lordship over the flock over which he was a faithful overseer. 23rd being first day had a large meeting in which the power of truth was eminently known amongst us to the melting and cementing of divers of our hearts, who were met. 25th. Had one appointed for us in which the states of many were laid open and things so clearly spoke to that our said Friend stood up and declared his surprise thereat and exhorted them who were in the practice of those things we had to testify against might thenceforward forsake the evil of their ways. Observed to them that we had been amongst them, huntswomen who had hunted them out of their dens and pits, with sundry useful observations upon that and other heads. 26th. Went to Grayrigg and had a meeting.

PLACES ELIZABETH HUDSON VISITED IN SCOTLAND AND NORTHERN ENGLAND

THE JOURNAL OF ELIZABETH HUDSON

PART III

The 27th, I parted from my dear companion and set my face towards Scotland, having drawings to visit those parts and my companion not finding any necessity on her mind to undertake such a tedious journey cheerfully gave me up to go without her, and a sober young woman, daughter to Thomas Rebanks, gave up to go with me and proved a very agreeable companion in all respects and thoroughly helpful, although she had no publick testimony to bear. Got to Shap that night and 28th, had a meeting at Strictland where I met Deborah Layton who was returning home from a religious visit into Cumberland and her company was acceptable to me. Lodged at a son's of Rowland Wilson[35] who had formerly visited America. I was led to speak to divers states and think truth favoured. 29th. Went to Alston [Aldston] Moor 16 long miles and bad road. 30th. Had two meetings both satisfactory. Was led to speak to the low and dejected a word of comfort. From Shap was drawn to write my companion the following letter—

Shap, the 28th of 5th mo. [July]

My Dear Companion ,

Although the time of our absence is yet but short and nothing happened so extraordinary to furnish the matter sufficient to compose a letter off to a common Friend, yet to one I hold so dear in the strictest bond of friendship cannot be at any loss for matter. And though it might appear trivial to one less dear, and not worth the acceptance of, yet flatter myself from our united friendship that almost anything from me will be acceptable to thee——

Therefore will tell thee that after we parted I found a strong struggle betwixt my affection to thee and duty to my master and for some [time] did not know which would get the mastery. As for philosophy, if I am master of any point of it at this juncture, affords no weapon powerful enough to subdue me to right reason or calm a mind involved with a tumult of jarring passions, nothing less than religion itself has such healing virtue in it, or could anything short of its powerful influence support me in my present situation, the prospect of service before me and thoughts of leaving thee, afford afflicting ideas, but oh the power of religion reflects such strength of argument that nothing can withstand it or oppose its decree, by it I find all passions of the mind subdued and made subject to the divine will, to act according to its appointment, in which passive state hard things are made easy and bitter things sweet. I never told thee half the distress of my mind on account of this journey but may now tell thee which do with pleasure that I am now made easy and hope it may turn out well though am far from thinking that all my exercises are at an end but hope that I shall be supported through them all, which is all I ask and I shall be content with my life, for a prey which hope will be granted by him who has the Treasure of wisdom and life in his disposal—I now beg thy care of thyself and that thou by no means hurry beyond thy strength, and observe I pray my parting request, not to leave me I plainly see shall not exceed three weeks in Scotland and as those meetings in Cumberland, do not

see them at present, but if it is the will of heaven I return shall timely let thee know my mind. Am thine
always in great affection. Eliza Hudson.

At Alston I met with our Friend Daniel Stanton,[36] my
countryman and fellow citizen who was on a religious visit to
these parts and we rejoiced in each other's company. Went
to Cornwood, seven long miles through boggy roads and had   *6th month*
a memorable meeting. (1st of 6th month.) I had many things
to speak to especially to such as had been enlightened, warning them to keep near to that which had been revealed to
them in the day of visitation. And went to Allendale and
had a meeting in which the power of Truth was revealed
amongst us to the highest degree I ever knew it and in which
my soul magnified the Lord and gave him the praise of his
own works. That night went to Hackforth [Hackford] upon
the Tyne and lodged at an inn. Next day rode fifty long miles
to Alwick and the next day had a large satisfactory meeting
mostly made up of them who were not Friends. I was let to   *Acts 10:25*
mention that meeting which the Apostle Peter had at the
house of Cornelius. 5th. Went forty miles to Kelso, the first
town in Scotland, and the next day had two meetings one
with Friends, the other with the people of other professions
which was very large. Next day rode thirty miles to Ormiston
to a Friend's house and lodged with them that night and next
day reached Edinburgh. 9th. Had a poor small meeting. 10th.
Set out for the north, crossed the ferry at Kinghorn, four miles.
The wind was very high and an extreme high sea rendered
our passage very dangerous and the more so as we were in an
open boat with a crowd of horses. I think fourteen or more
who were very unruly and several times by the violent tossing of the boat fell down to one side and with difficulty were
got up again. I believe the stoutest sailor aboard was struck
with fear. I am assured their faces gathered paleness and to

me it was a trying time for had not only my own life in danger but the two Friends, my companion and guide who were there altogether on my account which occasioned me great exercise and self examination when could honestly appeal to God that it was his honour and the good of souls I had most and indeed only in view in undertaking the present journey and to him did I humbly look for help in this my sore trial of flesh and spirit and in his abundant mercy he was pleased to afford it in the needful time and conducted us safe through the tossing waves of a troubled sea and preserved us from showing any unbecoming diffidence of that power whom the winds and seas obey —— The following I wrote to my companion, though had not answer to the former one, dated from Alston, the 30th of 5th mo. [July], 1749

My dear companion,

I have through mercy got this far on the long tedious journey that is before me and found some part of the way bad beyond conception of those that have never seen them and they tell me the ways are worse that I have yet to go. But as I do not believe these reports it gives me no concern. And should it prove so is not that good hand that has hitherto been with me the same today, yesterday, and forever, and did not I find that hand near for my support should fail in the present undertaking for indeed the weight of the work lies heavy upon my spirits. Am at this time ready to sink under it but as it's just before meeting perhaps it may be the effects of that exercise —— Since the above have been at two meetings, the first greatly to satisfaction, the latter in heavy silence. I believe the people's expectations were too much outward by reason of the favour of the morning, but it pleased the Lord to shut up the gospel treasures and then no man can open, and I find great peace in waiting on the Divine Will to be just what my master dictates I should be. Towards the close of the latter meeting unexpectedly came in Daniel Stanton who is to have a meeting here tomorrow and proposes going from hence to Penrith so on through Westmoreland to Kendal where he hopes to see thee as it's greatly his desire. Have had an opportunity of seeing and hearing Sally Smith but as I am so much pleased with Ellen's company do not repent missing Sally. Had it suited her to have travelled with me I am sure she could have been more agreeable but more of my opinion when I see thee. Pray tell Nelly's parents I am much indebted to them for their daughter's company and hope her going with me will not prove of any disadvantage to her. We are at a very agreeable Friend's house, one John Reays[37] who with his wife are quite kind. They send their love to thee and with many other Friends hereaway would have been glad to have seen thee but really the roads are so bad I think thou could not bear the fatigue of the journey hither. If there comes any letters to hand for me, thou may open them and let me know the substance of what is material therein and keep the originals until we meet. Let me know if thou heard from Elias, and if our letters got there safe, which shall be glad to hear. I once more beg thy care of thyself, keep thyself from too great, great hurry of spirits as I know thou cannot bear it. If D. W.[38] goes with thee perhaps she may use endeavours to urge thy travelling faster than is tolerable for thee to do but I know of no necessity thou art under to mind anybody in that respect. D. Stanton gives his dear love to thee in great degree. Whereof I conclude thy affectionate companion—Eliza Hudson.

The following is a copy of a letter from my companion in answer to the one I wrote her from Shap——

Dear Child—

Kendal, 1st day 6th mo.
[August] 1749

Thy favour of the 28th came to me which was acceptable and I am truly glad to hear thou are easy in the present undertaking. May Divine Providence protect and keep thee to the end of this journey. Be not anxious about me who am in the midst of Friends whose kindness is beyond expectation though the want of thy company makes everything insipid. If good providence had not interposed yesterday and favoured, the enemy would have got the better and overthrown me for I could get no sleep from the time thou left me until last night when I had the company of good Grace Chambers[39] whose husband gave her up to stay with me until today when this afternoon I intend to their house to be at their meeting next fourth day—Thee may judge the situation of my mind by my writing, there being no connection or sense in what I write—the only thing I ask is that God may bless thy soul with solid peace and crown thy labour with success that when thee and I meet it may be to our mutual comfort. But why do I thus beg when by experience find that disappointment is my lot and I must endeavour to resign unto that hand which knows but how to order all things. I thought to be left alone was hard and more than I could bear but yet if its the Divine will, with patience must submit. Intend to stay here till after the general meeting next third day week and then into Lancastershire and so on. I don't know where, like a poor lonely traveller, yet hope my great master will not suffer me to sink lower than is necessary. For my good, thee may see, I give thee up to do what is required of thee. Take care of thyself and write often to me. Grace Chambers has her love to thee and companion as is mine. In which I conclude thy affectionate Friend etc., Jane Hoskins.

I being greatly affected at this moving letter which filled me with fears lest she should do otherwise than well, and induced me again to try the fleece when found it most to make for peace to proceed and wrote the following answer.

> Edinburgh, the 8th of 6th month
> [August] 1749

My Dear Companion,

Thy dear letter of the 1st of 6th month came by the hand of Friend Miller. But thy account of taking my absence so hard distressed my very soul and has unfitted me for service and almost for anything for I do not think can write intelligible. But it's thee who knows what absence is from those who are dear in the best degree of friendship. I think I have all the aggravating circumstances that can combine together to weaken my resolution to go forward. The thought of leaving the best of companions and she mourning my absence and all the enjoyments of life rendered insipid; this comes nearer than the trouble of parting with thee. Were thou more easy and indifferent about me I could have reasoned myself into easy thoughts of absence, having thought a strong argument to weaken those bonds of affection, which, now I find thou in proportion to my love loves me, are too strong to render parting from thee as easy as my better judgment dictates. Since I left thee have through mercy been favoured in meetings, especially the border meetings in which Truth was pleased to own me and supported me through the exercises that fell to my lot, that at Kelso was a proving meeting yet favoured to go through. There's some the Lord has a regard to an especial manner with whom he is striving but oh the cross is their rock of offense and stone of stumbling. I was led to speak in a particular manner of the effects of the love of God to Christian fellowship and what the true union of soul consisted in. They appointed one for the people of the town to which they came in crowds and indeed the sight of them bowed my very soul and the more because I found myself very poor and no prospect appeared of having anything to say to answer the expectations of the people, who are hungering after words and quite at a loss in time of silence, being stranger to that blesssed principle of an instructor within. I think I was never more tried since I knew what the ministry was, and what increased my concern was least the anxious desires of the people should have that influence upon me to draw me forth in words without the qualification, but as waited in true singleness I hope a right spring opened and the people gave great attention.

I found the journeys at the meetings were laid out very hard, yet accomplished them all save yesterday's journey from Kelso to this city which we fell short of eight miles by reason of our guide's horse failing, so that I have no meeting here today but rest ourselves and horses which by no means is amiss, though tedious for want of thy agreeable company and I conscious that every day's rest is keeping just that day longer from thee who is dearer to me than any other temporal enjoyment. I propose hurrying as fast is advisable through this nation and as for Cumberland, I hope my good master don't require my doing nature such violence as to continue long from thee, so that as soon as this comes to hand pray write and let me know where I may meet with thee. Direct for me at Carlisle where I hope to be this day three weeks or sooner if possible. As for roads and entertainment, I can do mighty well with them and for the more material point when the Lord helpeth my infirmity, can do well also though without him can do nothing to any good purpose. I am but just got here and what with one thing and what with another I do not write fit to be seen so beg thou'd not let this be seen but it may light thy pipe over which thou may amuse thyself with the most pleasing thought thou canst muster up such as that thy bairn [child], using the north dialect, is well and that a few weeks will bring her to thee when thy leisure hours will be filled up with repetitions of one odd occurrence or other that has fell under her notice. Until when with entreaties thou not leave me, I rest thy very affectionate companion.

Eliza Hudson

Nelly is very good company and does bravely. Pray take care of thyself.

After taking some small refreshment road to Coupar:Fife. Lodged at an inn. Next day got to Henry Nippers and next day reached Urey, the ancient seat of the Barclay family, and had a hard meeting and next day road to Kingskettle. 15th. Had a comfortable meeting in her house at which was a daughter of our governor Gordon[40] and divers others who seemed tender spirited. 16th. Went back to Aberdeen and had a pretty thorough meeting, very large, chiefly other societies who were after some time brought down and subjected to the power of truth. Next day went to old Meldrum and had a very comfortable meeting though I did not find it my duty to speak save in prayer in the forepart of the meeting. And finding the time drew near of their six weeks meeting, consented to stay to it which was held the 20th at Inverurie where met a large company of Friends and others and it by the great condescension of our Great Lord proved a solid, lively refreshing season. My soul was made truly glad in the house of prayer and became truly humbled under the mollifying virtue of the word. That night we went back to Aberdeen and next day got to Stonehaven and had a hard meeting at a Friend's house, after which we rode to Urey and was kindly received by Robert Barclay, the grandson of old Robert Barclay who wrote that excellent treatise called his Apology. 23rd. Got to Henry Nipper's and lodged there that night and the next day reached Richard Holding's. Lodged that night and the next day went to Perth and lodged at Allen Christy's. 26th. Rode to Edinburgh which proved a hard day's journey and by reason of great delay at Queens Ferry occasioned by the boat man's taking in many cattle which not only very much incommoded us but rendered it somewhat dangerous, especially if they proved unruly as was to be feared, and perhaps had been the case had not that good hand which is ever full of blessings been reached forth to our help and conducted us safe over the water in which time my mind was greatly humbled under the renewed sense of the mercies of God being so often extended towards me what was not worthy of the least of them, which drew tears of reverent thankfulness from my eyes, and in the fullness of humility I at that awful time lifted up my soul in sweet meditation upon the outward creation of God, and blessed with all the powers of it, the great creator of all things.

Ps. 122:1

It was drawing to sunset when we got ashore and had six miles of bad roads to go to Edinburgh, so that it was within night by then we got half way, so had to ride the rest of the way in the night which was very tedious as we were strangers to it and by reason of the darkness of the night could not pick our way or go faster than our horses could walk, which brought us a good way within night by then we got to the city gates which are always shut at ten o'clock, when a great gun fires from the castle and then the inhabitants of the city think themselves at liberty to fling out of their windows all the filth that they have contracted the preceding day of what kind soever which poured down without mercy upon the heads of every unhappy stranger who has not learned the meaning of "Hold your hand" which all who pass through their streets had need call out with an audible voice.

Both myself and companion were terrified at the thought of our being necessitated to run this disagreeable gauntlet which looked likely would be our lot, for when we entered the gates our guide asked us where we'd go. We told him where our lodgings was, but had forgot the street and could not direct him to it and he being a stranger both to the Friend and in the city knew not where to take us but thought it best to take us to some inn and inquired for one and we were directed to one not far off to which we went and found it was past nine which served to increase our fears. We called for our landlady and asked if she knew the Friend where we lodged. She answered no nor did she own to the knowledge of any Friend, but let us understand we might have lodgings at her house, but a dark cloud came over me by which concluded it was not meet we should accept her offer, or had I freedom to let her know we would not, so that I was mightily straightened indeed and for some time could not resolve what course to take, as we were situated, but I looked to him who had oft been my helper and from whom I then received help.

I rung a bell and a man servant came up. I told him to bring us half a pint of wine which he did and then took an opportunity to ask him if he knew George Miller[41] or any other Quaker. He told us he knew Mr. Arisekin, the brewer. I asked him if he'd go with us there. He said he could not. I then desired he'd procure me some one that would carry a few lines to him, upon which he went downstairs, for we were shown up to a little private room that would not accommodate above two, and he soon sent us up a boy who said he would take a letter, so I wrote a few lines letting him know at what a loss we were and begged he'd either come to us or send somebody else for that we knew not where we were or in what sort of hands—and what greatly aggravated my distress was that when this boy opened the door to go out, I see divers others of these little rooms with men and women in them in such positions as give me an insight what sort of house we were in, and also of the necessity of our departure. The boy soon returned with a servant of Friend Arisekin's, with a lantern to light us to our lodgings which was not above two stone's throw of the house where we were. But our joy at entering under a roof where we could repose our weary limbs with safety is more fully felt than described. We were kindly received by our landlady who was all of the family who was up and just as we entered the clock struck ten. I took care to reward the faithful messenger, and forgot not an offering of my feeble prayer to him that is supremely good.

The next day being first day had two large good satisfactory refreshing meetings, the wing of Sovereign power being spread over that assembly to the melting of many hearts. 28th. Spent the day in visiting what few Friends are left in that city, in one of which families were on a visit one of Charles Ormston's daughters who I had seen at her father's, and had found my spirit nearly united to her both when absent as well as present when we outwardly conversed. I was made very sensible of her spiritual state and the strong struggle between nature and her heavenly monitor which some time after we parted I in a letter signified to her, and under somewhat of Divine authority warned her to obedience, to which she returned me the following answer————

My Dear Friend,

As thou was so kind as to mention in thy letter to my father that thou would be pleased to hear from me, now write a few lines with pleasure for a correspondence with thee would be highly acceptable to me, though I can't expect to be often favoured with letters from thee as things of a much high nature take up thy time and attention than to answer letters of common friendship, yet hope when thou can conveniently let me hear from thee thou wilt favour with a letter for assure thee it will always give me sensible pleasure to hear of thy welfare— My dear Friend I am much obliged to thee for thy good advice and kind wishes for me. May I be so happy as to mind it, but young people in Scotland are at a very great loss as there is but a few of our society in this county our conversation is too much amongst those that are not Friends.

29th. Took a Friendly leave of my Friends in Edinburgh and set out for Kelso which we reached that night and spent an agreeable evening at our kind Friend Charles Ormston's with divers other Friends. 30th. Got twelve miles on our journey towards Mayside. Lodged at an inn. This was one of the [most] unpleasant days journey I had in all my journeyings Northward. 1st of 7th month [September] reached it. 2nd. Had a meeting, not very lively. 3rd went to Sickside. 4th. Had a meeting at that place in the forepart of the day to solid satisfaction, after which rode through a very violent storm of wind and rain to Carlisle and had an extraordinary meeting in that divine goodness was pleased in a plentiful manner to pour down of his Heavenly Rain to the solid refreshment of my poor soul and comfort of divers of his people present — Here I missed my way by gratifying my own will, I having parted from my companion in great nearness of spirit which absence rather increased, grew impatient to see her, and being by a letter from her informed that she intended shortly to leave the North, too precipitately concluded to return to her to Kendal and leave all those meeting in Cumberland which had not visited, and in a day rode from Carlisle to Kendal where I found my companion ready to set out on the morrow, when fatigued as I was, I attended her the next day to Crook general meeting which was large and to many a com-

7th month

fortable meeting, but for my own part was much shut up and left by the divine presence. And that satisfaction which was wont to be betwixt my companion and self in our travels in each other's company grew less, which I attributed to her removal of affection to one who joined us to visit about two weeks meetings, who did me great unkindness, of whom I may say as the Apostle said respecting Alexander the coppersmith. During which time I suffered greatly both in meetings and out of meetings, so that my distress was often inexpressable, yet sunk not deep enough under the baptism of the judgments of the Lord who thus pleaded with me in order to convince me that obedience was better than any sacrifice, where I might have been instructed by the unerring oracle, not only what was the cause of his sending forth the cloud which spread over my tabernacle, but what would have prevailed with him to remove it, but instead thereof pursued the track laid out by my companion and left that truth [which] would have opened more clear had I kept a single eye to it. The inducement of my hinting any part of those unpleasant hours I spent with my companion, which till after this time were as few as I believe ever any had who travelled so long together as we did, is to incite if this ever should fall into the hands of others in like circumstances to a single eye to the Divine leader, not suffering our affections to any companion whatsoever to bias our enlightened judgments and draw us from pursuing that track truth directs us to follow, for tis not always consistent with the Divine will to indulge us in the choice of our helpmeets in this day more than in the Apostle's when the voice of the Spirit was "Separate, Barnabas and Saul for the work's sake whereunto I have appointed them," and I have reason to believe it would have been best for us to have parted, when the spirit parted us, for although we did not differ outwardly so as to have many words, yet I never after found our spirits united in gos-

2 Tim. 4:14

Acts 13:2

pel labour as had ever before subsisted, which made us truly dear to each other and helpmeets indeed. And I was in hopes it would have revived again, especially when the Friend parted from us who I thought the principle impediment to our fellowship as formerly, but this I leave and only say, I had a bitter cup to drink during her being with us, for although twas with me as I have hinted, I dearly loved my companion and could not properly bear the thoughts of parting personally, so kept on travelling and suffering in spirit which I kept to myself pretty much save what my countenance betrayed on which I believe deep sorrow was imprinted. From Crook we went to Hawkshead and had a dull meeting, and next day to Height meeting. 9th of 7th to Swarthmore Hall and had a meeting in which my companion had good service. 10th. Set out and got to Lancaster. 11th had two meetings. 12th went to William Backhouse's.[42] 14th had a meeting at Yealon to pretty good satisfaction though the cloud still over my tabernacle. 17th had two meetings and on the 18th set out for Liverpool. Got that night to Garstang accompanied by William Backhouse and Lidia Lancaster.[43] Here we lost our, to me, disagreeable companion who set out the next day with L.L. for London and my companion and I toward Preston where we had a meeting on the 19th in the which it pleased the Lord to renew his ancient kindness to my poor soul, who had sought him with many tears, which somewhat encouraged me to go forward though not quite clear of Cumberland. 20th. Had a meeting at Langtree which proved a close yet thorough good meeting. We were both led to speak home to those who had known the truth and had fell from it and to divers other states as they opened to us. 21st. Had a meeting at Ashton in which was hard work but favoured to divide the word. There was a word of consolation to the heavy hearted in Zion, encouragement for them who were seeking the right way of the Lord, as well as reproof for the backsliders in Israel. 22nd to Bickerstaffe and had a meeting in which close doctrine was preached for some who obeyed not the Truth, also it was sealed upon our spirits that the power of truth was at work and the anointing oil was near being poured on the heads of those whose outward appearance concealed it from those who look with an outward eye only. 23rd. Got to Liverpool where we had on first day two pretty good meetings. 25th. Set out for Penketh and on the 26th had a meeting at which was our Friend Samuel Fothergill.[44] That evening we went to Warrington and had a meeting which was large and my companion had an open time, I hope to service. As for me I set all the meeting in the depths of poverty. 28th. Went to Frandly, had a pretty satisfactory meeting. 29th to Morley where my companion had an extraordinary open opportunity but I was deeply dipped into suffering which often fell to my lot. 30th. Went to Manchester when on the first of eighth month [October] being first day we had two meetings, the morning meeting, dull and heavy but the afternoon proved better, the God and father of all our mercy was pleased to favour us his poor dependent children with a fresh supply of bread from his heavenly table and give us to hand forth; even the cup of consolation was not withheld. Oh how precious is the presence of the Lord in the eyes of his servants after times of desertion in which he has hid his mercy from us and as it were sealed up his blessings; these although painful yet are profitable dispensations as they tend to the reducement of the creature which is too apt to glory and deck itself in those jewels the Lord at times lends his ministers to dignify his testimony he gives them to bear with, which are never to be esteemed our own riches or ornaments to be put on at our pleasure, when we may think a proper time to appear most excellent to the people, but to be put on when he the owner thinks meet and likewise put off at his pleasure who hath not as yet seen meet to bind these his jewels so fast

8th month

upon us that they are not to come off at any time, but there is appointed to us times of unclothing when every excellency and spiritual ornament is taken off and lain up in the great treasure house, when our own vileness and nakedness appears not only to us poor stripped deserted soldiers of the Lord but perhaps all men who know not the hand of the Lord is in it & that for good, and that in his due appointed time when all that is of the creature is fully slain with all creaturely willings and turnings, and true subjection to the divine will in all things witnessed, that then the Lord will again arise for our help to unlock his Treasure house and hand forth the precious jewels that heretofore he thought good to intrust us with.

4th of 8th. Went to their weekday meetings both silent and in the evening had a good meeting at our lodgings in which was given us to see the Lord was at work in the hearts of the youth and I had to believe there was some of that house that would receive the anointing to the ministry if they kept faithful to the openings of life. 8th being first day there was of course two meetings to which my companion went, but my indisposition kept me at my lodgings in the morning which was what some thought providential as things turned out afterwards for Friend Hoskins was led in a particular manner to speak to them of that meeting which I heard nothing of until after the afternoon meeting when some Friends said it was well I was not at the meeting in the morning or they thought I should not have gone on so freely in the same line of doctrine as my companion had in the morning, great part whereof was word for word. She began "oh how is the fine gold changed" etc., so went on with a warning to the dead professors and in the afternoon I got up under great exercise of soul on the same account. I began, "And in that day seven women shall take hold of the skirts of one man saying we will eat our own bread and wear our own ap-

Lam. 4:1

188

parel but will be called by thy name to hide our reproach."
Next day we had a meeting at Stockport which was but small
yet Truth favoured the small handful. 11th. Had a meeting
at Mackelsfield. There was a variety of states spoke to in that
meeting. I was led in a particular manner to speak to some
one who had in their youth been visited but through un-
faithfulness had lost a good state and had committed great
abominations when a person got up and showed great uneasiness and seemed as if he would have gone out of meeting
but turned back, sat down and showed some disorder as if
greatly effected. After meeting the Friend where we lodged
came to me and said he was very sorry we had been at his
home for I was led so pertinently to speak to that man's state
who had behaved as I have mentioned that he feared he'd
say I had been told all that he had ever done, but glad I so
solemnly declared I had received no human intelligence concerning any one's state in that meeting which was a great
truth, and that person had so long declined meeting, that
the Friends did not expect him there if they had been disposed to tell his case. 12th. Rode to Middlewich and next day
had a meeting in which my companion had the principal
service which was satisfactory to Friends in general, but it
pleased the master of our assemblies to reduce me very low in
this meeting and give me to taste true poverty of spirit as also
at the close of it the promised blessing to the poor in Spirit.
15th. Had a meeting at Nantwich which was very large of
other people there being few Friends in that place, yet it
pleased the fountain of eternal goodness to favour us with
his living presence, which was blessedly known to the humbling of our hearts under a sense of his continued mercies to
us his poor handmaids. 16th. Rode to Chester. 17th had a
meeting which proved but dull and heavy. 18th. Had a meeting at Newtown in which was close work yet Truth favoured
us to discharge ourselves of that burden that lay upon our

Isa. 4:1

Matt. 5:3

minds to satisfaction. 22nd of 8th month had meeting at Morley in which my companion had good service and I believe it was to general satisfaction and edification of many who were not Friends. 20th. Went to Manchester again and next went to a meeting appointed for Edith Flower[45] in which truth favoured me. 26th. There was a marriage which we attended as also our Friend Samuel Fothergill. Stayed their first day meetings, and on the 3rd of 9th month [November] set out for Halifax and next day had two meetings which were large and the God and Father of all our comforts was pleased richly to favour by opening the Gospel Treasures and giving plentiful help to minister the word in its own power and authority to the subduing many hearts and begetting in us the voice of humble thanksgiving and praise. 6th. Went to Bradford and next day had meeting. Next day went to William Hind's and had a meeting at Rawdon to satisfaction. 12th I left my companion and went to Brighouse to their weekday meeting in which I found hard work, yet gracious help ariseth at times when we honestly lean to it in those pinching times which enabled me to get through—

9th month

14th. Went to Farefield where had though small yet comfortable meeting, the enlivening presence of almighty God being felt amongst us to the uniting of the hearts of the faithful. 15th had a good meeting at Netherdale. 16th to Aysgarth where had a small hard meeting yet not forsaken by the good hand who is pleased to remember the very dust of Zion and feed her poor with bread — 17th. Went back to my companion at Rawdon who I found in good health and my own soul in the enjoyment of sweet peace which is the crown of all our labours, whether great or small, and as I was sitting retiredly commemorating the mercies of God to my soul throughout those various dispensations in his wisdom he had visited me under, there arose an assent in my heart which at that time breathed forth the same language with

Addison, which I think not amiss to insert here.

1.   When all thy mercies, oh my God
      My rising soul surveys,
      Transported with the view I'm lost
      In wonder, love & praise

2.   Oh how shall words with equal warmth
      The gratitude declare
      That glows within my ravished heart
      But thou canst read it there.

3.   Thy providence my life sustained
      And all my wants redressed
      When in the silent womb I lay
      And hung upon the breast.

4.   To all my weak complaints and cries
      Thy mercy lent an ear
      Ere yet my feeble thought had learned
      To form themselves in prayer.

5.   Unnumbered comforts to my soul
      Thy tender care bestows
      Before my infant heart conceived
      From whom those comforts flowed.

6.   When in the slippery paths of youth
      With heedless steps I ran
      Thin arm unseen conveyed me safe
      And led me up to man.

7.   Through hidden dangers toils and death
      It gently cleared my way
      And through the pleasing paths of vice
      More to be feared than they.

8. When worm with sickness oft has thou
    With health renewed my face
    And when in sins and sorrow sunk
    Revived my soul with grace.

9. Thy bounteous hand with worldly bliss
    Has made my cup run oe'r
    And in a kind and faithful friend
    Has doubled all my store.

10. Ten thousand thousand precious gifts
    My daily thanks employ
    Nor is the least a cheerful heart
    To taste those gifts with joy.

11. Through every period of my life
    Thy goodness I'll pursue
    And after death in distant worlds
    The glorious theme renew.

12. When nature fails and day and night
    Divide thy work no more
    My ever grateful heart oh Lord
    Thy mercy shall adore.

13. Through all eternity to thee
    A joyful song I'll raise
    For oh eternity, too short
    To utter all thy praise.

THE JOURNAL OF ELIZABETH HUDSON

PART IV

We staid at our kind Friends William Hind's until the 19th when went to Bradford and had a meeting in which my companion had good service. 24th. Went to a meeting at same place appointed for Gerrard Hasson[46] of Ireland after which I set out for Leeds in order to proceed on my journey through the county of Durham, it not suiting my companion to travel in such bad weather being under some indisposition of body, so I left her at Benjamin Bartlet's in Bradford, and next day being first day had two meetings and the company of Daniel Stanton which proved two good meetings, and the same writ the underneath to my companion and received the following answer:

Leeds 25th of 9th month [November] 1749
My dear Friend,
    As I doubt not it giving thee pleasure to hear I got well here, thought proper just to hint as much though greatly cramped for time. The ways were extremely bad which kept us until evening on our way hither, where I met our dear countryman Daniel Stanton who sends his love to thee and Edmund Peckover with a request thou'd send his letter which I forgot to bring. He is favoured with health as is all our good Friends in this place, save Friend Horner who joins me in dear love to thee. I am sorry have to acquaint with the death of little Penn Barrow, which has filled the family with tears, and that dear Christy Hind cannot, though her will is good,

go with me, I had not freedom to urge much so am likely to go alone as to mortals. I must conclude which, so thy affectionate companion. E. H.

Bradford, the 25th of
9th mo. [Nov.] 1749.

Dear Child,

It was with pleasure I received thy favour and was glad you got well to Leeds though I understand thy horse was smooth shod which rendered it dangerous travelling. I beg thou wilt get him better done before thou sets out on thy journey for fear by his slipping thou shall receive hurt. Take good care of thyself and don't ride long journeys nor into the night. Consider it is now short days and bad weather. Let me hear often from thee and where I shall direct. Let not thy mind be over anxious about me but do thy master's business thoroughly that when we meet it may be to mutual comfort. May the good hand of divine providence be thy support to attend thee in all thy engagements in behalf of the great and good cause. Think on me when Truth favours thy soul. I am well and left amongst kind Friends—After thou was gone I thought it might not be improper to signify in writing unto Friends the true cause of our parting which I communicated to Edmund with which he was pleased and said it might have its service. I got him to copy it and have set my name to it. However whether there may be need for it or not in this journey, it may prove of use in case I die before we meet when thou gets home. I hope thou will not look on it with disrespect, if so light thy pipe with it and there it ends. Give my dear love to Friends, as if named and accept a large share from thy affectionate companion, Jane Hoskins.

I was deeply affected at the receipt of this kind letter to which I wrote an answer but have lost it with sundry others that passed between us in our several partings. The following is a copy of the certificate above mentioned.—

To all Friends into whose hands these may come, greetings.

Dear Friends, as I am incapable of travelling much this winter season and as my dear and worthy companion, Elizabeth Hudson, the bearer hereof, hath a concern on her mind to visit several places where we have not yet been, these may inform you that we have parted from each other for a small time for the work's sake in the unity of that Blessed Spirit and power which is the strength and preservation of all those who are truly engaged in the Lord's service. So desiring this good hand of providence may go along with and support her and bring her back safe to me again with the salutation of dear love I remain your sister in the unchangeable truth.

Jane Hoskins

Bradford, 25th of 9th mo. [Nov.] 1749

28th. Set out for Knaresborough. 29. Had a meeting to which came many that were not of our society. Some of them what the world calls persons of rank. The meeting I hope was well. I thought the Lord owned the testimony he gave me to bear. The people behaved very solidly and gave becoming attention to what my great and good master enabled me in his name to deliver. There was one poor man walked four miles to this meeting who had been for some time under strong conviction for his past conduct who met with a cup of consolation to his refreshment, in the best sense, which he expressed in these words, that he thought the time in that meeting well spent and although his coming was attended with great difficulty by reason of the bad roads and weather being a severe and wet season with frost, yet all was abundantly made up in that he had been reached in mercy—30th Went to Masham, had a very unsettled meeting, truth appeared to me to be at a very low ebb. Had close doctrine to deliver yet through merciful help was strengthened to discharge part of that load which lay upon my spirits both before I went to meeting and in the beginning of it. 1st of 10th mo. [December] went to Leyburn and had a meeting with Friends little to the relief of my poor depressed spirits which were with the day baptized into suffering with the oppressed seed of God which is in many parts of this nation where heretofore the name of the Lord was famous and his servants in repute, greatly kept under even the rubbish of this world's trash—not finding myself clear or at all eased by the former meeting, had freedom to propose to Friends the having another more publick, which they coolly consented to as the following letter to my companion will specify—

10th month

> Leyburn 30th
> of 9th mo.
> [Nov.] 1749

My Dear Companion,

I am now at George Bickerrick's where am kindly received, got thus far on my journey well, the roads better than I expected and the meetings thus far through divine goodness pretty well. Have had two here today, the latter with the people of the town to which many came and were sober, it's not usual in this place for them to go to Friends' meetings as in some other places but it came a weighty concern upon me to have a meeting with them which I mentioned to Friends at the close of

the first meeting, but they made some objections thereto,
I queried their reasons for their not freely consenting
having a secret sense they were not of sufficient weight
to remove from me the concern I was under as indeed
they proved, being these, that the people of that town
never came to meetings, or was it usual to invite them,
they being a raw, careless people about religion. These
reasons rather served to increase my burden and I replied was that their case and they stood in more need of
help to which some replied the people would not come
if they gave notice, they being disaffected to Friends. I
was in great strait but could not be easy without desiring Friends to give the invitation as from one that came
many thousand miles to see them and requested their
company and that then I should be clear when had done
what I apprehended my duty whether they came or not.
Upon this they, though with apparent reluctance, sent
out and contrary to their expectations great crowds came
at that short notice and soon filled the house, at the
sight whereof my soul was bowed in awful reverence to
the almighty helper of his poor dependent servants,
whose power soon overshadowed the assembly and truth
spread itself greatly to the rejoicing of my poor soul
which vented itself in many tears. I by no means repent
giving up to my duty though quite in a cross to my own
will. Friends seemed mightily pleased things turned out
so well, but what shall we say, have not they lost their
authority amongst the people that truth gives to them
that are faithful in its cause and feebleness and unbelief
entered which creates such backwardness to call in their
neighbors which should not deter us from that duty truth
points out for us to fill up our measure in, I have through
this day's favour come to this result that in future when
I find an impulse to such services shall not let little

matter or trivial objections prevent my endeavours therein. Pray take care of thyself and let me hear from thee, who am thine affectionately.   Eliza

Next day set out and reached Aysgarth it being their monthly meeting was to me a poor low time. I was brought into the bottom of Jordan. 3rd. Went to Bainbridge and was at their meeting but to little satisfaction occasioned through fear that I had been too forward in appearing in testimony in which I apprehended I was left to myself more than at other times and that that life and power was wanting which alone rendered ministry truly helpful to the people. After I sat down my spirit was covered with distress even to anguish, however was favoured to prostrate myself at the feet of my master who knew if I erred it was not owing to the wickedness of my heart, but too great readiness to grasp at vision, which is no qualification to preach for there's many openings for our own instruction only, and the states of meeting revealed to us at one time when perhaps it is for another day's service and sometimes as there is sundry states in most meetings it may be that we are opened in understanding to see them, but called upon to speak but to a few that tis necessary for us to wait not only for the word of vision but word of command when, and what part of the opening is for the people, for want of so doing we often mar the service of the day and heap bitterness of soul upon ourselves and were it not that the Lord is good and great in comparison to us poor creatures we should sink under the heavy weight of self condemnation but in his abundant mercy and for the service's sake he blots out the transgressions and receives our humble acknowledgments as an atonement or trespass offering. 4th. Went to Swaledale and had a silent meeting. 5th to Richmond and had a pretty good meeting. Here I met Garret Hessons [Hasson] from Ireland and next day was at a meeting appointed for him and finding my mind drawn forth to the people had a meeting with them to satisfaction. 7th to Raby to a meeting appointed for Thomas Nicholson[47] from Car [Carolina] in which had an opportunity that discharged me from having any appointed for me. It was a good meeting. Lodged at Joseph Taylor's and was agreeably entertained. 8th. Went to Bishop Auckland. I was at their meeting which was to me a good solid though silent meeting. 10th. Went to Durham to a funeral which was a large good meeting. 11th had a meeting with Friends. 12th. Went to New Castle. 13th had a meeting. 14th to Shields and had though small a very comfortable meeting and found after it the sweet fruits of obedience to season my spirit. There was a word of consolation for the low and dejected. The subject matter that offered, art thou he that should come or look we for another. Seventh day rode to Sunderland.

Luke 7:19

17th being first day was at two meetings, both of my satisfaction. Had at the latter the company of Fanny Paxton[48] much to my comfort. 18th. Got up before day and went to a meeting at Shotton which was a small, hard meeting. 19th. Set out some hours before day in order for Stockton, having twelve long miles to ride and bad roads with snow, rain and frost made it tedious and very late before we got to meeting. The Friends had met near two hours before we got to it and was forced to sit down in all my wet clothes though not many minutes before I had to stand on my feet and had spending service which occasioned me to sweat violently that in some parts of my body what with the rain and sweat had few dry threads, yet found no bad effects from it. Was much hurt by an imprudent Friend's relating an affair in my hearing which cramped me in going through what opened on my mind lest what I had heard might in some sort influence me and cause a mixture in the testimony. I was sorry I heard anything of it and think it a great diskindness done any gospel minister for Friends where we visit to mention any of these affairs in our hearing, for it makes the service much harder when matter opens suitable to cases we have had any account of, than when we get up and go in the innocency and has more reach on the parties when we can say in truth we have had no information.

20th to Yarm to which meeting several of the town's people came, but were greatly disappointed that there was no words, for I had none given me and had been taught that silence was better than words when the Lord was not in them, and found great peace in waiting the Lord's time and for his putting forth. It was matter of wonder to them that I should come so far and say nothing. Went that night to Dornlen where had a sitting in the Friends' family and the agreeable company of that dear worthy, elder James Wilson[49] who was a nursing father indeed. Next day had a good meeting after which went to visit J. Wilson's wife who had sunk too low under some affliction they had met with in their family which he, like a faithful servant, was made willing to receive at the hand of his master without saying what doest thou thus. I admired his patient submission and was made truly near to them and they to me—

Next day went to Northallerton and had a comfortable meeting. Next day rode to Thirsk. Called by the way to see a Friend who had met with great loss by the death of most of their cattle, and should have been glad to have found in them a more patient resignation to the divine will who sees meet to take away as well as give and had I sat with them I believe there was greater trials in readiness—

24th. Had meeting at Thirsk in which was lead to treat on the subject of the fall of our first parents, also of the promise that the seed of the woman should bruise the serpent's head and he should bruise the heel and how he began with Cain by infusing the spirit of jealousy into him that as his brother's offering was more acceptable than his to the Almighty that

Gen. 3:15

therefore he would remove him out of the way and then stand chief with sundry remarks there upon —

25th. Went to York and on our way called at an inn to refresh ourselves and horses after which had proposed to set forward but found a strong drought on my mind to stay and retire in spirit in the family and after some time a pretty many people of both sexes came and sat down in the room where I and my guide sat. Some seemed of light and airy tempers and scoffingly viewed my I suppose retired manner of sitting which was novel to them, whilst all the family was extraordinary busy in getting things ready for a grand dinner, I with some of the most solid kept still. When dinner was served in, an elderly sober woman sat down at the head of the table and desired me to sit next to her and her daughter on the other side of her who kept looking at me, tittering, until her mother checked her and called out for master somebody, I forget his name, who I afterwards understood was the parson of their parish to come and say grace. But he was too busy in the next room with a noisy company to answer the woman's request of saying grace which gave her visible uneasiness and she said do some of your gentlemen, say it, tis a shame to eat without it. They all excused themselves, then she turned to my guide and said, pray one of you say grace, upon which my mouth was opened in great dread and filial fear, which brought in the parson and all his jovial companions who were very much confounded in themselves, and after I had done the friendly woman helped me first and said something in favour of the prayer which I thought disgusted the priest, for he behaved very sour and wrathful to me, but my spirits were seasoned with my master's love, and my soul filled with that true peace which casteth out all fear, was not moved thereby save to pity. I offered him my plate which he refused to take in a complacent manner, the disposition he was in considered. There was a great angle on my spirit and I thought theirs were made subject. I found mine engaged to converse with them and the subject that offered was the then present calamity amongst the horned cattle. I addressed myself to the priest saying it was a distressing time amongst the poorer inhabitants and some of whom had lost their all and queried did the distemper rage thereaway. He told me yes. This gave rise to a great deal of solid conversation which all the company gave becoming attention, so after dinner some of the company withdrew to other apartments and after they were gone the woman above mentioned told me that the occasion of their meeting to wit that whilst her dear father lived it was his custom every Christmas to invite all his children, the minister, and some of his most intimate friends to dine with him. That since his death her eldest brother who kept that inn had followed that practice and that being that day so called was the cause of their meeting and that she was glad I happened to be with them, was obliged to me for my company, etc. and after some time we parted in great nearness of spirit and I under the plentiful enjoyment of peace rode to York and was kindly received by Friends who expressed their gladness that I was preserved in health and from an accident the weather having been very bad and which had caused great floods in many places that rendered travelling dangerous as well as very difficult.

26th. The Quarterly meeting began and held three days, all of which meetings I attended being at four meetings in [which] the Lord was graciously pleased to own his own seed and raised it into dominion, blessed be his holy name forever. 29th set out and got to Bradford where I found my dear companion. 31st went to their first day meeting. 3rd of 11th month [January] to their weekday meeting. 7th being first day had a large but not open meeting. My companion not being able to travel I found freedom to stay with her until the 14th when I went to Rawden [Rawdon] to see my worthy

11th month

Friend William Hind who had taken a severe illness that his life was despaired of, the effects of a cold he took in going with us to Bradford, which greatly affected me. I found him on the recovery but very weak and low and at his request staid with them until the next day evening, when returning late on the moor between them and Bradford, being a bright moonlight night, saw a man jump out of a fur bush who seized my horse by the bridle and held him fast, looking steadily upon me. The servant I had with me being some distance before, finding I stopped stood still and saw the man, but neither of us said anything to him, but I concluding it was a robber, put my hand on my purse, but thought I'd let him demand it, so did not pull it out but looked full in his face sometime until he let the bridle go, saying, I was not the person he wanted. I was glad to get rid of him on such easy terms, so rode as fast as I could, not a little frightened.—Got to my companion about ten o'clock at night. My companion being unwell I staid with her until the 19th, then we went to Leeds to their weekday meeting. 21st being first day went to two meetings. Here we met with our dear Friend S. Spavold[50] who was on a religious visit, whom we had before met at Lincoln Quarterly Meeting. I had good unity with him, he being a humble, sweet spirited man and lived under the influence of his master's love as much as any Friend I ever knew, which made him loving to all men and enabled him to deliver the sharpest testimonies in such a manner as gave no offense even to offenders so that he had great place in the minds of all, and as I travelled after him, found he was made a useful instrument in the Lord's hand to awaken and stir up many to righteousness, and we were brought near in spirit to each other, and in meetings where we were together, jointly laboured in the gospel service, without either standing or sitting in each other's way. This meeting was not so satisfactory as could desire, poor Samuel had very hard work and I sat in such great weakness, had it not in my power to help him, for find my daily experience that without Divine aid cannot even labour or travail in spirit, though sensible of the want of labourers in the harvest, yet sometimes there's sweet peace to the soul results from those comfortable expressions of our Lord's respecting the woman: let her alone, she has done what she could.

Mark 14:6-8

Stayed their weekday's meeting and on the first day following had two large good meetings in which my companion had the principal service, yet it pleased the Father of all our mercies to give me sweet access to the throne of grace in prayer. During our stay here many that were not Friends attended meetings with whom we had divers open meetings and several were under convincement and may the Lord bless and prosper his work begun in them to their thorough conversion, saith my soul.——

23rd. Left my companion and had a meeting at Wakefield

and next day to Pomfret [Pontefract] 25th. Had one at Burton, all but poor, low meetings. Returned to Leeds that night. 26th. We went to Gildersome. The meeting was hard at first but truth arose into greater dominion. Towards the latter part of the meeting we had peace. Returned to Leeds and stayed over first day when had two meetings at one of which there was a burial and a many that were not Friends attended, and the power of truth was eminently known amongst us this day and the good cause honoured, be it spoke with praise of him who is rich in loving kindness to his people and for whose sake he is pleased at times to give his ministers access to the treasures of wisdom and life and we with them made partakers of his bounty as at the banquet of wisdom and how doth the Lord's servants rejoice when the blessed truth riseth into dominion — We finding service here found it our duty to make this long stay to attend meetings in the most of which we found service to do and it proved a time of near uniting to many with whom our spirits were refreshed and we parted in the fellowship of the gospel and in an especial manner with our dear Friend and true fellow helper in the gospel William Longmire who was one with us in our heights and depths—

Set out for York the 3rd of 12th month [February], 1750 and reached it that night, and being first day went to two meetings, rested and visited Friends until 3rd day when began their preparative and next day their monthly meeting which we attended and on the 8th I set out, leaving my companion and had a small yet comfortable meeting at Huby. 9th. Had a meeting at Thorton in the Clay which proved a deep exercising meeting but the Lord was pleased in his wonted mercy to hand forth help in the time of need and bear up my sinking spirits and gave strength to discharge what lay as weight on my mind and hope I got through well. The subject that offered was from whence come these tares. 10th went to Malton and next day had a hard meeting. 13th to

12th month

Matt. 13:24

205

Pickering where met with Gerrard Hasson and had a large, satisfactory meeting after which I rode to our dear ancient Friend's John Richardson[51] who I had seen in my native country and found that good old man alive in the blessed truth. He was very free and open to speak and tell me his experience in the Christian race and work of the ministry which was pleasingly edifying and tended to encourage me to hold on in the way of truth.

15th. Had a meeting at Hutton in the Hole when I received a letter from my companion advising me of her intention to go to London by coach so I set out before day on the morrow and got to her by noon. 18th was at two meetings at York in which my companion had good service. 3rd of 1st month [March] set out on horseback and reached Doncaster that night and next day went to Warnsworth meeting where I thought I suffered greatly through the expectations of the peoples being so much outward depending on the poor instrument which was but an empty vessel until the Lord was pleased to fill my soul with his divine goodness and gave the word of command to distribute that he thought meet for the people to have, which I honestly kept to I hope, and I trust truth did not suffer by me. During the time of silence I sat in great agony of mind, not for words to please the itching ears of those who were anxious to hear me as was silent when there before, but my spirit was deeply engaged to wrestle for the enjoyment of that power which was before words were, and it pleased divine goodness who is complete in mercy and in loving kindness exceeds expression, to visit my soul as with the day spring from on high, thus doth the Lord arise for the sincere cries of the poor and cause their cup to run over, and lips to utter his praise, who is worthy forever ——

Next day I went back to Doncaster where met my companion in the stage coach and purposed to have kept her company but found it too hard to keep up with them so parted

PLACES ELIZABETH HUDSON VISITED IN MIDDLE ENGLAND

from her at Newark and took a turn into Lincolnshire to visit a few meetings I had not before, and accidentally met with a Friend who was so kind as to accompany me to our Friend Robert Massey's[52] who had seen at Lincoln Quarterly Meeting. The next day went to Broughton and had a meeting in which the Lord was pleased measurably to own my labour, blessed be his name. Next day had a meeting at Wadington and the company of my kind Friend Richard Snasidal. I was at this meeting very unexpectedly favoured and was led to speak of my small experience in the truth and to advise against evil communications. Here all those Friends who had accompanied me from Broughton left me and the next day went to Boston and on the 12th being first day had two meetings. At the morning meeting there was a marriage which drew a large number of the town's people together, who behaved with decency and I hope the meeting was well, the afternoon meeting was appointed for me, but did not answer any extraordinary purpose. 19th went to a meeting at Leek in which had close work but being assisted by the power of truth got through the service before me with a degree of solid satisfaction. Rode that day to Wainfleet. 14th had a very good meeting. 16th was at two more, being their monthly meeting 18th being first day went to Mumby Chapel where was a marriage and a large number of people, not Friends, there being but few thereaway, here I was not favoured with so large a degree of that life and power of the Gospel as at some other times, occasioned I thought by my getting up too soon, before the life rose up to its proper height, a fault I am not often guilty of and pray I never may err on that hand, for by so doing the life is slain and the poor creature left in great poverty and distress. I could not perceive Friends thought as I did but rather concluded all was well, and as for others they behaved soberly attentive, but all this did not prove a sufficient balm to my poor depressed soul, which was deprived of that sweet peace which is the seal of our mission. I sought it with tears and great humility of spirit and sought it not in vain for it pleased my merciful father to visit me again with his life giving presence who knew the sincerity of my heart, for could appeal to him in the midst of my affliction, that the motive was his honour. But I found by experience he was not always honoured in words, though faultless, or in wilful silence which ought to be guarded against as well as voluntary preaching, God's honour, consisting in our obedience to the immediate direction or influence of his holy spirit. Then whether there be words or not, few or many, his own works praise him, and he is glorified in and by us — I was greatly bowed in spirit after this slip and led into earnest desires to be preserved in the future. Went back to Wainfleet and although the Friends were earnestly pressing with me to have a meeting with the people, and I found some drought thereto, yet was fearful of being too forward in it, but sinking deep and waiting for direction therein, found freedom to have an evening meeting and there being general notice given, abundance of the town's people came. I was brought very low in this meeting and in that state sweetly comforted, being favoured to draw nigh the place of true feeding. Here would gladly have kept and enjoyed the sweets of divine refreshment but I found it was my master's will, I should not, for he saw meet to open my mouth and in measure withdraw that solace of soul I enjoyed in silence, for was drawn out to the libertines and dead professors for whom was deeply baptized even to taste their states and deplorable conditions. The subjects that offered to view were the parable of the ten virgins, the end of silence with its several uses, the advantage of being Christ's sheep to know his voice, these follow not the voice of the stranger. I found it very hard work getting through those several subjects, but truth I have cause to hope did not suffer that night. After I sat down I could not but

Matt. 25:1

John 10: 4-5

reflect what should be the cause why my enjoyment should lessen for speaking when was convinced it was my duty —— And it was livingly brought to my remembrance how it was with our blessed saviour when he left the bosom of his father and appeared in the flesh to go through the bitter baptism of the cross, for the dead in order to redeem mankind from the power of the second death. 20th. Set out for Lincoln Quarterly Meeting where I met with Thomas Nicholson. The meeting held two days in which time, had four meetings but had not any thing to offer save once in prayer. 22nd. After meeting set out and rode nine miles on our way toward Spalding which we reached the next day and had an evening meeting with the people of the town but the cloud resting on the tabernacle kept my peace. 24th. Went to Gadney to the burial of Samuel Mason, whose corpse was carried to meeting and accompanied by a great concourse of people and the Lord was pleased in his wanted goodness to favour with his presence. May humility ever possess my soul under an awful sense of his continued mercies to me in thus vouchsaving

of his Heavenly help in times of need when destitute of every help but what cometh from him only. 25th. Went to Wisbech and had two silent meetings. In the evening went to see a sick Friend and had a time in prayer. 26th went to Chatteris, had

a small silent meeting and that evening rode to Newton. 27th. Had a pretty good meeting and that night went to an evening meeting in Hadnam [Hadham] where had a large solid good meeting, though did not find it my duty to minister to the people, who were chiefly those of other societies, yet found freedom to stand up at the close of the meeting and give them some account of the reason for not speaking to them, after inviting them to meet me in that place which perhaps had raised their expectations to hear something. I had to tell them the nature of our ministry and from whence we received, to wit from the Lord by virtue of his holy spirit influencing our understandings to behold in the light thereof the states of those we minister to and it was for these illuminations every gospel minister waited, and that I had in that meeting thus waited in order if it was the will of the Lord I might receive this qualification, which for reasons best known to himself it was withheld and therefore dared not open my mouth. Withal commended their solid deportment and hoped they would not be discouraged by my silence from attending meetings which perhaps some other might in gospel love be drawn to appoint for them for though the Lord had seen meet to keep me silent yet another might have to communicate to them and if not it was as their own fault if they benefited not by them, for they might be made seasons of profit to their souls, whereby turning the eye of the mind inward they would find a teacher near that teaches as never man taught and that it was the end and design of all our ministry to bring people to that, of inward waiting upon God and that I had to believe the Lord would be found of them if they sought him. 27th set out for Royston, got there that night. Had a meeting in a Friend's family and next day had a publick meeting in which had close work, yet the Lord was pleased to assist me in the time of great trial and was helped to get through to satisfaction. 20th. Had a hard, silent meeting at Baldock. 1st

Elizabeth Hudson

1st month

of 1st month [March, 1750] had two meetings at Hitching, appeared at one of them. Next day went to Hertford and was at two meetings, it being their quarterly meeting, were met there by our Friend John Griffith,[53] after which rode to London and 4th went to Gracious Street meeting. 5th to Devonshire House to the burial of Ann Ilyam. 6th. At Gracious Meeting. 8th to two at same place. Stayed and visited

2nd month

meetings as they came in course until the 29th of 2nd month [April] when set out with my companion accompanying me for Barking where we had a large meeting and somewhat favoured with the anointing oil. My companion returned that night to London and next day I went to Waltham Abbey where met with dear M. Peisley[54] and we joined as companions to visit a few meetings between that and the yearly meeting, it not suiting my old companion to travel, or was her concern so extensive as mine appeared to me to be which often occasioned our parting for the work's sake. Had a large meeting but I thought it but a low time and the good that sprang up amongst us crushed by a Friend's hastily breaking up the meeting at the usual time. Went that night to David Barclay's at Bushill [Bush Hill], had a meeting with the family.

3rd month

1st of 3rd month [May] Parted our dear Friend Mary Weston[55] who returned to London in order to take shipping for America on a religious visit. We went that night to Hoddesdon. 2nd. Had a very hard meeting at Ware and that evening had a good meeting at Hertford. 3rd. Had an evening meeting at Stansted with the people much to our satisfaction. Divine Goodness condescended to own us with his life giving presence. 4th. Went to Bishop Stortford and had a pretty good meeting and a comfortable sitting in a Friend's summer house, which happened somewhat particular. We were asked after dinner to walk in the garden which we consented to and it well suited the retiredness of mind I was favoured with,

212

which drew me into silence and after a turn round a pleasant walk we entered a summer house, and sat down even the two or three, as in the presence of the Lord who was pleased to draw near and appear in the midst of us and gave us a testimony to bear for him and the benefit of retirement, in which the Lord meets with his people and teaches them himself—

5th. Returned back to Stansted in order to be there on the first day, our minds not being fully clear, had that evening a meeting in the family, and on first day had two meetings when divers Friends from London and parts adjacent met us in whom our souls rejoiced in the Lord in that he in the riches of his love was pleased to favour us together and cause the gospel power to flow in upon our souls which richly attended the word preached that with reverence and deep humility we might acknowledge it was in the demonstration of his spirit and with power, it was indeed a high tide, but the Lord's doings are ever marvelous in the eyes of his servants, and living praises flow towards his throne of grace, who thus is pleased to exalt his name amongst the people — 7th. Went to Buntingford and had a meeting with the people of the town in which the Lord owned us. 8th. To Saffron Walden, got dinner and went five miles to an evening meeting which we had drawings to appoint in a town where there were no Friends, to which many sober people came and a blessed season it proved for the Lord by his spirit came down amongst us. My spirit was deeply bowed under the weight of the service which that evening fell to my lot. The matter that opened was that passage where the good old patriarch sent his son Joseph to see how his brethren fared which had to spiritualize upon, the meeting held late which occasioned our being exposed to the night air for were obliged to return that night to Saffron Walden which gave me a violent cold which held me some days, yet through mercy was not prevented from attending meetings. 9th. Was at their weekday meeting which

Gen. 37:13-14

proved but a poor meeting, yet our master favoured our souls in a family meeting. 10th. We went to Royston where we had close work. 11th to Baldock had a meeting which was but dull and silent save for a few sharp yet living expressions my companion had to drop at the close of the meeting which I thought was enough to stir up some that were at ease in Zion and trusted in the mountains of Samaria— Went that evening to Ashwell and had a baptizing time with and for the dead professors. 12th. Went to Hitchin and on the 19th had two pretty satisfactory meetings in publick and one in the Friends family where we were to our comfort and consolation. 14th. Had a meeting at Luton. 15th. Went to Pollox Hill and had a meeting where was also our dear Friend Samuel Spavold and a hard day's work we all had of it yet strength was given us to discharge our selves of the burden that lay upon our minds. Went that night and had meeting at Ampthill. 16th. Went to Hog Sty End in which Samuel had the principal service and our spirits were nearly united in our gospel labours——and though I had near unity with him it pleased the all wise disposer of all good to suffer a dark cloud to cover my tabernacle. That night rode to B. How's. 17th had a meeting at Cranfield. 18th. Went and had a meeting at Sherrington, both silent and very poor. That night to Olney and had a meeting in which Molly was divinely favoured. That night went back to Newport-Pagpell and lodged there that night and rode next day to Dunstable. 20th. Had two meetings where met us Sarah Crawley,[56] a Friend of the ministry and divers others from divers parts but it pleased the Lord to prove my poor soul with poverty and give me to see he was about to lead me into the furnace, and with what strength I had I prayed for the baptism that I might abide under it all the appointed time with patience. 21st. Went to St. Albans where was also Samuel Spavold. We had two appointed meetings in which both Molly and myself were silent to the general amazement of the people who greatly censured us for calling them together as they called it and then not preach, but what gave us greatest pain was the uneasiness those under our name showed and indeed it's cause of exercise to think that material branch of our testimony is so little understood that of worshipping in silence and in it waiting on that divine teacher which cannot be removed into a corner. I was enlightened to see in some measure into the reason why Almighty God thus proves and tries his ministers, for such it must be esteemed to be, to find it our duty to be silent and to sit in poverty with the expectation of the people fixed upon us who at other times have had to minister in that ability our master gave and perhaps was what tickled their itching ears, and experience taught me to esteem it a great blessing when could patiently submit to every dispensation of the divine will whether it was to abase or to abound, and this disposition is certainly most pleasing to him who is all seeing and therefore knows what is best both for us and the people, and what will redown most to his honour, and to be fixed in this sentiment will mightily help to quiet the mind in the times of probation for the creaturely part is apt to be restless and uneasy under disappointments of this sort and here is a foundation for the enemy to build in and where he has often prevailed upon, even honest minds to go beyond the word of the Lord and caused them to run where the Lord sent them not, to their own confusion and oh the Death one wrong step of this sort brings upon the soul and what an humbling query is this to be sounded in the ear of the soul, who hath required that at thy hand? 22nd to Hempstead and had a meeting. 24th to Chesham and where our souls was greatly proved, nigh unto death for it seemed as if the powers of death and darkness were let loose and a spirit of division reigned amongst them few Friends that compose that meeting. We had a deep suffering time whilst with them

Isa. 1:12

215

yet the arm of the Lord secretly supported us under our sufferings with his precious seed. 25th to Amersham where the
Lord has a living seed but it lies low and it requires deep
wading to minister properly to it yet we may say the Lord is
abundant in mercy to his church and ministers in visiting
and revisiting of them with his powerful presence and life by
which all that abide in it are kept living and fruitful. 27th to
Tring and had a hard difficult meeting. 28th to Avensbury
[Aylesbury] 29th at Wyecombe 30th at Chorleywood. 31st
at Jordans, all proved but low meetings and indeed great was
the poverty that clothed my spirits in these meetings and it
look as though my service was over and I was brought so low
I concluded I would go up to London and take shipping for
mine own home, but with this conclusion such a cloud of
darkness covered my tabernacle, attended with such deep
distress as proved too heavy for my tender frame to bear and
occasioned great indisposition, yet was in the midst of all my
weakness enabled to look the right way for I knew the Lord
was not slow to hear and therefore I cried to him both night
and day that he might direct my steps aright. And in his own
time he was graciously pleased to cause light to spring up and
I in an acceptable time found that saying fulfilled in me that
they that sit in darkness should see a great light and by virtue
of its blessed influence my way was opened to me as clear as
though a plan were drawn and spread before my natural eyes.
I received the intelligence with great thanksgiving and gave
up cheerfully even body and spirit as into the hand of him
who formed me and called into his vineyard.

Isa. 9:2
Matt. 4:16

THE JOURNAL OF ELIZABETH HUDSON

PART V

1st of 4th month [June] went to Uxbridge where divers Friends with vacant seats in a coach met us in order to accompany us to London, which we reached that night and here I met my old companion after her return from visiting Bristol. 3rd came on the yearly meeting. First day I went to Devonshire House in the morning and in the afternoon to Peal where it pleased the Lord to favour me in an abundant manner. 2nd day morning at a ministers' meeting and in the afternoon went to their woman's meeting. 3rd day to Park and in the afternoon to Peal. 4th day to Gracious Street, afternoon to Wapping. 5th day went to a woman's meeting held in Devonshire House, afternoon to a meeting for worship at the same place, and in the evening I went to the Park where in the forepart of the meeting a Methodist stood up and in a fiery zeal spoke not much to edification which hurt the meeting for a while, but through the extendings of immortal goodness truth arose into dominion and several of the Lord's ministers were favoured and the meeting ended well. An awful sense of the goodness of God rested on my spirits and bowed me low beneath his glorious throne. 6th day I went to Devonshire House and Peal, and on the seventh day was the parting meeting but I was not able to attend it through indisposition, having attended all those meetings in great weakness of body and for the work's sake had lived very low, not allowing myself to eat meat or drink anything but water during the course of the yearly meeting in order to keep my spirits free and lively, having sometimes found an inconvenience attend going to meetings after full

217

meals, as I also did from this too great abstinence, for by when the meeting was over I was so weak and low was obliged to keep house some few days, yet by the 14th was well enough to set out on my journey under great weight of spirit, for had no companion to bear a part with me in this so great an undertaking, it not suiting my own companion to travel on horseback or did she find a necessity upon her to visit the nation so generally as I did, she having been there once before, but was kind enough to go with me as far as Canterbury where we parted in true gospel love. She returned to London and I had two pretty good meetings amongst the few Friends there. 18th. Went to St. Margaret's in order to have a meeting with the town's people there being but one person in the town that bear at that time our name, and the Friend that was with me told me the people of this place were prejudiced against Friends for which reason none had been there to visit them for some years, which somewhat discouraged me, and made me try the fleece again when had to believe it was my duty to offer myself, so I told the Friend if he was free we would go to some inn in the town and inquire for that woman who bore our name, and we would consult her, which proposal was agreeable to the Friend so to St. Margaret's we went very thoughtfully for the Friend, my guide, was one of the ministry and accordingly must bear some part of the weight of the undertaking. We put up at an inn and one of our first questions was whether there was ever a Quaker in that town. Our landlady said there was a woman, a Quaker that went out to nurse people but she could not tell where to find her for that she was seldom long in a place but she sent one to inquire for her and accordingly sent a person who found her in a little time and the poor woman being so overjoyed to hear of Friends coming there again, was not long before she came to us with great pleasure in her countenance. I told her I had a desire to have a meeting if I thought the people would come, and asked her opinion. She told me she believed they would and that she'd go and give them notice. So we concluded to meet that evening to which a pretty many people came and behaved soberly. My spirit was deeply baptized under the weight of the gospel power, but truth favouring hard things were made easy— After meeting a man and his wife came up to me and in great brokenness of spirit told me he had great unity with me and that he had never felt so great a degree of the power of truth as under the testimony I had delivered and that it was the truth indeed. They both wept very much and desired I would go lodge with them with uncommon earnestness. I weighed it and found freedom to go and abide the time. I stayed at his house but I kept inward and what conversation we had was serious and in the course of it he told me the manner of his first being reached by the good hand, which as it's something particular shall give it in his own words: A poor man who he had known in good circumstances came to his house with some

pottery ware to sell. He thought to himself this poor man must certainly be very dejected to be reduced to this mean way of life. I pity him. How is it possible he can bear it? I'll ask him in and see how it's with him. Upon which he invited him in and he accepted the invitation and appeared with a serene, cheerful countenance which was a surprise to him and he put the question to him, how

was it possible he could keep up his spirits under the change of circumstances he had the misfortune of. The poor man solidly replied he had a great reason to be content, for though he had lost his outward substance yet had Christ given him for an inheritance, which words he said pierced his very soul and filled him with these reflections: Sure Christ is a great blessing when he can thus comfort in the midst of poverty. Lord what know I of this enjoyment of Christ which begets such sweet peace in the mind. And these thoughts wrought mightily upon him and he burst out into tears under the consideration of his living so long a stranger to his redeemer, and the poor man was touched with his distress and kneeled down and prayed and he observed to me that during the time of prayer he found great calmness cover his spirits, and from that time he was drawn from all outward performances of religious duties, could not pray when he would as heretofore he used to do but was frequently drawn into silence and in that he could sometimes pray but this was very different to his former manner of prayer and then he was convinced of the deadness of the public worshippers and the emptiness of their ministry who could preach in their own wiles and own time, and could not now go to hear them or join in worship with them so declined all places of public worship and on first days sat down in his family in silence which induced several others to join him in it, and in this situation he was when I had that meeting with them. I heard him with attention and had to encourage him to continue this silent waiting and to guard against that spirit which would perhaps draw him into action before the Lord's appointed time, for I was jealous his great love and zeal for the cause of truth might without further qualification, influence him to act a part he was not under an absolute necessity to meddle with, that of exhorting others. Some hints of this sort were offered and taken in good part by him, and he owned there was some reason for my fears of this sort, and he hoped he should in the future cease from all the creaturely willings and runnings and lean upon his master. He and his wife was very tender and next day I set out for Deal, and he accompanied me part of the way and just at parting he told me of a sober young woman at Sandwich, a town we were to ride through, who used frequently to come all the way from that town to his house to sit down with the two or three, and wished I could see her, or that she could go to any meeting with me. I told him I did not know how I should be disposed of but if I found any drawings on my mind to have a meeting in the town where she lived I should give up to it, and so we parted. He went home and my guide and I forward to where truth sent me, and just before we got to Sandwich the Friend with me asked if inclined to a meeting. I told him I had been weighing it, but thought I was clear of it, but found a warm desire revived to see that young woman the man had mentioned to me. He said our road did not lead us through the town but just by one end of it, yet to please me he would go into it, but was at a loss to find her out, we having both of us forgot her name or did we know what part she lived in. I paused upon it a while and told him he would oblige me if he'd take me to one of the inns, which he willingly did without knowing what I had in view. As soon as I got in I asked the landlord if there was not a young woman in that town that had declined to go to public worship. O yes, says the man, it's Miss Baker and she suffers enough for it. I told him I should take it kind if he would send for her which he readily did and she as readily came. I felt as she entered the room love to spring in my heart towards her and I was made dear to her and we embraced each other affectionately, but was neither of us forward to enter into words but she sat some time silent when had freedom to tell her of the meeting I had had the day before, and that a friend of hers had told me something of of

Gospel Love flow forth toward her which had induced me to send for her, though did not find I had much to say to her. Her answer was she felt that accompanying my spirit which was beyond words, withal asked me what profession of religion I was a member of. I told her was one of them called Quakers and that I had come several thousand miles to visit that nation and found the love of God of such universal extent that it would that all might be brought to the knowledge of truth and in consequence thereof I was going to Deal to have a meeting. She said she should rejoice if there was any room to encourage me to have a meeting there, but there was none, for that their hearts were too hard and spirits bitter, but that if she could she'd go to Deal meeting but she doubted getting time enough for that, she must go on foot, her parents were so exasperated against her for her change of sentiments and conduct that if they knew she was going to any place of worship with dissenters they would not suffer her to ride, having forbid their servants any way assisting her in such cases, and as much as in them lay discouraged her from pursuing that path I trust the Lord by his invisible power had turned her feet in, and had given a measure of his Holy spirit for a light to them to which I believe she kept a steadfast eye upon amidst all her outward discouragements, for outward helps she had none. But providentially the truly valuable works of that worthy servant of Christ Isaac Penington[57] had fell in her way and was made greatly helpful to her in her seeking state, but she was so great a stranger to Friends that she knew not of such a people or what profession of religion that author bore, but was, she told me in one in faith with him, and she desired to know if I was one that held with that doctrine. I told her yes, that he was a Quaker and one whose works we owned. She told me she had oft desired that if here was such a people she might be brought acquainted with them, for it was with such she had unity and that it came in her mind soon after she see me I was one and was glad I was sent to her. I told her I should be glad to have her company at the next meeting. So we parted and I set out for Deal and put up at a person's house who had made profession with us but had gone out and there being no other, the meeting had dropped for some years. I think he told me the meeting house had not been opened for ten years and that in all that time no Friend but that indefatigable labourer in the gospel service, Benjamin Holms,[58] had had a meeting. That he lay under great disadvantage on account of his situation, having no Friends near him, etc. We got some little refreshment whilst the meeting was appointing and then went to it and indeed it looked as if it had not been used for half a century before. However it's often manifest to us who seek the Lord that he is to be found, and that he confines not his presence to stately temples made with mens hands or is the place meet in required by him, who is everywhere present with his, and this day he was pleased to bow the heavens and come down. I was made a rich partaker of his merciful goodness which administered strength in the needful time when many light and airy spirits were meet with us, perhaps out of a vain curiosity, but the power of truth prevailed over their lightness and there was renewed cause of thankfulness. After meeting the young woman above mentioned lovingly came up to me and embraced me, desiring some of my company, and in order to gratify her I went to an inn and we went to a private room and soon entered into religious conversation, in the course of which she asked me many questions relating to our principles and practice which I according to my abilities received satisfied her, in particular respecting our ministry, which I told her was from God and not of man and by his appointment some were engaged in the manner I now was, to go up and down from land to land, not counting their lives dear or their near enjoyments in life, but willingly gave them up for the service's sake, and the good of souls which we sought, being filled with that universal love of God which would gather all through Christ. She said it was love in perfection that could draw me from a comfortable home in such perilous times and induce me to submit to such hardships as I must of course go through and she thought the weight of such meetings was none of the least, for she was led to bear part of the burden of that meeting in which she had deeply sympathized with me and had it not been for the people, most of whom, she feared, were strangers to the benefit of silent meetings she should have been glad to have sat all the time in silence for that was awful indeed and in that I was made truly near to her and to her it was the most edifying part of the meeting but for the people's sake she was willing to lose part of that sweet enjoyment she sat under, and at last prayed something might be given suitable for the people. I was so sensible of the help of her spirit I could do no less than acknowledge it. She pulled a purse out of her pocket and told me by what I had said touching the nature of our ministry she was convinced we preached not for hire or did she offer me anything on that score but as travelling was expensive perhaps I might be strengthened especially as I was led to visit places where there was none of our people, and if she could administer her substance to enable me to discharge that duty she freely gave it. I told her I took her offer kind, but I was under no necessity to accept of it for that it was a rule with us ministers not to make the gospel chargeable to any but more especially when we had of our own which through mercy I had and freely parted with it for the service's sake.[59] She told me she hoped I did not take it amiss. I told her, by no means, I looked on it as an evidence of her love to me and the cause I was engaged in and so with mutual love and good wishes for each other we parted. Went to Dover that night and next day had a satisfactory meeting in which was led to speak upon the consequences attending our giving way to our unbridled passions, and the advantage of bringing them under subjection, at which time was present a gay young man that gave great attention and after meeting told one of the Friends I had preached to him, and he appeared affected, and I understood there was occasion for it, he was an inhabitant of France and had fled from justice having fought a duel and killed a man. 20th. Went and had a meeting at Folkstone where it pleased the fountain of all good to fill my soul with his love and enabled me fully to discharge that which opened upon my mind to be for the benefit of others, and in his name indeed I spake for it was not mine own, I don't know that I was ever more favoured with the gift of utterance, yet with a reverent mind I give the praise to him to whom tis due, who for the work's sake is thus pleased at times to cause the heavens to drop down as dew and fill his ministers as clouds with rain and through them water his heritage, and yet there is no cause of boasting for without him we can do nothing that is good or praiseworthy, contrariwise we are poor and weak, destitute of every comfort and of consequence incapable of administering any to others wherefore it is our incumbent duty, to keep a constant guard over our own hearts lest after these times of reigning with the seed a spirit that would exalt the creaturely part in us should lift up its head, and boast itself as though it had done something extraordinary and so build up self upon the sandy foundation of imaginary excellences that we poor creatures are singularly endowed with above others of our fellow helpers in the work. I have often thought it unsafe to look much at our services or draw comparisons between our gifts and the gifts of others, by reason of the easy possibility there is for us to give wrong judgment in matters where self is so deeply interested. Perhaps that natural partiality with which we view ourselves and what we do, may place our performances in a fairer light than they will bear, and this may cast such a shade over others that it will be no hard matter for us to give self the preference, which if once concluded on as due will be looked for from others. This sort of sentiment if indulged in will introduce into the mind a long train of unprofitable suggestions which will disqualify us for the ministry of the word which teaches each to prefer an other to himself and that none should think more highly of himself than he ought —

22nd. Rode to Ashford and on the 24th had two meetings. 25th to Cranbrook, all three poor meetings, 26th to Garner Street and had a pretty satisfactory meeting. 27th to Lewes and had a solid meeting, truth measurably favoured us. 28th. Went to Brighthelmston [Brighton] and as I went through the town my heart yearned toward the poor, to whom I thought I felt the gospel sound, and I was made willing to propose to the Friends my desire to have a meeting with them, with which they readily acquiesced, and a messenger was sent to invite the poor of the town, and this request arose in my heart: Lord, if it is right, dispose their minds to come to meeting. The which request was answered, for though the notice was short, the meeting house was soon filled and great was my travail of spirit for them, I think I never in my life was brought into a more deep and humble prostration even of body, soul and spirit before Almighty God than in this meeting, or had at any time greater awfulness of spirit which evidenced to me the Lord looks not as man looks, for these poor and despised men of the earth were as dear to him as the king upon his throne and I believe had he been present I should not have stood under a more reverent awe than I did amongst them. It fell my lot as it often did to sit a great while under the weight of the service before I dared stand up, which lead a Friend who was not remarkable for his gift of discerning to conclude I'd have nothing to say and therefore as he told us he thought he might in the freedom stand up and speak a few words, the principal end whereof was to apologize for my silence, when if he had kept his seat but a few minutes he would have been convinced apologies of that nature were needless. Whilst he was speaking there was a general restlessness and there was some room to fear the meeting would have been hurt, but through mercy it turned out better than was expected, for he stood not long. The subject that opened upon my mind was the words of our Lord when he was manifest in the flesh, to wit, There is no man can come unto me except the father draw him, and I had to tell them that the call of the Lord was gone forth to the ends of the earth in order to draw all men to Christ and that the call was in a particular manner to them there met, and I had to tell them what his call was and where it was to be heard and the necessity there was for all mankind to give heed thereto. The people behaved very solidly and I thought Divine good hovered over us and by the blessed descendings of life it was made a profitable season to many, I believe. 29th. Went to Arundel and had a meeting but not much to satisfaction. Next day rode to Chichester and on the 1st of 5th month [July] being first day had two meetings which were large and the Lord of life and endless glory arose and was found of those that sought him

5th month

and them that sought him not for it proved an awakening season to some that had lived as without him in the world. My soul reverently bowed under the awful power of truth which clothed my spirit as with a garment and enabled me to speak well of its ways and leadings and to make thankful mention of his mercies who is the God of Truth. My spirit was nearly united to those few Friends that composed this meeting as was theirs to me and in the Lord we mutually rejoiced. After meeting I received a message that the Duke of Richmond's stewart's [steward's] wife, who had been his housekeeper at his seat near that place, requesting me to visit her and accordingly next day I went, accompanied by some Friends. She received me very lovingly and after some time she told me she had been at those two meetings above mentioned, and that what she had heard had put her upon searching the scriptures upon which she opened a large Bible where she had turned down leaves at most of the passages I had treated upon, and said she did not know there was any such passages before and she said there was something in her seemed to bear witness to the truth of them, and looking up to me as she read said, miss. You have a good memory or you could not have repeated so many texts with so great exactness, which observation gave me opportunity to declare to her the nature of our ministry which depends not upon the strength of memory. I told her as to memory, it was of little use to a gospel minister, for they relied not upon it but upon the immediate revelation of the spirit of God which brought these scriptures to our remembrance which perhaps we had not read or thought on for many years, and that had been the case with me that day. She said with visible surprise, why did not you know before you came to meeting what you should say. I told her I did not know that I should preach for some time after I sat down in meeting, much less what I should say, which was not shown me until I was on my feet, and that when I had delivered one sentence I knew not the next, which had been the case in a remarkable manner in that meeting for I had stood up under the weight of the gospel power and all those openings I had had during silence were removed from me and other matter brought to my remembrance which I delivered without any premeditation thereupon. She shut the Bible and acknowledged to the power which she said had reached to her in those meetings in such sort she had never felt under any ministry before, and proceeded to give me some account of her former life and of her present state. She had as above mentioned lived with the Duke, in the highest station of servitude, and circumstanced so as to have opportunity to partake largely of those pleasures the world and worldly minds admits and indulges themselves in, but she observed to me all those things had no solid satisfaction in them and her mind for some time past had lost the relish thereof and she found a strong draught of desire to retire from them and the world and as she grew in years a preparation for another life appeared as an incumbent duty for which reason she had prevailed on her husband to take a house in Chichester and she had then retired to it, being content to live on the profits of her husband's station, which as stewart [steward] brought them a competency and with that she had more peace than in the enjoyment of greater abundance, when her mind was more in the hurry of the world, and hearing there was one come from another country to have a meeting, she had a desire to go to hear what they had to say, but without any great expectations of being edified, especially as I was a woman of whose preaching she had no opinion at all, and as to the Quakers in general her mind was prejudiced against them, but as she acknowledged for want of knowing them better, for she had thought them an unconversable, simple people, and was indeed ashamed to go to their meeting or be seen with them, but such a desire was begot in her

to see and hear one that came so many thousand miles prevailed over all objections that rose in her mind, and she said
she was greatly disappointed in us as a people and that she
was fully convinced we were not what she thought us, for
that all her wisdom appeared as foolishness to that wisdom
which she beheld the gospel clothed with, and those who
preached it appeared wise in her eyes indeed, and confessed
to the truth of the doctrine with great tenderness, and wished
she might have strength to conform her life to the just, though
strict rules of it which she saw would introduce her into a life
of self denial and draw on her the contempt and censure of
her old acquaintance but that she said she could easily sur-
mount, if she was sure she was right, and that she should
stand her ground. To these observations which I solidly attended to I had to remark that I commended her search into
the scriptures to see how far the doctrine I had delivered
corresponded therewith as also her retirement from the world
and spirit of it which was at enmity with all true religion and
had a tendency to weaken our desires and growth in it, and
as to a sudden conformity to our mode of religion I'd have
her deeply weigh it and if she found the spirit of truth, which
had I thought touched her mind, called her to it, I could
assure her that she would have strength to comply with its
dictates for that I had found by experience every manifestation of divine light which pointed out any religious duty
brought strength to do that duty, and by our obedience, hard
things were made easy, but I left it with her in charge to eye
the light that makes manifest, and labour for strength to follow its dictates, signifying that was the end of our ministry to
bring people to a belief of, and obedience to the inward manifestations of grace in their hearts and more our desire than
bringing to this or the other mode or form of religion which
without the life and power of it, which would work a change
in us, was of none effect, to all of which she assented, and

before we parted she said she wished the Duke her master could have such an opportunity with me as she had, but remarked the disadvantage such great men of the Earth laboured under, who if they were favoured with religious sentiments, the grandeur these stations necessitated them to keep up and intercourse with such as seldom thought or conversed on spiritual things, banished them their breasts or stifled them there which she thought was the case with her Lord Duke as she called him, who she said was a religious man for one in his high station, and when at his seat frequently went alone in her garden and made it his practice every day to read in the Bible, for which he always kept one in a summer house, in his garden, and she proposed to me to go and see him, and to make it more easy she said than to be introduced in such a formal manner visiting men in his station required she'd introduce me as a foreigner curious to see his gardens which would be readily admitted of, and as she knew his hours for walking we could easily throw ourselves in his way when she knew he would have the curiosity to ask who I was, when she could inform him who I was and from whence I came which would naturally introduce me to his notice who was one courteous to strangers, and by this means she proposed our having a religious conference. I looked at it and found love in my heart abundantly to flow towards him and ability arise in my heart by the power of him who taught that we should pray for all men, for Kings and them in authority, to pray for him, and nothing but a cowardly fear kept me from complying with this her solicitous request. He soon after this died suddenly at Godalming on his journey to London and I made no doubt but his secret love to religion gave him place with God the Father who is the author of all religion. 3rd. Had a meeting at Shipley. 4th Had a meeting at Horsham in which was silent. 5th. Had a pretty good meeting at Ifield. 6th. Went to Ryegate and had a very hard meeting. Rode that night to

Dorking where the next day my companion with several other Friends from London met me and being first day had two meetings, the latter with the people of the town, both of which through the extendings of immortal goodness proved solid satisfactory meetings, after which my companion returned to London and poor me left alone as to mortals, yet for the work's sake patiently submitted to this separation. 10th. Went to Capell, had a hard meeting though some thought well of the service. 12th went to Guildford and had a silent, hard meeting. 13th had a meeting at Godalming but not finding myself clear stayed until first day and had a large meeting and more satisfactory although had some close service. Whilst I was on my feet and under the exercise of my gift, I found such an ebb of the gospel power as that dared not proceed in words, though the matter that had opened in the life continued after the life had withdrawn, upon which I made a full stop yet had not freedom to sit down, which drew the eyes of all the meeting upon me save one whose eyes sleep had closed, whom I fixed with mine eye upon and instantly a word arose in my heart to him and I called out to him to awake and attend to the service I hoped he had come about and then craved the help of his, and every other spirits, letting them know the work was hard and that I had need thereof which sufficiently roused him and thought fixed him in his proper exercise when had liberty and strength to return to the subject I had digressed from and I thought truth measurably favoured. That night rode to Alton. Next day had a meeting at Trivil in which was silent save in prayer. Returned to Alton, 18th was at their weekday meeting in which had the cup of consolation handed to my poor soul. 19th to Basingstoke and had a hard silent meeting. 20th went to Whitchurch. 21st being first day was at a meeting in the fore part of the day which proved a dull, heavy, silent meeting. Afternoon rode seven miles to Andover and had an evening meeting which was large and comfortable—the Lord's silencing power was eminently known amongst us to the melting of our hearts ever blessed be his Holy name who is thus in the riches of his love condescending to visit the low estates of his people and did manifest his might in being my strength in weakness and riches in poverty. 22nd rode to Salisbury and in the evening had a poor low meeting and yet was preserved in patience as it's meet we should learn to know how to be abased as well as to abound. 23rd. Went to Romsey and had a small meeting. 24th. Went to South Hampton and had a small, hard silent meeting. 25th rode to Portsmouth. 26th had a large satisfactory meeting where several Friends from Chichester met me to our mutual comfort. 27th went to Uxbridge. 28th being first day rode 15 miles to Ringwood and had two meetings, not very extraordinary either way, and finding some drawings went to Lemington and had a meeting in the court house where met abundance of people that were not Friends, there being but one family of Friends there. They for the most part were people of note in the world who behaved soberly but divers ordinary persons crowded in and by pressing to get in, for the house, large as it was could not contain them all, made some disturbances which somewhat discomposed the meeting, yet after I got up all was quiet, but I found not too large a degree of divine life accompany me as at some other times, which discouraged me so that I stood not long and humbly hope truth did not suffer. After meeting some of the better sort of people sent me word they were sorry I met with any disturbance, but assured me it was only some bad people, and if I would have another meeting they would come to it and take care that none of these bad people should get in, but I not finding necessity on my mind declined it —

About this time I received divers consolatory letters from several of my dear and worthy Friends which were truly helpful to me in my low and deeply bowed state for as I was without any companion to bear a part of the weight of so great an undertaking it of consequence fell the heavier upon myself, one of which I think worthy a place here. It was from my dear Friend Mary Smith[60] with whom I had contracted a near friendship when in London first, and it continued until her death which was not long after her return from Jersey to which place she was going when she wrote me the following letter:

Southampton, 6 mo.
[August] 2nd, 1750

My Dearest Eliza,

It was in my heart to write to thee by the bearer had I not received thine from Lymington this morning, as supposing he might meet or convey it to thee, our vessel is likely to sail on the 4th or 5th of this instant, but the weather is unsettled and at times stormy and rough with the wind quite against us. Cloudy Gay's wife with a sober young man from London is going over with us. We came pretty easy along as to the water, but now being at our port fears crowd in and diffidence attack the poor frail creature. Methinks the latter part of thy dear letter hath given me a little cheer up. I note the contents throughout and perceive the steps thou takes sundry precautions with respect to the ministry, seeking and desirous to know the proper and right season when to speak or keep silent when to offer or not offer. Its a blessed thing indeed to know and practice this, and that is most truly done I think without prescribed or fixed rules. As to us, our safety then is to be open or shut, little or great, both with respect to our service and peace insuring each being in their degrees, settling down in the holy submission lest by too much reasoning and distress the way becomes intricate and dark to us—

I have known something of this troubled experience therefore conclude settling in the quiet habitation

234

is best, in which concerning the present case we see our error or mistakes and do in truth and sincerity repent of them and so merciful and benign is our great Lord and Master who is filled with clemency, love and compassion to our weaknesses not willfully committed, that we need not be so distressed or anxious. The latter is occasioned variously, first as from an apprehension of things not centering in reality by presupposition a misconduct by suggesting our auditory dead or depressed in the divine sense that just before appeared fresh in it, when probably it may not be so, but admit it should, the fault may not altogether lie at the minister's door but contrarywise from a digression of travel and watchfulness in them. And as thou justly observes, places differ, time and seasons alter with the publishers as the present states and conditions of the people are which our great I am is not a stranger to, though we may be, and if the people's capacities are low and dark in proportion are the arisings or manifestations of the Divine gift in us at that time —— And no wonder if he that sometimes when we are extraordinary clothed and honoured with singular majesty to which many humbly endeavor to acknowledge, insinuate that we are somebody, should also on the other hand lead the poor creature to depression and bear down below due measure. Thou may find occasion to remark the observations in thy present journey, who like an Elisha alone, will meet with contracted waters and Jordan undivided, but as thy cry is continued: Where is the Lord God of Elijah? trusting in the power whether the degree be less or more in the use of the mantle, the Holy gift; separation and way will be made and thou will pass safely over, and though the sons of the prophets are not with thee and other children not well instructed in the deep and great sciences of

Christianity, may cry, go up thou bold head, as thinking because thou passes their courts in silence, thou are not suitably qualified or properly called to the work, for let me say there are such novices now both on the right hand and on the left, but the truly apostolical and nobly honoured ministers of Christ, who are filled with evangelical virtue, pass quietly and submissively through all and rejoice to be counted worthy to suffer or to reign for his worthy name's sake, and hence is verified the saying of the wise man that wisdom is more moving than anything, it quietly passes through all things, it being the brightness of the power of God, and pure influence flowing from the almighty.

Oh holy armor to God's people, his chosen and anointed ones inclusive indeed of the breastplate of righteousness, of the helmet of salvation and noble sword of the spirit, wherewith they are enabled to withstand all the fiery darts, all the trials arising from truths and our enemies. May the Lord God of my Life thus secure, surround, and graciously protect his faithful servants and tender handmaids in this day of soul travel and go before them in the Ark of his Covenant that their labours may tend to his honour and the exaltation of his name on Earth, and ever keep us in deep humility and bowedness of spirit as in his holy presence, amen, saith my spirit in reverence with thine and I am in his love and heavenly life my dearly beloved Eliza and truly valued friend, think in a deep and solemn manner.—

M. Smith

P. S. Do not my dear travel too hard but take some care of thy poor body, knowing it is not very hardy. Let me repeat the apostle's advice to his son, Timothy, take a little wine or what else is necessary for thy stomach's sake and thine own infirmities. My companion and all present join the salutation of dear love. Farewell Dearly, and if we are favoured to return shall be glad to hear from thee.

Just before I left London I received the following from the same hand in answer to one I wrote when under great straits in my mind on sundry account which though out of order as to time I judge will not be unacceptable should this be read, in which is manifest her Christian love towards her master's servants.

My Dearest Eliza,

This morning received thy letter, indeed unexpected but not unpleasant. Yes, let me say I read it with inward pleasure and fervor arises in my heart to the God of my life that thou may be preserved to pursue thy known duty with holy, immovable integrity, that naught indeed may be kept back but all given freely without reserve to the call and motion of him that is drawing into the furnace for pure gold. We read the firing pot is for silver but the furnace for gold, the choice and more noble species, etc. and as thou, dear favoured lamb, abide the operating refining thou'll come forth brighter and brighter to the eclipsing of many who are at best but tarnished silver or impure gold that want refining. I am made to remember the useful instruments in the outward house or sanctuary, sundry of which for precious service were formed of pure, beaten and perfect good, such as the snuffers, tongs, and candlestick, prime instruments of one refined solid metal that hath a solemn and most teaching relation to the spiritual work and preparation of the instruments of service in the spiritual house or church of Christ our Lord. I pray God so strengthen thy loins of deep travail and bind up the truly broken that thee may be enabled and fortified to bear the various dispensations and sundry baptisms that he in his infinite wisdom and consummation to his secret will is leading his dear children and people through in the glorious gospel day, and oh what are our manifold deepenings, humblings, and abasements for but that no flesh shall glory in his presence or boast in any acquirements or parts whatever. Oh! this coming under the great Potter's hand, this abiding in the house of mental labour and soul work, how excellent it is in the resignation to it when the thing formed dare not say to him that formed it, why hast thou made or fashioned me, thus passivity, filial submission, and supine subjection is imparted in these observations of the Almighty by his holy prophet to wit: shall the axe boast itself against him that heweth therewith, or the saw magnify itself against him that shaketh with it, and so also of the rod and staff as may be seen by the text, by all of which is fully demonstrated the variety of instruments with their several and singular uses, and no instrument can perform its due service whether intended by the great workman for one or the other of the above mentioned, until it's really made so to will one of these, and as the work of such, spiritually understood is supernatural, so indeed is the government and application of them to their appointed services by a hand supernatural. They cannot handle or apply themselves, therefore the whole system of the matter calls aloud for submission. May we be truly and become as weaned children, weaned and brought off from the breast of our old mother, the world, the fashions and dresses of it, and as there is a fallowing that hand that's near, and Light which is discovered, I am certain it will be so here, little things will magnify and become a burden and the right eye being opened sees clearly and properly distinguishes objects, which I am thankful to find that the eye salve hath been readministered by a renewed touch to thee. It brings fresh to my remembrance my early day in the Truth, being one that was made to witness the essential and saving powers of life and virtue of religion before the form thereof, and after my mouth was opened sometime and had travelled a little and as thou observes I think as greatly favoured if not more so then as now, some little matters relating to dress and other things I had not left off or got through or did I consider them closely needful as that Truth required them at my hands to be laid down, so did not much regard the remarks others made of my own conformity in so strict and primitive a plainness not exclusive of the genteel as well as gay part. The latter in my nature I was adverse to but that of a genteel cut and grand taste I was itching after, but can truly and thankfully say when the Lord was pleased by the further manifestations of his light and truth in my heart, discovered these to be superfluous and unnecessary branches, and gave me to see that the inclination toward and love of them was the little foxes that would endanger if not spoil the vines which although they bear goodly yet were they tender grapes. I consulted not with the flesh and blood nor formed one request for them as I remember, but delivered them up to the great requirer and my body and soul to be ornamented as he pleased. I very well call to mind the seasons when these dresses would no longer serve, but solid adorning such as the holy Christian women formerly were under, must be my clothing, and likewise saw the absolute necessity and weight of this regulation and further conformity to the divine will of God that works and leavens into the nature and image of his blessed

Song of
Sol. 2:15

son Jesus Christ, our holy and perfect pattern, and that brightness of example to accompany precept was now loudly called for that the instrument or trumpet should be all of a piece, otherwise it could not duly call all the assembly together into proper solemnity, and I justly believe had I withstood the call in these, seeming, to mere fond nature, trivial matters, I had blocked up my solemn way and service, but that became and still is I trust dearer to me than life itself. Oh! what a right hand or right eye could I not then have plucked out or parted with rather than fallen short of acceptance with God and his true hearted people, and have dwindled in my growth, the day of mine espousals was precious and here, my dear Eliza, I was led into great plainness and singular conduct as in some measure natural to the true work of the soul's regeneration, not stiff, formal, pharisaical which is hateful, but conscientiously concerned and bowed under an awful tendering sense of what manner of persons we ought to be, especially us ministers that have at times the word of deep reproof and exhortation to others and liable to the word of holy command to be instant in season and out of season. And under these humbling considerations and circumstances I have judged it highly prudent and indeed necessary to be strictly retired in families where my lot has been cast, nor hath it been altogether owing to my own prudence, for I really believe many a time had I attempted a freedom in conversation on matters indifferent to my solemn concern and function, there had been a mark sat on me and become confounded, though the temptations thereto hath been many, and I do hearby confess I have been astonished and filled with wonder to behold the jocularity, the fluency and freedom of some others under the like concern and holy calling, which hath filled me with sorrow when I had none visible to utter it to, and have not this sort of behavior hurt the right thing, especially in many of our favoured youth to whom it looks to me there is a day of fresh visitation offered by keeping that alive in them which unmortified nature loves which ought in my conception to be exampled as well as precepted to the yoke, But oh! my Dear Child, we had need to cry for wisdom and an understanding Heart to go in and out before the people, that so if happily we may steer without error either on the right hand or on the left that indeed only is profitable to direct aright, where, when and to whom it is required to be recluse or open so as to use a little truth like freedom in the innocence and sweetness of the lamb, for dispensations differ and grounds vary, all are not alike, we have to work upon, therefore let's learn to be skillful. Some there are that a little openness and innocent freedom will mightily take with, and it facilitates the way for the tenders of truth, with others a more austere, awful behavior is most suitably adopted and here, the truly engaged become in a religious way all things to all men, if so be they gain ground to the blessed truth and yes its glory, and this also may be aptly termed patiently bearing the ark, taking their growths the children and little ones that cannot go deep and fast. Oh! the unutterable patience of the true priests, the temperance and forebearance of the Lord's servants under their trials and services amidst the people; Moses, standing in the gap, and Aaron interceding even for the rebellious and murmuring one. May the Lord's ministers, prophets and servants in our day be clothed with the like precious faith, courage, conduct, patience, and magnanimity, prayeth my soul who, though one of the least and most unworthy in Israel, yet abundantly desires and travels for its common wealth and that in her beloved tribes she may arise gloriously with ancient splendor and be as a standard to the nations, that Kings and much people may yet come to the Light of Zion and princes to the brightness of her arising glory, honour and high praises be given to our God and let us my dear Eliza, utter then aloud when clothed in the congregations of his people, saith thy very near and true friend and let us remember one another for good etc desire that love, fellowship and union may increase and be continued and the accuser of the brethren cast out— oh holy love and fellowship is that of the saints, I am with endeared love to thee and to friend Hoskins.

Thy Mary Smith.

This dear Friend and truly Christian woman got safe to Jersey and stayed in the service of truth many months, labouring diligently as by accounts I received from others, but fell under great indisposition of body which was feared by many would take her out of time before she could reach her native country, but it pleased the Lord to length out her day longer than was expected, so that she got home but did not live long after. I was got to my own country before she died yet the distance of place did not lessen the thoughts of the loss I sustained by her death or alleviate my grief, for was very sensibly touched when the ungrateful account reached me of it. She was a warm and faithful Friend, as well as a diligent labourer in the vineyard of our Lord and Master, who by the influence of his Holy Spirit of wisdom, made her skillful in that business her hands found to do in it.

THE JOURNAL OF ELIZABETH HUDSON

PART VI

From Lymington on the 30th I went to Poole in Dorchester and had a meeting the same day in which was silent, sitting under great discouragement on account of the aforesaid meeting and was brought into close examination and deep distress lest I had run unsent into that particular service, and thus it pleased the master of our assemblies to dip me deep into suffering, which tended greatly to the humbling of the creature, which for some time lay low before him, who hath it equally in his power to kill or make alive, to bring down to the grave and raise up again, which in his wanted mercy he was pleased to do with regard to me his poor servant, whose view were his honour. 3rd of 6th mo. [August] went to Weymouth, had an evening meeting which was a poor, hard time. 4th. Went to Bridport and put up at the house of our dear ancient Friend Samuel Bownas[61] who was then on a religious visit to some neighbouring meetings so that had not the desired pleasure of his company, which was a disappointment to me who had conceived hopes of some consolation or solid benefit from his Christian experience for had thought to open my state to him, but thus it pleased providence who will in his own time teach his people himself to cut off any reliance upon human help, and he was graciously pleased as I turned the eye of my mind towards him singly, to appear as a ph[illegible] of value, who mercifully bound up the broken hearted and strengthened of that which was ready to die. 5th had a good meeting and next day set out for Exeter when on my way thither I met our Friend Samuel on his return home. 7th had a hard meeting but

6th month

Luke 2:35

243

through divine help got through the close service before me
to tolerable satisfaction and found peace in obedience. 8th
rode to Bowey. 9th. Had an evening meeting in which was
drawn to silence to the surprise of those present who were
mostly of other societies who after about an hour and a half's
waiting withdrew, leaving those few that were Friends to
ourselves who was to witness sweet peace together at North
Townbushel and rode that afternoon to Totness, had a seasonable opportunity by the incomes of refreshing goodness
in the Friend's family where I lodged. 11th. Went to
Kingsbridge and had an evening meeting in which sat silent,
next day set out for Plymouth, lodged by the way at a Friend's
house. 13th being first day got with hard riding through wet
weather to Plymouth Meeting, got late there and had particular hard service yet peace in the discharge of duty. Next
day had a hard silent meeting at Looe, where some forward
unsent messengers hurt the cause. Next day was at Austle
where our ancient Friend Samuel Hopwood[62] had the service. 16th. Rode to Penzance, had a meeting on the 17th which
was a low time. That night had a meeting at market town,
had a satisfactory meeting, the subject that offered was that
scripture, there is not a thought in my heart or a word on my
tongue but thou knoweth altogether, oh Lord, which had a
reach upon a young man that happened to be there from
some distant part of the country, some things being opened
to his state. 18th returned back to Penryn. 19th being first
day had a morning meeting at Falmouth and the afternoon
at Penryn where the master of our assembly was pleased graciously to favour with his life giving presence which was
matter of great joy to my poor soul which had been deeply
baptized into death and suffering for the oppression of the
pure seed of Good which lay as slain in many places, this
meeting proved a refreshing season to Friends and had a tendency to unite us in gospel fellowship and was a fresh confir-

mation that the Lord was with me, his poor minister, whose
trials at times were great and needed heavenly help from day
to day to wade through the various dispensations of providence and to keep in the proper median in heights and depths.
20th. Parted with Friends in them parts and set out accompanied by Andrew Kingson and wife in order for the circular
yearly meeting to be held by appointment at Ilminister. Got
to Parry [Perran] that night and next day had a meeting at
Lescard [Liskeard] which was hard to an extreme degree and
again brought me into deep affliction which was for a time so
heavy I could take no refreshment of any kind but rather
sought a release if it were the will of God, Oh the inward
bemoanings and cries to him who is all powerful is not to be
expressed. I sought retirement that I might pour out my tears
unseen of men. 22nd. Rode to Oakhampton but was too low
to have a meeting appointed so next day proceeded on our
journey by Exeter and reached Ilminister the 25th late at
night and put up at an inn, there being no Friends in the
town, and here to my great satisfaction I met with many solid
weighty Friends of the ministry who were as a reviving cordial to my dejected spirit, to wit, S. Hopwood who had met
one on the road and accompanied me here, S. Bownas, J.
Churchman,[63] and companion from my country whom I rejoiced to see, J. Hunt[64] from London, my particular acquaintance, with divers others of the ministry. The meetings were
held in the town hall from the 26th through the 28th in
which time had 6 meetings, one of them held in the street in
the market place where truth favoured us who had the service of that day, as also in all the meetings there was witnessed heavenly help and we had renewedly to rejoice in the
Lord and one in another. The meetings were all large and
attended by divers in high stations of life, who expressed great
satisfaction which was evident by their frequent and solid
attendance. After the meetings were over Friends parted in

thankful tenderness and returned to their several homes and services. I set out in company with S. Hopwood and J. Hunt for Bristol. Lodged that night at an inn and spent an agreeable evening together. Reached the city next day and put up at my Friend's Richard Champions,[65] where I stayed to rest my weary carcass being much spent in this last journey, having sundry meetings near Bristol and mostly attended them in the city as they came in course until the 21th of 7th month [September] when set out for Wales, Hester Brag accompanying me. We got to Curlin that night in Wales, lodged at an inn and next day had a satisfactory meeting in their free school house which privilege was granted us by a clergyman in whose power that house was, the school being entirely under his direction, a rare instance of brotherly kindness in one of that function. 23rd. Went to Pontypool and next day had 2 meetings, both hard, afflicting meetings. 25th. Went to Cardiff, put up at an inn, there being no Friends in that town, at the entrance of which I got a bad fall from my horse which sprained both my wrists and otherwise bruised me so that was in great pain as soon as we lighted from our horse. The people at the inn told us that our Friend Samuel Hopwood had had a public meeting in the town hall and was gone to a private meeting appointed to be held at a friendly persons' house, one of those called Methodists. Although I was wet, weary and bruised, found a strong draught to the meeting aforesaid so we requested one of the waiters at the inn to show us the house, which they readily did and when we came there we found the house full so we crept in unobserved and got behind the door out of sight for was fearful of interrupting Samuel's service, not expecting any to fall to my share, but had not sat long before I found my mind engaged toward that auditory and when I conceived the concern fully ripe, I stood up to the great surprise of the people, especially those Friends who had accompanied Samuel from neighbouring meetings, none of whom had ever seen me or heard of our being in those parts as they told us after the meeting was over. Also that one of the young men had put out his hand to pull me down, supposing me to be one out of unity as they had heard no tidings of any Friend being that way, but as he owned to me, he was so smitten he had no power to do it, and that a few words convinced him of my mission. After I had delivered what I had on my mind I looked round the meeting for Samuel, but could not see him or any other qualified to answer the service of said meeting so that I with others thought it providential our being thus drawn to that place. I as soon as had opportunity inquired for Samuel and was informed he was taken ill just as meeting set in and was, as he afterwards told me, made quite easy about it, but was greatly rejoiced when he heard how things turned out, for truth rose high amongst us, and I found great peace to flow as the reward of my obedience to the divine call at that time to that particular service, and concluded it good at all times to follow the leadings of the Heavenly motion. During the meeting I was not sensible of much pain but after it was over I found I was considerably hurt, yet not free to lie idle so had a meeting appointed next day to be held in the town hall which was pretty satisfactory as being attended with an evidence of divine help. That night rode to Treverige, and next day had a comfortable meeting with the few Friends in those parts. I found my spirit sweetly seasoned with a larger degree of divine love than common, which greatly enlarged my heart towards them. 28th. Went to Cowbridge and that day had a very satisfactory meeting in the town hall. Next day set out for Swansea and reached it that night. Put up at our Friend's James Griffith; whose family received us lovingly and used some proper means to relieve me from the painful effects of my fall, which answered the end desired. Here we stayed amongst our kind Friends, visiting several families in some of which we had service as well as in their more public meetings which we attended as they came in course until the 9th of 8th month [October.] Then set out for Caermarthen and reached it that night and next day had a dull meeting with the few Friends there. 11th. Went to Lawn, and had a meeting with the people of the town in which the power of truth was eminently known to the humbling our spirits and baptizing many who acknowledged the visitation and spake well of the way of truth with tears. My soul and all that was living within me bowed down in reverence to him who is alone mighty to save and ascribed greatness with glory to him with his dear son the Lamb who thus is pleased at times to give us cause of triumph in him, and maketh manifest the savour of his knowledge by us, his instruments, who are nothing without him, but he all fullness without us. 12th. Set out for Jamestown and in our way thither passed through Tenby, a pretty large town, and as we rode through the streets a lively concern covered my spirit, to have a meeting there amongst the inhabitants, but having no man guide or any meeting place, and ignorant what sort of people they were or whether it might be suffered or not, with divers reasonings with flesh and blood, I spake nothing of it to my companion or the other woman Friend that accompanied us, until we had got about a mile from the town, when the weight increased to that degree was forced to submit to what I apprehended a divine call though in fear and trembling. I proposed it to my companion who readily fell in with it and also encouraged me to give up freely so we turned back and put up at an inn which my mind found the greatest freedom to; for as we passed by several, I found not freedom to enter I still kept on till I came to the door of this, when was ready to say, peace be to this house which we cheerfully entered and sat down in peace whilst our woman guide went about three miles to a Friend, so called to desire his company, for we all thought it a great

undertaking for us 3 women only to appoint a meeting in a place where perhaps none had ever been. And as soon as well could, I desired to speak with our landlady who readily came to us with a good natured countenance which seem a further encouragement to us, to propose the meeting to her, and my companion leaving it to me to settle the matter, I first told her my inducement to visit them parts and asked her if she was willing we should have a meeting in her house, and whether she thought the people if invited would favour us with their company, to which she kindly replied we were welcome to her house and her man who knew the town well should go about and let them know there was to be a meeting, to which she doubted not but that many would come —
— And by then all things were got ready. Our guide returned but no man Friend with her. So that we had none to trust or in the least to depend upon but our heavenly helper, and on him alone my expectation was placed, yet he was pleased to try me very nearly by withdrawing his supporting presence for some hours before the people gathered, which brought me very low and into deep travails of spirit before him with whom I then covenanted that if he'd be with me and support his own cause so that his truth suffered not, or cause given to speak evil of his ways, I'd by his help more fully give myself up to do his will than heretofore I had done, to go wheresoever held send, yea be his servant forever. Oh the deep contrition and humiliation of spirit in which I sat during the gathering of this meeting, the inward labor and travail is not to be expressed, or the agonizing of mind that at last seized me; all this while the people flocking in until the house was full and the yard also crowded, insomuch that they, by pushing at the window, broke it in so many places that it was judged best to set open all the windows and doors that they might both hear and see, without which also they are not content. After about an hour's silence spent in the manner above mentioned,

such a senselessness seized me as I knew not how to describe, attended with such a dead pain in my head and a fullness as if some blood vessel there would burst, insomuch as I knew not but the hour of my dissolution was come, when my nose gushed out a bleeding freely, and at that juncture my companion for the first time since we were together stood up, I believe under a right motion for as in an instant I found relief as if the healing virtue of our lord was poured forth and I grew strong in him and as was my distress so now was my joy in the Lord undescribable. I could say in truth, my soul magnified him and rejoiced in God my saviour. She stood not long but was lively, though what she said I was hardly capable of attending to from the sudden resurrection of life in me. Her voice drew the people more than the room could hold so that we were pressed hard and I found their breaths very suffocating to me, and had hardly room to stand up when my time came, which was as soon as she had done and by that time my nose stopped bleeding so stood up in the lively demonstration of the spirit of truth being with me which gave ability to speak in his name and the meeting ended in a fresh feeling sense of his goodness, etc. The people withdrew, well satisfied and the reward of peace crowned our labours and after some time we got some and may say I partook not of these outward blessings unthankfully but remembered from whence all these good things comes. We lodged there that night and next day cheerfully paid our kind hostess more than she demanded for I was not easy without getting her window mended, which cost 2/6 although she more than once desired I would not pay for it, telling me we were welcome to her house and were not accountable for what the people did. However as this was most easy to me, valued not paying damages had they been larger. Set out after breakfast and got to Jamestown and had a hard little meeting after which went that night to Haverfordwest with our woman guide only and had a stormy passage over the water which put us in some fear, and not without some danger for it was with difficulty we persuaded the ferry man to take us over, he having refused divers others who were then making merry at the inn at which had we stayed we must have took up our lodging, but when had viewed the company and considered our circumstances as having no man thought it not quite safe to stay with such an ungodly company as they appeared to be so told my companion my mind with regard to going forward, but she being somewhat fearful I did not care to press it until way was made in her own mind and and after some time she grew uneasy and told me she had rather venture than stay there, which gave me pleasure, so we asked the man if he would row us over the river. He said it was not safe, for that boat was not safe being old and weak. I then stepped to the water which was near the house to look at it to see if his unwillingness proceeded from real danger or desire to have us stay at the inn, when espied a fine larger new boat, a little distance which I thought would safely take us over, I then asked if he could not take us in that. He replied that was the King's boat which he dare not meddle with, but could we get that she would carry us safe enough, and whilst we were in discourse, an officer who had a right over that boat came by, which, when I understood, I applied to him for the use of it which he readily granted, so that our way opened beyond expectation so that after a boisterous passage got safe over and Haverford late in the night etc. Next day being first had two meetings but found truth but low which kept me low. Next day visited several Friends and the next day went to Pied Stone and had a meeting. 17th. Returned to Caermarthen and on the 18th had a meeting with the people of the town to good satisfaction. They behaved soberly and we did no harm I hope. 19th had a meeting at Penplace in which had hard service, things as to the life of religion are but low.

20. Had a meeting at a place called Llangadock at an inn where we put up, at an hour's warning, we having no design when we lighted off our horses, but soon after I sat down, I found my mind drawn to silence and in that a flow of divine love to the people of the town which breathed forth towards them in desire for their growth in the knowledge of the truth as it is in Jesus and waiting deeply found the concern live and grow strong in the Life when found liberty to mention it to them with me who own their unity with me in the concern, so then we proposed it to our landlady who freely offered us her house and sent out to invite the people who at that short notice came and a tendering, heart melting season it proved to divers that were not Friends, whose tears ran like water and the gospel went forth freely and met with an open door. I was humbly thankful for this seasonable refreshment of the love of God. Got that night to Pennybank, where next day had a suffering time, sitting throughout the meeting in a dead, senseless condition, by which was renewedly convinced that every good comes from our Heavenly helper, without whom we can do nothing or get anything that is of an Heavenly nature. My poverty of spirit was great which kept me low and depending in the simplicity of waiting as at the King's gate, who was at times pleased to dignify as with princely robes and then again strip them off and leave destitute of every royal ornament, even reduce to want and beggary, and this for wise ends, seemed somewhat like the Dove. Could find no rest in this place so prevailed with my landlord to set us on our journey as far as the next town which was Landoverry [Llandovery], where we put up at an inn. Here our guide left us and I found peace in this place and some little service, in the following respect. I desired fire to be made in a private room which whilst it was doing sat down by the fire where two well dressed men sat busy in discourse jocosely, from which I endeavored to retire, but unexpect-

edly found it my place to sit there, although their conversation was so unsanctified, I found my spirit wounded and yet love in my heart to the men, especially to one of them to whom I thought I found the visitation of divine love extended. I sat still and after some time a word rose in my heart, which had great place and drew from him that I felt most love to a confession to the truth and that he was often checked for his profanity which proceeded rather from wantonness or custom than from a bad heart. I told him I believed he spake the truth, but that such bad customs must be watched against and that I would not have him trifle with these gentle reproofs, lest he become hardened or to this purpose for which he thanked me for my good advice, as he termed it and my companion and I left them to go to our own room with mutual good wishes for each other's welfare, and for this little service I had peace. Here my kind companion met with a letter from her husband, informing her of his indisposition and desire to have her return home as soon as possible, which was a considerable trial to me, and proved a fresh instance to drive me yet more near to my inward helper who is with his in all places, and frequently makes his power more eminently known when we are most destitute of human comfort. Next day set out for Thomas Floyd's with hopes to reach his house that night, but could not by reason of the weather which proved very cold and stormy with sleety snow and rain and wind full in our faces with the additional difficulty of very high mountains before us, which had not the divine presence been abundantly near to bear up my spirits, had thought this a hard day's service, but such was the refreshing virtue of it, that all the sufferings of the flesh were buried in insensibility under the lively enjoyment of heavenly love, which filled my heart to that exalted degree that could scarce forebear singing aloud the praises of him whose awful presence filleth Heaven yea, the Heaven of Heavens cannot contain

Elizabeth Hudson

him, but by his abundant mercy the poor inhabitants of the earth are made partakers of his goodness and lively impressions of his life giving presence, I then could say by happy experience;

> Thy mercies sweeten every soil
> Makes every region please
> The hoary Appian hill it warms
> And smooths the roughest seas

And for many miles I rode in raptures of devotion avoiding conversing with those with me lest I should loose the Heavenly Treasure, in which was refreshment for both body and mind for this day we travelled mostly without food, it being a barren part of the country and thinly settled and at those places we called could get nothing save at one place

254

some sour beer with bad cheese without bread which I could not partake of so travelled that day until evening with only a drought of water and indeed nature seemed not to want anything else. It continuing all day tempestuous weather could not seasonably reach our intended lodgings so put up at an inn at a little town 3 miles short, but reached it next morning and had a meeting with the few Friends there. 25th. Went to Talbot and had a hard meeting. Next day 27th had a tedious day's journey over snowy mountains with pinching cold to John Goodwin's which we reached late at night, and met with a kind reception with the renewed touches of divine love which sweetens all our bitter cups. Next day had a satisfactory meeting. 29th. Set out for Delobron [Dolobran] but could not reach it that night so put up at an inn 2 miles short of it but got in good time to the quarterly meeting held at Delobron at which was but 4 besides myself and guide and I the only woman, I much depressed in spirit at the view opened to me, of the decline of Friends in these parts, here once being a pretty large meeting duly kept up but now dropped save once a quarter, and that in common poorly attended. We lodged that night with one that was no Friend but kind to them when any put up at their house, which is situated near the meeting house; set out next morning with a man Friend who had attended the meeting from Shrewsbury to which place I went that night and next day was at their weekday meeting in which had an humbling time in prayer. Next visited two Friends who were confined in the castle for non payment of church taxes so called, where we had a meeting in which truth favoured us with a comfortable season. 4th of 9th month [November] went to Coalbrookdale, being the first day rode hard to reach meeting which proved hard and silent. 5th. Went to Dudley and next day had a meeting not much to satisfaction. 7th went, though much indisposed, to Birmingham. 8th. Had a comfortable meeting, stayed until

9th month

255

the 11th when went to E. Clark's [66] and next day had a meeting in their new meeting house which was small yet the few met were not without some degree of evidence that the master of our assemblies was near both in a word or reproof to the gainsayers and stiffnecked, and consolation to the mourner in Zion. Went that night home with those Friends who were so kind as to meet me from Coventry and had a meeting there. Next day 14th had a meeting at Warwick. 15th to Henly [Henley] and had a meeting, all three poor low meetings scarce able to live. After which returned to Birmingham where stayed their first day meetings which were large and graciously favoured. 19th Went to Browngrove, and had an evening meeting I thought to poor purpose. 20th. Set out for Worcester in order to attend their quarterly meeting which were large though suffering meetings to the living ministers who found it hard work to get and keep near the spring of divine life. Stayed over their first day meetings to little purpose unless suffering in spirit answered any good end. 26th set out for Evesham and next day had a meeting in which our heavenly helper was pleased to manifest himself in humbling mercy, vouchsafing to break and bless the heavenly bread amongst us. I thankfully received this divine nourishment which was as a precious cordial to my poor sorrow sunken soul and sure I am the mess of pottage the prophet received when in the lion's den could not be more acceptable to him than this renewed visitation of life was to me for had had to drink deep draughts of the cup of suffering by which was brought very low both in body and mind, yet was preserved in the spirit of patience under the hand of him who knows best after what manner to fashion the vessels of his house, and what uses to put them to when fashioned. From hence I went to Tewkesbury although greatly indisposed in body and the cloud was again cast over my spirits so that could not journey on, spiritually speaking. Had a dull

Dan.6:19

256

hard, meeting from hence to Gloucester where had a small silent meeting save at the close, pretty free access to the Throne of Grace in prayer. Next day went to Painswick, had an evening meeting. Next day rode to Nailsworth and on the following day was at two hard meetings. Next day went to Sodbury and had an uncomfortable journey by reason of bad weather being very cold and mirey. The following day had a suffering meeting, after which found my disorders increase with so great dejection of spirits, being shut up with regard to further service that concluded it best go forward towards Bristol where I always found an open door in all respects. Lodged as usual at my kind Friend Richard Champion's and on account of my bodily weakness put myself under the direction of a skillful doctor whose prescriptions answered the desired effect so that I was enabled to attend most of their meetings as they came in course in divers of which the Lord owned us, and blessed my soul with an evidence that although it was his pleasure to dip me deep into suffering, I was not forsaken by him, who is our Life and by the gracious renewings of it we live, whilst here and in the time of my great suffering in spirit I often was earnest with the Lord to show me the cause thereof as I was not conscious to myself of having wilfully offended in either doing or leaving undone what had been clearly revealed to be a duty but had as far as I knew been faithful, and abundantly desired to be preserved in steadfast obedience to the divine call and as I continued seeking and desiring to know the cause, Holland would at times appear before me with a kind of feeble drought toward it which nature trembled at the view of and gave too much into reasoning upon my incapacity for such an undertaking especially as it was to a nation of another language which I understood not or could I be understood by them save by an interpreter. Whether looking too much at difficulty or imprudently divulging it to an injudicious Friend who gave it birth untimely I cannot tell, but such a perplexing mist came over my understanding from that time that could see no way clear and about that time receiving letters from my companion acquainting me with her determined purpose to go home the first good opportunity and urged me to come to some conclusion rather wishing it might be to return home with her, this added to the strong draught of natural affection I bear my native country and relatives there gave an imprudent bias to my mind which was not in so settled a state as to be capable to form a right judgment in a matter of such great concernment so that in concluding to return home in that cloudy state I ushered myself further into the wilderness and was an inlet to many tribulations which swiftly followed one on the back of another until I was almost swallowed up, being for the most part covered with sadness and clouds of heavy

12th month darkness, and in this situation set out on the 6th of 12th month [February] when set out for Bath had a meeting. Next day 8th went to a meeting at Bradford. 10th. Had a meeting at Melksham so on to the Devizes, Lavington, Bruton House, Calne and Chippenham, in all of which meetings sufferings fell to my lot though sometimes truth favoured. 17th had a meeting at Penswick. 13th to Cosham. 20th at Sutton. 21st at Cirencester, 22nd to Benham, 24th had a meeting Milton. 26th. Went to Witney where the glorious son of Righteousness appeared again to my humiliation, comfort and consolation, but after meeting the cloud again covered my tabernacle. 27th. Went and had a meeting same day at Charlbury. 28th to Chipping Norton where I received a few lines from my much esteemed Friend Edmund Peckover,[67] advising me of his having appointed a meeting that night at Long Compton and also of his great desire to see me if possible, and my desire to see him being equal, as soon as meeting was over set out and got there in good time which was joyful meeting to us all. Edmund had an extraordinary time in meeting to the edification of many. 1st of 1st month [March] went to a meeting which had been appointed for me at Todmarton to which many that were not Friends came, but the distress of my spirit and poverty is not to be expressed in words, and when I lifted up my head which had for some time been down and beheld the people all seekingly with their expectation fixed upon the poor instrument whose condition none knew but him to whom all hearts are open and secrets known—oh the unutterable anguish of soul that seized me insomuch that I could not forbear pleading with the Lord either to lighten my load or remove me from hence, and yet in the midst of my distress a desire sprang in my heart the Lord in mercy would be pleased to feed the multitude although I were not found worthy to be the instrument to hand forth the morsel he might bless, when very unexpectedly to me who but dear Edmund should I see under the meeting house door, and as I sensibly felt clothed with the gospel spirit, which seemed to revive that little spark of life that yet lived in me, even to kindle into a kind of flame of love and adoration of God our Father who was then manifesting his regard to his cause on earth which he had engaged his instruments in and although it was meet with his will to bind my spirit as in fetters of iron and shut up my way for whom this meeting was appointed, yet should concern another, many miles distant whose face was turned another way to come to that meeting, which was the case, was cause of awful marvel and melted me in tears, which run down like rain and as I sat under this watery baptism with my eye to our holy head, sweet silence came over me and in it the waters were divided and an unexpected passage made through Jordan even when she overflowed her banks, and this by virtue of the holy mantle, or gift of the holy spirit of the Lord God of Elijah which seasoned my spirit, and gave strength to stand up and to speak a few words in his name, which I believe settled the minds of the people and prepared the way for the superior service of my Friend to whom I cheerfully gave the right hand of fellowship and his master blessed the cause in his hand that day and it was a day worthy to be remembered amoung the high days when the Lord's servant may say in truth the Lord reigns in Zion. After meeting he told me that he could not proceed on his journey without coming to that meeting, which shows to us that a kind providence is over all. 2nd of 1st month, had an evening meeting at Hook Norton in which was largely concerned. Next day went to Sibford being first the meeting was large and none of the worst. 4th. Went to their monthly meeting held at Avensbury [Aylesbury] where our worthy Friend Benjamin Kidd[68] met me and truth measurably favoured us together. 5th. Went to South Newton and had a good meeting. 6th to Shetford in which after deep exercise was favoured. 7th to a meeting at Warwickshire and that evening rode to Banbury and put up at my particular Friends B. Kidd's who with his wife received me kindly and was sensible the God of peace was with them which rendered my stay with them agreeable to me as well as profitable in the best sense for during my stay he was divers times opened to speak of his experience which was large in the things of God, having been for many years an able minister of the word. Had travelled in divers parts of the world in the exercise of his gift to which I believe he was faithful to an exemplary degree and he in this, the close of his day reaped the fruits of his faithfulness for the Lord was near to him in his bodily decline and though that waxed feeble yet his inward man was strengthened in the lord, etc. He could speak well of the way of truth and had to rest under its shadow with great delight in the approach of immortality for it proved nearer than any of his friends expected, for he daily wasted and departed this life very soon after he expressed his sense of its being nearer than there was any reason to suppose from any outward appearance to me before we parted with many precious truths I treasured up. 8th. Was at their weekday meeting at Banbury and next day went to Avensbury [Aylesbury] again and had a large, good meeting after which went back to Banbury and next day parted with my dear friend, and set out through Northamptonshire for London, expecting the vessel my companion had taken her passage in and the which I proposed to take mine. Had meetings at Eden, Northampton, Malton, Wellingboro, Hitching and so to London, when finding the ship not ready to sail and no great draught to stay in the city, set out with Sarah Beck,[69] an innocent and exemplary Friend, though not public at that time, in order to visit some meetings I had not been at in Essex, Suffolk, Huntingtonshire and Cambridgeshire, etc. Being straited for time was forced to hurry, taking one or two meetings a day in [which] my companion was a faithful helpmeet, travelling in spirit according to her measure, and was affectionately tender to me in my sufferings which she had a sensible feeling of. After had performed this visit returned to London where stayed visiting meetings as they came in course until the 27th of 3rd month [May] when set out and reached Gravesend that night and next day went on board the ship Carolina, Stephen Messnard master, when after tumbling eight weeks in the Downs and at sea we landed at Philadelphia where I found all our family much as I left them and met with an affectionate welcome from my parents and other relations. During our passage about two weeks before we made our capes, being favoured with fine weather and brisk gales in our favour, was looking with pleasure at the fair prospect we had before us of our soon arriving at our desired port when my mind was led to look back at the last meeting I was in Ratcliff in London a little before we left the city. The meeting was large and I found it my place to appear and have reason to think was greatly favoured when in the course of

3rd month

my service was led to mention something of our speedy departure and that there then was opened to my view a prospect of an exercising visage to me, it presented with a dark cloud before me, what it might be, or how it might please God to dispose or deal with me I knew not, but that grievous sufferings awaited me I was confirmed of beyond a doubt which at that time so deeply affected me, could not but request the prayers of the living, a thing I seldom or ever publicly craved before. At that time I did not know but it might be our lot to be cast away, yet as to that was made perfectly resigned to the disposal of that almighty power by whom the worlds were made — and in the remembrance of this sight was desirous to see into the cause of it, what it should be I was to suffer as the voyage until then had been prosperous and no ways more disagreeable than might have been expected from a crowded cabin of variety of dispositions, some of them none of the easiest, when such a scene opened to my view as was almost more than nature could live under. I laid myself down on my bed in perfect agony of spirit which vented itself in a flood of tears, when my companion came down to my cabin, a thing she seldom did in the daytime, it being always her practice to stay upon deck and mine to stay below. She came up to me, and taking hold of my hand, thus addressed me, my dear what is it ails thee? I could not immediately enter upon the subject for real grief, or did I at once conclude it proper, but after weighing the matter, told her if she would sit down I would tell her that part of the cause which related to herself. She seemed much affected and was tender. I told her I had then opened to me as clear as the sun in the firmament that when I got home there would be such spirits raised up against me as would perhaps lay me waste in the truth which would certainly be the case if the Lord did not powerfully oppose for my help, and that she would with one other who I named to her, convey the fuel to kindle the fire, the heat of which I then felt. I never shall forget her astonished looks. After some time I still weeping, she said to this purpose, "the Lord forbid, that cannot be, thy conduct has been such that malice itself cannot blast thy reputation." I looking at her with a fixed countenance said, "do thou stand to that and all will be well," upon which she kissed me hastily, and suddenly left me, from which time the Lord only knows the trials I met with, divers ways being much deserted by divine good, and greatly depressed at which I had clearly seen would be my portion, which cut off much of that joy I might have had at the prospect of soon seeing my native country and near relations and friends whom I affectionately loved after an absence of three years and three months, exclusive of the time our being at sea. Should any doubt the truth of this relation, as perhaps some may who hate me without cause, Shall just say that at time I write this I am confined to my chamber under great indisposition of body and from some prospect of my future change, am desirous of being found before God, doing justly to all men, and can thankfully say I can now forgive all men, which has been the most difficult lesson to me, our Lord has prescribed his followers to learn.

Some little time after I got home, went to Plymouth and Horsham to meet my dearly beloved Friend Mary Weston,[70] who was then on her religious visit to Friends in these parts. My obligations to her were many for her kind treatment of me whilst at London. I was always affectionately received by her and her kind husband at their home where I spent many of my leisure hours, sometimes to real profit. Once in particular, not long before she took this journey to America, there being with me there M. P., M. Smith[71] and companion with other Friends, fell into silence when M. Smith appeared in an extra manner, upon the passage of Ruth's, following her mother-in-law, commenting upon Ruth's great attach-

Ruth 2:14

ment to her, and what she met with in consequence thereof, to wit in the field of Boze, where her sop was dipped in vinegar. Had never heard that passage so commented upon before, she spoke with great authority and clearness and we were truly baptized under her ministry. After meeting she took me in her arms, and said dear Eliza, thou wilt have thy sop dipped in vinegar. Our meeting was pleasant to us, and her service acceptable in those meetings. After Horsham meeting, I returned home and in a few days went to pay my dear Friends at Fair Hill a visit, where I was affectionately received by my valued Friends I. Norris[72] and his sister Betty, and his children who were always near to me. When here I remembered a comfortable assurance I had been favoured with when in Sussex in old England I being then at a Friend's house after a meeting I had thereaway and it being a pleasant place in the cool of the evening walked out in order to enjoy a little retirement which is very difficult to get in this journeying among Friends being desirous of our company. As I was in his gravel walk which fronted his house much as that does at I. Norris's, and this place in other respects resembling that brought the Friends there fresh to remembrance, and this thought rose in my heart when shall I be favoured to see that beloved spot and immediately was said in my heart, by this day twelve months thou shalt be there. There was such an assurance with it as brought great tenderness over me, so that when I joined the company a Friend present inquired into the cause of my being thus affected. I told him home was brought fresh into my memory and perhaps by that twelve months I might be there. This for the present was comfortably confirming but it passed away and I seldom if ever thought of it until now when I saw the performance of that assurance. Soon after this came our quarterly meeting which was large and satisfactory, when had the opportunity to see many of my particular friends from the country which gave me joy. I then went to visit my dear friend and relation Hannah Cooper,[73] who had in my absence buried her beloved husband, my uncle by marriage who had always been affectionately tender to me. I found her greatly declined in her health, and upon seeing me much affected with her loss, as it was brought fresh to her remembrance ———— Soon after this visit I went to Merion Meeting where I met with our worthy Friend J. Evans[74] from North Wales, whom I was rejoiced to see. The meeting was large, many going from town with me, and proved a humbling time. John had the principal service to my great satisfaction for I really loved and honoured him for the work's sake, he being an able minister of the gospel of our Lord, and one that delighted to see truth prosper in any. I may indeed say he was my nursing father.

The fall following when the time of our yearly meeting came the prospect of its being larger than common, Friends concluded to hold a meeting in the State House, that on first day my companion and I attended, which was large and hope well. The meetings throughout the whole was to me satisfactory, yet not without my exercises in them. In the eighth month following I had in my heart to visit my Friends at Wilmington and my near Friend Esther White[75] offered to go with me. Also my Friend A. Morris[76] accompanied us, where my meeting with dear E. Shipley [Elizabeth Shipley][77] was joyous to both. In this journey my husband that now is, first acquainted me with his intentions of offering himself to me as a suitor for marriage which I was to take under consideration, his former wife being then deceased about eight months; but we did not keep company upon that score for some time after, which affair I think I duly weighed, and in the second month following concluded to accomplish, but before that was done, between the monthly meetings in which we proposed our marriage, I performed a visit to Friends within the verge of our quarterly meeting, Elizabeth Morgan[78] being my companion from North Wales where had a large favoured meeting and solid satisfaction in J. E.'s [John Evans] family. From hence we went to Providence and to William Evans Pott's furnace, Oley, and so over the blue mountains and back to the forest, taking the meetings thereon which took up the best part of three weeks, in which journey we travelled hard yet it was made easy to me, having an agreeable companion and Friends everywhere exceeding kind, especially our worthy ancient Friend E. Hugh [Hugh Ellis],[79] a lively minister of the gospel, one of a tender spirit, lively and instructive in conversation, which rendered our stay at his house edifying. After these meetings was over returned home, a few days

before our monthly meeting where we were left to our liberty to conclude our marriage, which was solemnized on the 30th of 2nd month, 1752 at our meeting house at Philadelphia. We were favoured with the company of our esteemed Friend William Hammans[80] from Duck Creek and Elizabeth Shipley who had come on purpose to attend our marriage. The meeting was large and the public service weighty and particularly suitable to the occasion. I had a good meeting which had the tendency to confirm me I was right in the present undertaking ——

Some little time before our marriage went with Mary Weston to Haddonfield and Burlington Quarterly Meetings where was also Sara Thompson and had good service at divers meetings at one of which was Governor Belcher[81] who invited us all to dinner with him, and he and family behaved very respectfully. Here I had the pleasure of seeing his wife's son and his wife who had been my mates and had been kindly useful to me on board. After the meetings were over I returned home in company with I. T. and others. About six weeks after our marriage my husband went with me to the marriage of Gidion Bickerdike with Hannah Watson at Trenton where was a large meeting. The fall following, our yearly meeting being held at Burlington, went in company with E. Shipley to it, taking Haddonfield in our way where we had an extra meeting, through the extendings of Divine regard manifested to us. The subject treated of that was the necessity of Divine revelation respecting religion, and urged that alone being the foundation on which Christ had built his church and by which we come to be members of it. We went home with a Friend who had lately been made an elder to lodge that night who, as we were sitting still in the evening, seriously put the question to us, did we really believe that Divine revelation was yet continued to people in our day. I was startled at the query but was not forward to answer it as my elder Friend was present who turned toward him and replied, "I think my companion today has said enough as confirms she believes in it and I will assure thee, I do." The next day we got to the meeting of ministers. The meetings were in general very large and many of them divinely favoured, particularly that at Bristol. We had one in the evening at T. Marriott's[82] where was a large number of Friends in which the power of truth was in great dominion. It might in truth be said to be a feast of fall things with wine well refined. My soul was humbled under the sense of God's love and reverently bowed before him, giving him the praise of his works which are marvelous in our eyes. After this meeting we returned home, my husband having come to accompany me. The remaining part of this winter was under necessity to abide at home. The spring following my first son was born, on the 10th of 3rd month, March being the year 1753, was named William Hudson Morris. The first journey after my recovery was to Lancaster whence had proposed to go to West River Yearly Meeting but whilst I was here the drought had so far died away thought it best to return home lest after all the fatiguing of such a long journey I might instead of the reward of peace be queried with after this humbling manner, who hath required this at thy hand? After being at one meeting and visiting my particular Friend S. Wright,[83] returned home, when soon after was brought under great exercise of mind from various causes, both within and without, insomuch as I was fearful I should make shipwreck of faith. No language is sufficient to set forth to the full what my soul passed through for many months, such unspeakable poverty of spirit with failure of inward strength, and almost all outward help, when, through the complicated provocations and temptations I then met with, I stood in the greatest need that in any stage of life had done, I was bereft of all outward consolation, even those with whom I had taken sweet council became estranged from me, and I really believe it was the will of God to thus enclose me in a veil of darkness from the sight of my Friends that I should not in the day of proving make man my refuge or flesh my arm, for our Lord is a jealous God and will have the praise for his own works, which are marvellous indeed. I then thought it hard, and from the view of times past, greatly lamented the present both night and day, each furnishing fresh cause of complaint, for was frequently scared with dreams and affrighted with the visions of the night. Insomuch that when it was night I wished for the morning and as the day abated not my exercises, again I longed for night, and thus was I led along as in the night, not being favoured to see the hand which supported me in the day of trial. I would frequently retire alone to seek the Lord as in days past, but in vain did I seek him who had his face hid from me. As to prayer I could not even form words or in any attempt find access to the throne of grace. After this afflicting manner I passed many tedious months, until one night as I was in my bed wrestling with all the power I had until I felt a deprivation of my outward faculties, and such terror of destruction as was more than could have long lived under, for it was as if was near going out of life, which if I had but been favoured with an evidence of acceptance with God would have been joyous to me, but it being otherwise with me dared not seek it. I thought I was going out of life and cried to God in the bitterness of my soul and he graciously heard even from heaven, his holy habitation, and speak peace be still, may I never forget the mercy, there was calm and in it a holy submission to the dispensation of Almighty God, and renewed strength to trust should it please him that the fig should not blossom neither should there be fruit on the vine, the labour of the olive fail and the field should give no meat, the flock should be cut from the fold and there should be no food in the states, yet I will rejoice in the Lord and joy in the God of

Heb. 11:1

salvation. From this time I walked by faith, and not by light, for had now to support me was the substance of things hoped for and evidence of things not seen. The first meeting after this sore baptism was at the Bank Street Meeting House at the time of the spring meeting. Of an evening I went to it poor and low, with little expectation of any great enjoyment, or did I ask great things in that day, a crumb from the table was sufficient. But he who is glorious in holiness, fearful in day and worketh wonders in the Earth appeared in his ancient being and mightily favoured with presence to the humbling of many hearts present. I then thought my captivity was turned as the streams of the south, and was exceedingly fearful of doing anything that should offend my maker, and cause his displeasure any more, but, for what cause I knew not, the cloud was cast over my tent again, but I was kept in the patience, and suffered in silence, for no mortal knew in all this time how it was with me, but made various conjectures upon my silence in meetings foreign from the true cause, all which I patiently rested under from a lively hope at times was favoured with, that I should see better days. During the gloomy season I several times went to country meetings in hopes that the change of place might produce a change of state, as Haddonfield, Evesham, Burlington Yearly Meeting, Concord Quarterly meeting, Wilmington and divers other places. But to no great purpose. There still remained a void unfilled, that nothing but the divine presence could fill. About this time it opened in my mind, as what would be most likely to settle my mind to retire into the country as I could not in the state I was in properly attend to the cares of so large a family as I was then the head of, or was the daily concourse of people about business pleasant to me. I longed to be released from those outward encumberances, that my mind might be at leisure, to pursue the object of my wishes, to wit, a quiet habitation in the truth. My husband fell in with this proposal much readier than I expected, and sundry circumstances concurred to lead to it I believe by the interposition of providence. We left the city in the latter part of the year 1756 and settled at our place in Southwark, soon after which was visited with a severe fit of illness which brought me very low and before I recovered my husband fell ill with a nervous fever which brought him to the brink of the grave and upon me grievous exercise. However it pleased the restorer of paths to walk in to remove this threatening storm, by raising him up which I thought singular favour, yet suffered other trials to befall us of various [illegible] which through mercy I was enabled to bear with resignation, as believing they would all work together for good if I kept my eye single to the master, who knoweth how to rule his own household, which he ever governeth in wisdom. I had about this time some drawings to visit a few meetings in the Jerseys with my dear Elizabeth Shipley, but for reasons I am a stranger to, was discouraged therefrom by some who I knew it would nothing avail me to strive against, so submitted to give the matter up, though it tended to increase my inward sufferings for a time. After continuing two years at the farm our health not recovering thought it best to let it and leave off all business which some favourable turns in our circumstances admitted of. We then went to that place we had formerly kept as a country house, to which moved in 1758 where we enjoyed better health and had less care upon me. At this place I had my second son Luke who was born April 10th and the 4th of the week just seven year and one month being 1760. After the birth of this son was favoured with a better state of health than had been blessed with for some years, by which means got more to meetings both at home and abroad. In about six weeks after my son's birth my well esteemed Friend Grace Lloyd[84] departed this life. I went to her burial at Chester where had a large solid meeting. She had been always tender

1st month

11th month

and loving to me which rendered her death a real loss to me. The next day I returned home and attended to the care of my little nursery, went but little out except to meetings at home and near home such as Fair Hill, Germantown, Haddonfield. 1st month, January, 1761 was proclaimed our present King George 3rd, his royal grandfather having full of years departed this life 25th of 9th month, having filled the exalted station with honour alloted him by that providence by whom Kings rule and princes decree justice. For years his mild government and love of peace rendered him the beloved object of his subject's affections who greatly lament his loss.

Being invited to attend the funeral of my cousin, William Evans, my husband accompanied me to Evesham meeting house where we meet the company who came with the corpse for internment. After which we had a meeting which was large and satisfactory. Next day came to Haddonfield meeting where was a marriage in which meeting truth measurably favoured us, after which returned home. 11th month, 28th, my third son was born and deceased the week following in a fit. I was brought very low by heavy bodily complaints which confined me sometime to home. As every manifest interposition of providence in our favour calls for our humble acknowledgements to the director of it I cannot but mention with gratitude what I esteem such in a singular manner. My oldest son going into the next room from where I was sitting and in a few minutes I heard a gun go off and a little girl I had living with me screamed and then ceased. I was greatly alarmed and run to where they were. Found her lying flat on the floor speechless with fright and my son little better. He not knowing that the gun was charged held it up toward her .....

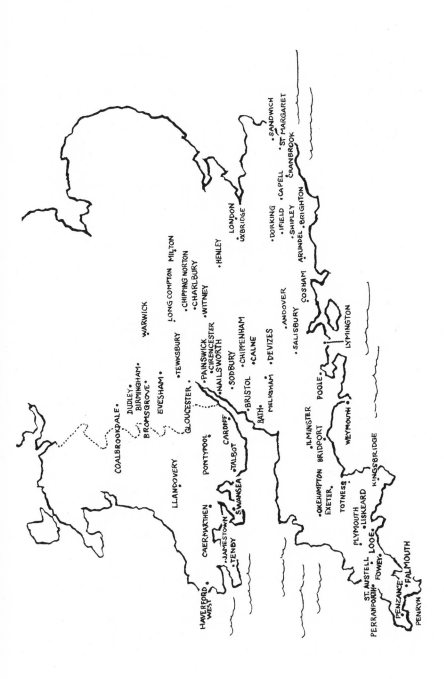

Places Elizabeth Hudson visited in southwest England and Wales

THE JOURNAL OF ELIZABETH HUDSON

Notes – Introduction

1. Frederick Tolles, *Meeting House and Counting House: the Quaker Merchants of Colonial Philadelphia 1682-1763* (University of North Carolina Press, 1948).

2. Elizabeth Hudson's *Journal*, Part II, 151. Quaker Collection, Haverford College (hereafter cited as QCHC).

Notes – Part I

3. Edmund Peckover (1695-1767); Samuel Hopwood (1674-1760); and John Haslam (1690-1773) were three British Quaker ministers who traveled in the American colonies at this time. "Dictionary of Quaker Biography," (hereafter cited as DQB), QCHC.

4. Christopher Wilson (1704-1761) of Cumberland and Eleazar Sheldon of Dublin (approximately 1702-1760) also visited the American colonies in 1744. DQB.

5. Elizabeth Hudson might have meant Elizabeth Stephens of Third Haven, Maryland, who was on a religious visit to the Philadelphia Yearly Meeting area. *Minutes*, Ministers and Elders, Philadelphia Yearly Meeting 1-19-1742/43. Microfilm, QCHC.

6. Isaac Norris, II (1701-1766) was a prominent Quaker merchant and statesmen, whose library at Fairhill was prized. His sister Betty, Elizabeth's friend, lived with him. DQB.

7. Millicent Somers Townsend (1685-1762) of Egg Harbor, New Jersey, was recognized in 1723 as a minister. DQB.

8. John Shotwell was a member of Rahway New Jersey Monthly Meeting and of a large Quaker family. *Records*, Rahway and Plainfield Meetings, published by New York Yearly Meeting Records.

9. K. B. is possibly Keziah Baker, a minister of Rye, New York; P. D. is likely Peter Davis (1680-1776) of Rhode Island who was traveling in the ministry in this area and subsequently went to England. "A Register of the Names of Publick Friends that have visited New England since the year 1656." QCHC.

10. Born in England in 1693, Jane Fenn came to Pennsylvania as an indentured servant in 1712, and became a Quaker, traveling in the ministry in 1722 in the colonies and in 1725 to Barbados. In 1727 she made a trip to Great Britain, traveling with Abigail Bowles, a minister of Ireland. In 1738 she married Joseph Hoskins. "Life of Jane Hoskens(sic)" in *Friends Library* (Philadelphia, Rakestraw, 1837) 1: 463.

11. For J. Evans, please see Susanna Morris's *Journal*, Part III, note 40.

12. John Griffith (1713-1776) was born in Radnorshire and in 1726 emigrated to Pennsylvania, where he became a traveling minister. D.F. is possibly David Ferris (1707-1779) of Wilmington, Delaware, who joined Friends in 1733 and became a minister. DQB.

13. For S. Nottingham, please see Susanna Morris's *Journal*, Part III, note 56.

14. Margaret Bowne was prominent in New York Yearly Meeting. Please see *Women's Minutes*, 1757, Haviland Room, New York Yearly Meeting.

15. Thomas Gawthorp (1709-1780), a British Friend, made four trips to America as a minister. John Griffith and Peter Davis were both en route to Great Britain as ministers. DQB. "Ministering Friends of America who have visited foreign parts in Truth's Service," QCHC.

Notes – Part II

16. Joseph Fade was a prominent member of Ireland Yearly Meeting and a descendant of James Fade, a pioneer Irish Quaker.

Mentioned as a property owner in Olive C. Goodbody, *Guide of Irish Quaker Records: 1654-1860* (Dublin, 1967).

17. For M. Peisley, please see Susanna Morris's *Journal*, Introduction, note 9.

18. Abigail Bowles Watson (1685-1752) became a minister in 1725, and that year visited the American colonies traveling with Jane Fenn. She also visited Great Britain four times. DQB.

19. John Turner of Lurgan was a Quaker minister in Ireland, mentioned in the "Memoirs of Samuel Fothergill" in 1744, and in the "Life of Thomas Story," *Friends Library*, 1: 120; 9: 120; 10:361.

20. James Gough (1712-1780), an Irish minister, became the superintendent of the Friends School in Dublin. DQB.

21. Sarah Artis was a traveling minister. Mary Kirby (1709-1779) of Norfolk became a minister at age 30 and traveled widely in the ministry. In 1758 she visited the American colonies. DQB.

22. Richard Champion's home in Bristol was a haven for Friends. In 1710 he married Esther Palmer of Long Island, one of the early American traveling women ministers, who had come to England on a religious visit that year. She died in 1714 of smallpox. "Ministering Friends," 2, QCHC.

23. Benjamin Kidd (1692-1751) of Yorkshire traveled extensively in the ministry, including a trip to the American colonies in 1723 -24. DQB.

24. Israel Pemberton, Jr. (1715-1779), a prominent Philadelphia merchant, a clerk of Philadelphia Yearly Meeting, and a well-known philanthropist, was known as "the King of the Quakers." DQB.

25. Daniel Weston (1707-1755) of London, a cooper, was married to Mary Pace, the minister and was himself a minister. Joseph Row (1722-1792), a London weaver, was an elder and frequently entertained foreign guests at yearly meeting time. DQB.

26. For S. Bownas, please see Susanna Morris's *Journal*, Part III, note 47.

27. Isaac Sharpless (1702-1784) was a popular minister in Great Britain. DQB.

28. Isaac Thompson was a British traveling minister who accompanied Samuel Bownas on his travels in 1699. Mary Neale mentions him in her journal in 1748. *Friends Library* vol. 3:13; vol. 11:80.

29. Charles Norris (1712-1766) was a Philadelphia merchant and a brother of Elizabeth Hudson's friend, Elizabeth Norris. DQB.

30. For Edmund Peckover, please see Elizabeth Hudson's *Journal*, Part I, note 3.

31. For John Wilson, please see Susanna Morris's *Journal*, Part I, note 19.

32. John Haslam (1690–1773) of Yorkshire was host to John Woolman on his 1772 journey. Henry J. Cadbury, *John Woolman in England* (London: Friends Historical Society, 1971), 53.

33. William Longmire (?–1763), a British minister. *Friends Library* vol. 9: 97–101.

34. For John Griffith, please see Susanna Morris's *Journal*, Part I, note 19.

Notes - Part III

35. Rowland Wilson, a traveling minister, visited the American colonies in 1727. DQB.

36. Daniel Stanton (1708-1770) of Philadelphia was a minister for forty-three years. On this trip he had accompanied Samuel Nottingham, another minister, to Barbados and then to Ireland and Great Britain. DQB.

37. Sarah Dixon Reays (1711-1755), wife of John Reays, was a minister who traveled to Scotland and Ireland. DQB.

38. Elizabeth Hudson may have meant Deborah Wilson (1687-1754) who was a traveling minister and wife of John Wilson.

39. Grace Chambers (1713-1762), born in Durham, England, married and became a traveling minister. *Piety Promoted.*, 8th part, 391.

40. Patrick Gordon (1644-1736) was governor of the Province of Pennyslvania, 1726-1736. James C. Wilson and John Fiske, eds., *Cyclopedia of American Biography* (New York: Appleton and Company, 1886), vol. 2:278–279.

41. George Miller (1682-1761), a manufacturer of linens, was a prominent Edinburgh Quaker. Thomas Areskine (Elizabeth Hudson spelled his name Arisekin) was his son-in-law. DQB.

42. William Backhouse (1695-1761) was a yarn merchant and a Quaker minister who visited the American colonies in 1735. DQB.

43. Lydia Rawlinson Lancaster (1682-1761) was a minister for fifty-three years. She had visited the American colonies in 1719. DQB. The disagreeable companion may have been Deborah Wilson.

44. Samuel Fothergill (1715-1772) of Warrington was a shop-keeper and a Quaker minister. He subsequently traveled in the American colonies in 1754. DQB.

45. Edith Flower (1701-1755), a minister from 1745, never married, and traveled throughout England and Ireland. DQB

Notes - Part IV

46. Gerrard van Hasson (1695-1772) was born in Holland, but moved to Ireland in 1737. A minister, he traveled in both Great Britain and Ireland, visiting families. DQB.

47. Thomas Nicholson (1715-1780) was an American traveling minister from Little River, North Carolina. He visited England from 1749 to 1751 traveling over 2500 miles on horseback. DQB.

48. Frances Henshaw Paxton Dodshon (1714-1793), a British minister, wrote an account of her spiritual pilgrimage, *Some account of the convincement and religious experience of Frances Dodshon*, Warrington, England, 1803. DQB.

49. James Wilson (1677-1769), a British minister, became a convinced Friend in 1707. DQB.

50. Samuel Spavold (1708-1795), a ship joiner, traveled extensively in the ministry, including a trip to the American colonies in 1757. DQB.

51. John Richardson (1667-1753), a traveling minister, visited the American colonies in 1700 and 1731. DQB.

52. Robert Massey was clerk of Lincoln Quarterly Meeting and a member of an old Lincolnshire Quaker family. Susan Davies, *Quakerism in Lincolnshire* (Yard Publishing Services, 1989) 71.

53. For John Griffith, please see Susanna Morris's *Journal*, Introduction, note 3.

54. For M. Peisley, please see Susanna Morris's *Journal*, Introduction, note 9.

55. For Mary Weston, please see Susanna Morris's *Journal*, Introduction, note 6.

56. Sarah Crawley (1717-1799) traveled in Ireland and Great Britain in the ministry. She also wrote *Piety Promoted*, edited by John Gurney Bevan, London, 1810, 113.

Notes - Part V

57. Isaac Penington (1616-1679), a founder of the Religious Society of Friends, wrote copiously about the new religion. William Braithwaite, *The Beginnings of Quakerism*, edited by Henry J. Cadbury (Cambridge, 1970), 504.

58. Benjamin Holmes was a traveling minister. Benjamin Johnson of Hanover County, Virginia, was converted to Quakerism by

this minister in 1717. John Smith, "The Lives of the Ministers of the Gospel among the People called Quakers," unpublished MMS, 1770, vol. 2: 397.

59. This reference bears out the fact the Elizabeth Hudson was wealthy enough to provide her own traveling expenses.

60. Mary Smith (1712-1751), a traveling minister, was born in Norfolk and became a convinced Friend. She visited the Island of Jersey in 1750, and died shortly thereafter. DQB.

Notes - Part VI

61. For Samuel Bownas, please see Susanna Morris's *Journal*, Part III, note 47.

62. Samuel Hopwood (1674-1760) became a minister in 1699, and visited the American colonies in 1741. He returned to England in 1746 and continued his travels in the ministry until 1754. DQB.

63. For John Churchman, please see Susanna Morris's *Journal*, Part III, note 37.

64. John Hunt (1712-1778), born in Great Britain, first came to the American colonies in 1738 with John Churchman. In 1756 he and Christopher Wilson were sent by London Yearly Meeting to look into the management of Indian affairs. He later emigrated to Pennsylvania and was one of the Quakers banished to Winchester, Virginia, during the Revolutionary War. DQB.

65. For Richard Champion, please see Elizabeth Hudson's *Journal*, Part II, note 22.

66. Eleanor Clark (1705?-1756), a British traveling minister, was convinced in 1746. DQB.

67. For Edmund Peckover, please see Elizabeth Hudson's *Journal*, Part I, note 3.

68. For Benjamin Kidd, please see Elizabeth Hudson's *Journal*, Part II, note 23.

69. Sarah Sims Beck (1715-1799), of Canterbury, became a minister at age thirty-seven and later visited Ireland and Scotland.

70. For Mary Weston, please see Susanna Morris's *Journal*, Introduction, note 6.

71. For Mary Peisley, please see Susanna Morris's *Journal*, Introduction, note 9. For Mary Smith, please see Elizabeth Hudson's *Journal*, Part V, note 60.

72. For Isaac Norris and Betty Norris, please see Elizabeth Hudson's *Journal*, Part I, note 6.

73. Hannah Dent Cooper (?-1754) of Yorkshire traveled as a minister in England and Wales and visited the American colonies in 1732. She married Joseph Cooper in 1733. He died in 1749. DQB.

74. For John Evans, please see Susanna Morris's *Journal*, Part III, note 40.

75. Esther Canby White (1700-1777) of Wilmington became a minister in 1717. In 1743 she traveled to England in the ministry with Elizabeth Shipley (1690-1777) of London Grove, also a minister.

76. Anthony Morris, Jr. (1705-1780) oversaw the Morris family brewery and extended the family's real estate holdings. He was an overseer of the Philadelphia public schools and a contributor to Pennsylvania Hospital. In 1730 he married Sarah Powell and together they had seven children.

77. For Elizabeth Shipley, please see note 75 above.

78. For Elizabeth Morgan, please see Susanna Morris's *Journal*, Introduction, note 5.

79. Elizabeth Hudson may have meant Hugh Ellis (1687-1764), born in Wales, emigrated in 1700 to Pennsylvania, and settled in Gwynedd. He became a minister in 1722. DQB.

80. For William Hammans, please see Susanna Morris's *Journal*, Part II, note 30.

81. Jonathan Belcher was governor of New Jersey from 1747 to 1757. Allen Johnson and Dumas Malone, eds., *Dictionary of American Biography* (New York: Scribners, 1931), 143–144.

82. Thomas Marriott, a member of Falls Meeting, was the husband of Mary Marriott, a traveling Friend. As Mary Foulke, she traveled with Susanna Morris in 1728. John Smith, "The Lives of the Ministers of the Gospels among the People called Quakers," unpublished MMS, 1770, vol. 2: 479.

83. Susanna Wright (1697-1784) was a poet, scientist, and frontier woman. James, *Notable American Women, 1607–1950*, editors, Edward T. James, Janet Wilson James, and Paul S. Boyer (Cambridge: Belknap Press, 1950), vol. 3:688–870.

84. Grace Lloyd (1680-1760) was a prominent member of Chester Monthly Meeting and clerk of the Philadelphia Women's Yearly Meeting. She had taken Jane Fenn into her home and encouraged her in her ministry. DQB.

THE JOURNAL

of

ANN MOORE
1710 – 1783

ANN MOORE
1710-1783

Ann Herbert Moore was born in Bucks County, Pennsylvania, on the 16th of 9th month (November) 1710. Her mother may have been a Friend, but her father evidently was not. Her mother died when she was an infant, and she was placed with a Quaker family in Newtown, Bucks County, Pennsylvania, who also raised several other orphans. She had a rather rudimentary education, as evidenced by her handwriting and spelling. She was, however, well-educated in the Bible, and early showed a religious bent. In or around 1735, she married Walter Moore, a widowed Friend with two small children,[1] and following this marriage, in 1738 she applied for and was accepted into membership in Buckingham Meeting. Later that year she became a recognized minister and frequently, thereafter, attended the meetings of ministers and elders of Philadelphia Yearly Meeting. In 1743 she transferred her membership to Middletown Meeting.[2]

Walter Moore was described as a man "not being of regular habits" and was often under meeting discipline, perhaps for drinking. Whatever the problem, the family moved frequently, and experienced poverty as a result. The two had five additional children.[3] They lived for a while in Bucks County near Middletown, then moved in 1746 to Fairfax, Maryland, where they joined Fairfax Meeting, although Walter was under meeting discipline. From here, in 1748, Ann made her first major trip as a traveling minister, and later that year Walter's daughter, Sarah, married Allen Farquhar. In 1750 they moved back to Pennsylvania, and joined Abington Meeting as a family. From Abington, Ann made a trip in the ministry in 1752, visiting Friends in Maryland and Virginia.

Unfortunately, her husband's problems did not improve, and he was disowned from membership by Abington. In 1753 they moved to Gunpowder, Maryland, and remained there for almost thirty years.[4]

The small country meetings, such as Gunpowder, often did not have a single minister in their midst, and were dependent upon the traveling ministers for spiritual sustenance. Shortly after the Moores moved to Gunpowder, two traveling women ministers, Mary Peisley from Ireland and Catherine Payton from Great Britain paid the meeting a visit, and may have inspired Ann to think about traveling more widely. After the birth of another child, Mary, in September of 1754, Ann began to visit local meetings, and in 1756 embarked on the first of the longer journeys recorded in her journal. In this case she felt called to visit the British army at Albany.[5]

Perhaps one factor in this call was the fact that her stepson, Thomas Moore, had enlisted. She spoke of him as "my poor captive son" but was unable to persuade or arrange for him to leave military life. In 1763 she wrote to Israel Pemberton about him, asking him to intercede. Ann Moore always felt that people might criticize her for the backsliding ways of her husband and son. "You were acquainted with my great and deep exercises on some of your accounts; being much blamed by some and others mocking and seeming to rejoice at the anguish of my poor afflicted soul, which made me conclude it would avail nothing for me to go this journey. As I could not rule my own family, nor persuade my Friends at home to walk orderly, what good could I do abroad?

Thus the unwearied enemy, who knew my weak side, got in at unawares," she wrote in her journal when making a trip in 1760. Her weak side, she thought, was fearing what others might think. However, she came to feel that this was a cross she must bear, and that it did not excuse her from Holy Obedience. Because of her husband's problems she had little money of her own, and needed help with her journeys, a fact that she mentions periodically in her journal, and which is attested to by the Philadelphia Yearly Meeting of Women buying the supplies for her trip to England.[6]

Her journal in her own hand is in the possession of the widow of a descendant, Rosalie Douglas of Indianapolis. It is too fragile to be copied or borrowed. Mr. and Mrs. Douglas have made a transcript of this manuscript, but because the manuscript itself is partially illegible, and they did not have access to Quaker names, it is not entirely accurate. A manuscript copy by her daughter, Rachel Price, is on file at the Friends Historical Library, Swarthmore. There is also one small section of manuscript in Moore's original handwriting, written in 1775, which is not included in the Price manuscript. I have transcribed the Price manuscript, with the one exception of the 1775 section.

This journal is remarkable for the lengths to which Ann Moore was willing to go to be obedient, and her constant openness to the guidance of the Holy Spirit. It is also worth study for the valor with which she defended women's right to preach against several clerical attackers. A strong pacifist, she insisted on preaching to the British army during the French and Indian war, and later, she traveled to and from New York in 1778, with Alice Jackson as companion, getting permission from General Anthony Wayne to cross the Hudson despite the presence of British troops. On the way back from Long Island she encountered soldiers but did not let them deter her from her ministerial duties.

Like many of her contemporaries, Ann Moore believed that dreams were a source of Divine revelation. The accounts of her various dreams and how they seemed to reveal her future course are quite remarkable. Around 1780, she moved from Gunpowder to Baltimore, and there she died on November 11, 1783.

THE JOURNAL OF ANN MOORE

PART I

*Her journey from Maryland to Pennsylvania, Albany, in
the Province of New York,
and some parts of New England.*

I set forward on this journey the 29th of 8th month, 1756
accompanied by Ruth Holland.[7] We rode about fifty miles
this day and lodged at James Brookes's. The next day at Sandy
Spring meeting which was a a solid, good meeting, wherein
my heart and soul was comforted. In the evening we had a
sweet, comfortable meeting in James Brookes's house, his wife
not being able to go to meeting she having been helpless
about three weeks with the rheumatism. From thence we went
home with William Ballenger and staid that night. The next
day attended their meeting which was close and heavy. In
the evening we crossed the River Potomac, and the day following at Fairfax Meeting, which was a sweet, heavenly meeting. From thence we went with several Friends to Mary
Janney's[8] and dined, in the evening we crossed the River
Potomac again, and lodged at William Matthews's.[9] The next
day we went to Monoquesy Meeting; this was a hard close
meeting, darkness seemed to cover the earth, and gross darkness the people. Yea, I thought I never was made more sensible of the darkness of Egypt; but, oh! the Lord was pleased
to give me a renewed cause to praise his great and holy name,
who arose by his ancient love and power, and divided the
light from the darkness, giving power to divide the word
aright, and to set forth the state of the meeting; several things
being mentioned among them which is contrary to our holy
profession. And when I signified to a Friend that I was ready

to admire that such things should be mentioned among us as a people, he told me it belonged to some professing with us; this was cause of sorrow of heart, to think that ever any that had been acquainted with the peaceful government of Jesus Christ, should join with wars and fightings, bloodshed and revenge.

From this meeting, I went home with Richard Richardson, and dined, and from thence with several Friends went to Fredericktown over which my heart mourned and could not be easy without having a meeting there; which I had the next day to good satisfaction; after which accompanied by several Friends we proceeded to Pipe Creek, where I met three of my dear and well beloved daughters; one of them being married, she and her husband went with me to a Friend's house where one was nursing and the third, with some Friends from the meeting I belonged to, came there on purpose to meet me.

We were glad to see each other and sat down together in silence together with the sick Friend to wait upon the Lord, and blessed be his great and holy name, he was pleased to manifest his ancient love among us to the comforting of our hearts.

From thence in company with several Friends I returned to my son-in-law Allen Farquhar's and staid there that night; next day was at their meeting at Pipe Creek, which I think was a solid, good meeting. I also staid that night with my children, and the succeeding next day with my dear companion Ruth Holland and some other Friends I set forward for the back meetings in Pennsylvania where we had several meetings, most of which were dry and heavy, except one that was held in a Friend's house, this was sweet and comfortable.

After this meeting, we went to Yorktown and dined; unaccompanied by any Friends we came to Wright's Ferry[10] and lodged; next morning we crossed the River Susquehanna, no

Friends being with us—I thought the Friends so called at the ferry were too rich in the things of this world, to have any time to go with us, poor pilgrims. So we pursued our journey to Lancaster alone, (my mare fell down by the way, but through divine mercy I was preserved from being much hurt) where we were kindly received, and had a sweet, solid meeting there, and when we left it they took care to provide us with good company to Maiden Creek and Oley Exeter meetings, which were sweet and good; and we had a comfortable sitting with Abigail Willis, who had buried her only son a few days before.

From thence came forward towards Burlington. Lodged one night at John Pott's, and two at Isaac Bolton's; then proceeded to attend the yearly meeting at Burlington where I met many of my old acquaintances, dear and loving Friends. This was a large solid, good meeting.

From this place we traveled to New York, and one meeting there, then crossed the Sound of Long Island, where we had many sweet comfortable meetings and Friends were kind and loving to us.

Leaving this Island we returned to the Main; but my not feeling easy to go on without visiting the city once more, not withstanding we were then twenty miles beyond it, we came to it again, where we met two women Friends who had been on a religious visit to New England, and some other places. Jane Hoskins[11] and Susanna Brown;[12] whom we had before met on Long Island; they being about to return home, gave us an opportunity of writing to our Friends. We now had another meeting in this city, which would have been to good satisfaction had there not been an unskillful blow struck by an instrument that came from Rhode Island, which marred the work, and brought a cloud over the meeting, after which we went to Mamaroneck on the Main, having one yearly meeting and five hundred miles and upwards.

Ann Moore

From this place we set forwards on our journey accompanied by John Cornell,[13] a choice young man; were at eighteen meetings more, divers of them good solid meetings notwithstanding we were sometimes brought down to the bottom of Jordan. Yet blessed be the Lord, he gave us from thence memorials to bring up for his honour, for the renewing of our strength and comforting the mourners in Zion. One of the before mentioned meetings was a quarterly meeting at Oblong where we met our dear Friends, Esther White and Grace Fisher[14] from Philadelphia. This was a solid, good meeting with several of other persuasions being present who behaved sober and still.

After this meeting went with my dear companion and other Friends to Zebulon Ferris's and dined; after dinner as I was reading a passage in The Rise and Progress of Friends in Ireland,[15] my dear companion came and said to me, Shall we return to James Tripp's where we had lodged several nights. The Lord knowing what he was about, laid the weight upon her, for he is a merciful God who knew the weakness of my body and the tenderness of my heart so that he kept his intention in his mind out of my sight, for when we got there, behold, all the rooms of the house were full, my heart seemed easy and cheerful but something moved softly on my mind to contrive for the people to sit down. Then I sat down with them, poor and empty, but truly given up to the will of the Lord, to be disposed of as he might see fit. Thus I sat until the blessing of his sweet spirit fell upon my companion and bowed her heart in awful prayer. Then did the living Lord God smite my heart, and awaken all my senses to set forth his praises and merciful dealings with his people. And oh! may praises be given to his blessed name forever, who gave us a full reward for all our trouble.

During our stay at Oblong the Friends where we lodged buried a daughter who left eight children; and notwithstanding their trouble was great, yet they were very kind to us; and oh saith my Soul! may the Lord bless them, and their poor motherless grandchildren, and feed their souls with living bread as freely as they fed us poor servants with temporal bread.

Previous to this quarterly meeting I was so concerned to go to Albany that I could not rest day nor night, until I freely gave up to go, which I did and rose one morning about a week before the quarterly meeting, with that intention; but before I was dressed my heart grew easy and rested in sweet peace which gave me to think that the Lord would accept the will for the deed. But oh! alas! the last day of the quarterly meeting, as I was walking up the hill to the meeting house, I seemed translated into heavenly joys and as though I saw myself standing in Albany by the army and heard the general, when he saw us, command his army to shout for joy, and give glory to the God of Heaven, who had remembered us; with much more which I forebear to mention.

From this time my concern increased, and grew so heavy that I found there I must go, notwithstanding I sought out all the little places where ever Friends had had meetings. But alas! this would not do, my heart was as yet heavy, and ran towards the British army at Albany, and by no means could I see my way home, though I strove much and the more I looked towards home, the darker I grew until I freely gave up, then my heart grew easy, for blessed be his worthy name, he made way for me, opened the hearts of my dear Friends at Oblong and Oswego who provided horses for us, and three of them went with us, Joseph Irish, David Hoag, and Allen Moore.[16]

And on the 14th of 11th month, 1756, we set out for Albany and went cheerfully on. We had not rode many miles before I saw the mountains covered with snow, but I can truly say my heart was filled with the Father's love which overflowed in the secret thereof, to give praises to my holy and

11th month

293

ever blessed master who had so mercifully favoured me in opening the way before me. And oh! may praises be given to him whose mercies endure forever.

We rode this day about five and twenty miles, stopped at Jacob Maule's, a Dutchman who entertained us as kindly as if he had been our brother though he professed not with us. May the Lord, saith my soul, in blessing bless him and in multiplying, multiply of his mercies to him and his forever. For I think there is a blessing due to him and all such who entertain the Lord's servants, for they that do it to the least of his, do it unto him.

Matt. 25:45

We had a meeting in his house which was greatly to his satisfaction. From there we proceeded to Albany and had to admire how the Lord provided for us, we meeting with kind entertainment by the way, and when we got opposite the city we stopped at a house wherein was an old man who discoursed very kindly with us and said to the people of the house and others that was standing by, These are Friends, they call themselves so, and indeed they are Friends to all mankind, and a quiet peaceable people they are.

After putting up our horses we crossed the North River to the city, wherein we were all strangers; yet we found a house where we were kindly used; and this evening, which is the 16th of the 11th Month, we sent a few lines to the Earl of Lowdon,[17] to know if we might have a meeting with him which he readily granted and a sweet time it was. He was put in mind who was the preserver of all mankind, to which he readily agreed, returning us thanks which I know through divine mercy belongs to God alone who willeth not the death of him that dieth; but rather would that he return, repent, and live. Thus do his mercies endure forever. Oh that all men would be so wise as to bow to the adorable name of God whose mercies endure forever. But notwithstanding we were so highly favoured two or three of the Friends who went with

11th month

us let in fear by reason of the smallpox being in the town, which darkened the work in my view and caused a cloud to come over me and the work, and made me afraid to go on remembering Israel was not to move while the cloud was on the tabernacle, therefore we returned back, but the weight of the work under which I had travelled for many months fell on a young Friend that was with us so that he was scarcely able to mount his horse. I saw his countenance was fallen but he did not open his mind to me until we had rode several miles, and then he mentioned to me how it was with him when I told him I should be exceedingly glad if he had spoke but one word on behalf of the cause. I was ready but none of you speaking one word, discouraged me and made the work seem foolish in my view I could not go on. He said he thought he could not have come away until it came in his mind that perhaps I might write to them. Then he came after us, and we rode on almost to Oswego; then the weight fell on me again and no way could I see home, without returning to the city of Albany again, and great cause have I to praise the name of the Lord who prepared a way the second time for us to visit that city which no Friend had visited before us.

The above-mentioned Friend and Zebulon Ferris, returned there with us, these two young men being endued with a measure of that pure spirit wherewith David was when he went out against the uncircumcised Philistines, who said, "Why should any man's heart fail him?" Thus was these two striplings clothed with the valour for the Lord, and his truth upon the earth. Their hearts being filled with zeal for God they proclaimed in the streets a meeting to be held by the people called Quakers in the city hall. Thus did the Lord make them instruments in his holy hand for our help in his work. May the Lord, saith my soul, preserve them in holy awe that they may be as fixed stars in the firmament of his glory.

1 Sam. 17:32

Isa. 61:3

We had five meetings in this city of Albany and had the answer of sweet peace for our labour. Yea "beauty for the ashes and oil of joy for mourning." So did our holy master reward an hundred fold in this world and if we hold on in well doing to the end, life eternal in the world to come.

From this place we returned towards home and at the ferry, met about 250 soldiers who were marching towards the city. When we came in sight of them, the love of the Lord to their souls filled my heart in such a manner that I seemed not clear without desiring them to stand still which the captain refused, saying, I can't nor I shan't for nobody. Then did my peace return to me again, and I went cheerfully on, feeling myself clear of both them and the city. And notwithstanding the weather was cold and the roads rough, yet all was made so easy that my heart often arose with such secret joy that I had to admire the wonderful works of the Lord towards me a poor simple handmaid. We rode pleasantly on, and had one meeting among a raw people between the city and the settlements of Friends where my beloved and holy master was pleased to give strength unto me his poor handmaid to speak well of his name.

From thence we came to Oswego where we had a good sweet meeting, then came to the old Center Oblong where our dear Friends received us very kindly. We staid here three days and had two meetings which were in the main good meetings especially the farewell one which the Lord crowned with the diadem of his love.

12th month

This being the 5th of 12th month, 1756, we have rode one thousand and ninety-four miles, and attended one yearly meeting and seventy-six smaller ones. The next day in company with several Friends we left Oblong and got to Samuel Field's that night, having been at one meeting on our way there where we staid until the succeeding day; then came to Joshua Cornell's. On the road way my mare fell down and threw me and though I was stunned for some time and continued weak many days, yet through the care of two very kind Friends who accompanied us, and the Friends whose house they took us to, I mended fast, so that I was but one day still. This made my dear Friends unwilling that I should return home on this creature, therefore they provided another more suitable for me. So great was their care over me, or rather so great may I say, was the care of my ever blessed master over me. Who would not serve Him, whose mercies endure forever?

From Joshua Cornell's we went to Mamaroneck Meeting, which was sweet and comfortable; We staid two nights at John Stephenson's near the meeting house, who with his wife were very kind to me. He with William Mott[18] accompanied us to New York, where we staid two nights and had two meetings, one in the meeting house and one in the house of the widow Bowne's which were comfortable meetings.

On the 13th of 12th month, in company with Joseph Delaplaine[19] and John Haydock we quit this city, crossed the bay and came to Joseph Shotwell's[20] at Rahway; next day had a meeting there and the day following went to Plainfield meeting; these were heavy sorrowful meetings to me, owing to an expression of a near and dear friend of mine whom I had a good esteem for. He reading some of the letters which my Friends had wrote me, said it made him think of James Nayler which struck me to the heart, and laid me very low that I could not readily recover, it being my weak side soon to be cast down especially by near and dear Friends who I trust are watching over me for my good.[21]

From Plainfield we went to John Webster's and dined, then home with Abner Hampton and lodged that night. Next day rode to Whippaney and had a meeting at Mendham, lodged at William Schooley's, whose son Robert, and Benjamin Shotwell, went with us to the Great Meadows to Richard Lundy's;[22] staid there one night and attended their meeting at Hardwick the forepart of which was a very low baptizing time, but towards the conclusion I was favoured to witness the arising of that ancient love which gives victory over the world, death, and hell and under the influence thereof we were favoured with a sweet, comfortable season. From this meeting we went to Robert Wilson's where we were weatherbound some time. From thence we travelled with the before mentioned Friends Benjamin Shotwell and Ebenezer Wilson to Samuel Large's[23] at Kingwood. Staid there three nights and had two meetings, one in the meeting house and one at Samuel Large's which were good satisfactory meetings wherein Benjamin Shotwell appeared for the first time in public. From thence our well esteemed Samuel Large took us in his sleigh to the next meeting, which was about fourteen miles, and within six miles of the Kingsess ferry. Next day we crossed the Delaware River, and came to John Scarborough's at Buckingham, and the day following attended their meeting, which was small, sweet and solid.

After this meeting we went to John Watson's[24] and staid there two nights. From thence accompanied by John Watson junior we came to Philadelphia, where our dear Friends received us kindly. Here we staid one meeting and then in company with Edward Stabler[25] from Great Britain set forwards toward my home, lodging two nights at Joshua Johnson's at London Grove and attended one meeting there, the early part of which was close and heavy, but ended well. From this meeting we went to Joshua Pusey's[26] and dined, from thence to James Brown at Nottingham, where we lodged that night. From there we came to William Coxe's where we were kindly received, though the master of the house was not at home, he having gone in company with John Hunt from England toward Virginia, who was travelling in the service of truth.

We lodged this night at William Coxe's and when retired to bed my mind was turned inward in a very solid weighty manner, and made renewedly to remember my own weakness, desiring my sweet and holy master might be pleased to give me strength to bear with patience whatever he may suffer me to be tried with on my return home, where we arrived the 4th of the 1st month, 1757, (having had ninety-one meetings) and through divine mercy found my family well, thanksgiving and praises him who is the strength of his people who was pleased to go before us and open the way to the praises of his own name who is God over all, blessed for ever. Amen.

1st month

PLACES ANN MOORE VISITED IN PENNSYLVANIA, NEW JERSEY, CONNECTICUT AND NEW YORK

THE JOURNAL OF ANN MOORE

PART II

An Account of Ann Moore's Travels, Travails and Exercises whilst on a journey from Maryland to Pennsylvania, New Jersey, Some Parts of the Province of New York and Albany.

I set out from home on a journey to Pennsylvania and some parts of New Jersey, the 3rd of 12th month, 1757 not knowing it would be required of me to visit some parts of the Province of New York and Albany, as it afterwards turned out. First visited the back meetings of Friends in Pennsylvania. Lodging one night at George Matthew's, two at Allen Farquhar's, one at John Everitt's[27] one at John Mickle's, one at Alexander Underwood's[28] one at William Griffey's, one at John Garrison's and three at Nathan Hewes's in Yorktown. Then crossed the River Susquehanna, and lodged three nights at Isaac Whitelock's, one at James Smith's, and one at Joseph Dickinson's one at John Clemson's, and two at Robert Miller's, and one at Robert Valentine's, one at Samuel Lightfoot's, one at Dennis Whelons (the last of whom was so kind as to present me a choice book, called *No Cross No Crown*,[29] three at Benjamin Pearson's in Reading and, one at Ellis Hewes, one at Thomas Lee's, one at Joseph Walker's and one at William Edwards's[30] and one at Morris Morris's,[31] and two at Steven Twinings's.

It being by this time the 4th of the 1st month, 1758 we having visited twenty-seven meetings, mostly to our satisfaction. This day we crossed the River Delaware at Pursley's Ferry near Durham and rode that day to Oxford and staid one night. Then we went to Great Meadows, and attended

12th month

1st month

301

one meeting there; from thence to Samuel Schooley's and had one meeting in his house. From this place we came to the Drowned Lands and had a meeting in Elijah Collard's house. From thence to Rockaway, a road and place rightly named for it was the rockiest way that I ever rode in all my life for so great a distance. We had one meeting at this place where we were weatherbound one day. From thence to Rahway, when I hoped to have returned, towards home, but alas! when I gave up thereunto my heart grew heavy and it seemed my breath would have been taken from me, yea all my body was filled with sickness as if present death was approaching which brought great heaviness on my heart and mind and great was the strait I then was in, under which my flesh and bones trembled, fearing I should offend the Lord; also a fear of offending my dear and tender brethren because my certificate extended not so far as my concern, I being insensibly led along beyond my expectation, notwithstanding an awful fear struck me soon after my certificate was signed that I should go further than I had before been apprized of, which occasioned me to say something thereof to some of the elders, who said they wished to have had one word more in the certificate but desired me not to come home uneasy for that one word being left out.[32]

Now solemnly weighing the matter before the awful judge of heaven, my spirits being melted down I cried out in the secret of my heart, O Lord, what shall I do? This being all I seemed to have power to say at that time. But in a little time he gave me strength as to write a little of my mind to the Friends present, and a young Friend whom the Lord had provided, insensibly to himself, to go with us. These dear Friends seeing but sensibly feeling with me, some of the pain of heart and anguish of heart I underwent, encouraged me in a very tender manner and provided for the journey and the 17th of the 1st month, 1758 we set our faces toward the north and I have to say that the blessing of the Lord went with us, which filled my heart with praises and thanksgiving in the secret thereof, as I rode on the highway, to him who lives forever and ever who never leaves nor forsakes them that put their trust in him.

After leaving Rahway, we rode about eleven miles and stopped at a tavern in Newark, where the people seemed very kind and discoursed very freely with us; and as I sat and took a steady view of the old folks, and their sons who were grown up, I saw there was something in them that might be wrought upon, which gave me strength to ask them if there were any people called Quakers in that town. They answered no. I then inquired of them if they thought we could have a meeting among them. They answered yes, they believed readily, so one of the young men went with our Friends to the justices, to see if we might have the court house to meet in which he readily granted, and told them he would stand between them and the rest of the justices, as it would be difficult for them to go to all of them, and that he would attend himself for the encouragement of others, and would cause the bell to be rung at the hour appointed for gathering, which he did though our Friends did not request it but left him at his liberty.

At this meeting there was a considerable number of people who behaved very well, all things considered, excepting one man who was drunk; he made some disturbance, but the magistrates spoke to him, and told him if he was not more peaceable he would send him to jail. This behavior of the justice was so commendable, that I could not forebear speaking in praise thereof in that place. This town is settled with a lot of civilized people who I think are worth visiting.

After meeting we returned to the inn and had a sweet sitting with the ancient people of the house, their sons and divers other young persons who were there. When we parted they wished us well, and desired us to call and see them if we came that way again. From this place we rode towards the North, without having the least knowledge of any Friends living that way, otherwise than by the secret suggestions in my own mind, pointed out this way to me; on which having rode several miles we came to a ferry, near which was a great road leading more northward, when my dear Friends turned to me and said, which way now? Then I stood a little while to feel which way the Truth, my guide would direct me, which pointed toward the great road, and after riding several miles thereon, I said to one of the Friends of our company, I do believe there are some Friends living this way; he said he believed not, for he had not heard of any; to which I replied, that maybe neither have I, yet I do think there are some. Shortly after this a man overtook us, who seemed free and affable, and after some conversation he inquired which way we were going. I then asked him if there were any Friends, the people called Quakers, living that way. To which he answered yes, about eight or seven miles out of this road you are now travelling. This was a great comfort to me renewing my love to my good guide who had bent my mind so strongly toward the North. We then rode cheerfully on, speaking to each other in praise of our blessed guide who leads in the paths we know not of. Thus he is pleased in mercy to send his pastors to his tender lambs in the wilderness to feed them that they may grow in grace and in the knowledge of God and be saved.

This night we came to a tavern where we met a very kind young man who lived near these Friends we had heard of and on the 19th of 1st month he conducted us to a Friend's house and on the 20th we had a meeting therein in which the truth was set over the heads of its opposers to the satisfaction of the living among us. There being some of that spirit in the meeting who strive to oppose the blessed truth of our God which is going forth to gather sons from far and daughters from the very ends of the earth. The people being invited to Christ, the true and living way and not to give their money for that which is not bread nor their labour for that which satisfieth not but to come and buy wine and milk without money and without price and to not to be so weak as to hire such as were worse than themselves to direct them the way of life and peace. And there being a Presbyterian priest present, who hearing the way described without money, it touched his interest, which raised that lying spirit in him which covets money more than the welfare of souls.

After this meeting as we set at dinner he began to vent himself, asking me where I lived. I civilly told him. Have you, said he, read Paul's works? I answered *yes*. Well, said he, and what do you with that text, ma'm, or don't you choose to meddle with it? I told him I took it as it was; if he had said so in one place, he in another recommended several women as fellow labourers in the church; and the prophet spoke of the day that was to come, when the Lord would pour out of his spirit upon sons and upon daughters, on servants and handmaids and I did not think it was reasonable to suppose the scripture contradicted itself. But he still sticking close to that text of scripture where Paul said, "I suffer not a woman to speak in the church," and that word *a woman* excluded all women and he was sure that the Lord never sends any women. I asked him if he was sure that the Lord did not send me. He said, *Yes*, I am sure he did not nor no other women. I then asked him, by what was he sure that the Lord sent me not? By the word of God, said he. Seeing, said I, Thou art so sure that the Lord sent me not I desire the favour of thee to inform me who and what it is that fits and qualifies a man to be a gospel minister. Why, said he, The Lord, by the influence and revealing power of his spirit. Well, said I, Now we agree on one thing and if so why could he not qualify a female as

Joel 2:28-29

1 Tim. 2:12

well as a male, in as much as male and female is one in the
Lord Jesus and without him none can do anything. I know
he can, said he, but *can* and *will* are two things; he can drown
the world, but he won't. I told him that was nothing to the
purpose, he had confessed the truth and that was enough.
He seeing himself shut up, and strove to turn and twist
another way; and after a great deal of frothy discourse, he
said, though a man may have all the qualifications the Lord
can give him it's not sufficient. I then queried with him what
more could be done; why, said he, the laying on of hands of
the Presbytery, as said in the Bible. I desired him to show me
that place but he excused himself saying time won't allow thereof.

Well said I, if not, I desire thee nor nobody may be offended at me; if they don't like what I have to say, leave it. I
don't want their silver nor their gold. Ah, said he. money is
the case. You knew I was a minister and intended it for me. I
answered, thou art mistaken again for, I assure thee I knew
not there was a minister in the meeting, so that is as false a
conception as the other. With that several persons being there
and seeing him so mistaken could not forbear laughing, and
he finding himself mistaken walked into another room, where
Benjamin Parvin[33] who travelled with us, went with him,
and after asking him many other questions he queried with
Benjamin if he had peace of conscience accompanying us?
to which he replied, *Yes.* I never enjoyed greater peace in all
my life. Well, said the priest, you are under a delusion, or I
am greatly mistaken. There being with the priest, a doctor, a
young man of tender spirit, after the priest left the room, he
seemed to want to vindicate his cause. I looked steadfastly in
his face and said, "Young man, there is that in thee that tells
thee better, why will thou dwell in a dead faith, is the Devil
stronger than God?" No, said he, well said I, why can't thou
not have a living faith, for did I believe I must unavoidably
live in sin all my days I never would hire a man to preach for

me. After some more loving discourse he said he wished he could have some more conversation with us but time not permitting he took his leave of us and desired we might meet again in a place of peace, where we might never more be parted.

He then left us and the next morning set forward on our journey, when William Noble, a Friend, went with us about ten or twelve miles, to put us on the right road, the snow being very deep and not broke for the most part of that distance. He was so kind as to accompany us to the great road where we could not miss our way, which we took very kind. Then he returned and we went on to Nathaniel Sands's where we staid that night, and next day had a sweet comfortable meeting there, they being the offspring of Friends; they acknowledged their great satisfaction with our visit and behaved very kind and loving to us greatly desiring they might be remembered both by us and other servants of the Lord, by us and all Friends that might travel that way. I told them I did believe they would be remembered both by us and other servants of the Lord if they would stand faithful for the truth and would not balk the testimony, for it is faithfulness that he delighteth in.

From thence we travelled to Lattentown and a very cold day it was, and very cold hard meetings we had at that place, one at the Widow Latten's and one at her son-in-law's. From thence we went to John Fowler's and had a good satisfactory meeting, then went to Doctor Jones's and had a meeting there, after which we went to New Windsor, and had a satisfactory meeting there, and then back to the doctor's and staid that night and the next day we had another meeting at the doctor's who was one of the offspring of Friends but he has gone off so far that I fear he will not be gathered to them again.

From thence we went to Joshua Sands's and next day had a large satisfactory meeting considering the place. At this place there was a country schoolmaster, who strove to vindicate the cause of the devil, but his foundation being so sandy he soon run aground and caused himself to be laughed at. Scorn and derision is the portion that all such will have in the end who rise up against the blessed truth of God, but blessed and happy forever shall all those be who stand up for the truth and seek true judgment.

From this place we set forward, leaving all that did profess with us, and went on towards the North, travelling through very deep snow but were preserved from falling or any hurt, though the creatures often blundered on their knees. We were favoured with two very kind Friends who were very careful of us, and we met with good entertainment for our money, which we esteemed a favour, a favour indeed, which divers of our early Friends and worthy elders many times could not obtain, and the desire of my heart is, that we who have survived them may prize this the day of great mercy and dwell humble before him who is the giver of these and all other mercies.

We travelled on until we came to a place called the New Parts, [possibly New Paltz] where we staid all night, though the heads of the family were not at home, we spent the evening to good satisfaction, part in solid discourse with their sons, and the remainder in reading.

Next morning having signified our willingness to have a meeting in this town, some of the people thereof was very desirous we should, they went and sought a house for us to meet in, and after meeting some came and desired to know if we would have another meeting after dinner, we told them no; and the poor man where we lodged requested us to stay and dine with him, which we did, and when taking our leave of him, we offered him pay, but he would not take it, but wished us well and desired that God in mercy might go along with us and prosper our journey. Thus we parted in much love and tenderness. After this we came to Esopus that evening, and finding it was the mind of heaven that we should stay and have a meeting there, our brethren who accompanied us went to the sheriff to ask the grant of the court house to meet in which he readily agreed granting the hour was appointed and the people acquainted therewith, but the priests and deacons hearing thereof were offended and caused the sheriff to come and tell us we must not have it, for which he expressed his sorrow, and strove to get a private room but all being bribed by the priest made some excuse, so we prepared to go on. But God who loves man's welfare better than man doeth himself, moved on the minds of several young men who were so sorry to think we were like to go away without having a meeting, that they sent one who had a sword by his side, to tell us that there was several sober young men of the town and several of the soldiers that would be very glad to hear us, and desired us to meet with them in the market house, as that could not harm anybody.

Our dear Friends seeing the earnest desire of these young men went to the colonel to see if he could be assistant to us. He seemed surprised to find that any should be against our having the court house and said, it could not be offense to any unless they were bigots, and desired them to tell the sheriff from him, to let us have the court house but if he would not, we should have his barn and welcome, rather than we should be disappointed, of which they informed the sheriff, but it proved in vain, so we met in the Colonel Horsbrook's barn, to which meeting he and the sheriff came with a multitude more, and a good satisfactory meeting it was, considering the time and place. But I have one remark to make concerning this meeting. My good master from whom I expect all my reward gave me sweet peace which came with me out of the barn. When we returned to where we had lodged the landlady offered me some money, and I supposing our Friends had overpaid the reckoning and that there was some change remaining, asked her what it was for. Why said she, you must have some, I looked for the plate in the meeting intending to have gathered some for you there. I told him [her] *no*, by no means, we never received money for preaching. No! replied she, why its our way. I then informed her we maintain our poor, and if any of our ministers were poor we helped them as we did the rest of our poor, but paid none for preaching; so we parted in love she and her husband wishing us well, and that God might bless us and give us a prosperous journey.

It being near sunset when we left this town of Esopus, we rode about nine miles, and having missed our road, and night overtaken us we stopped at a small house, where we were kindly used. Next day we travelled within twenty-nine miles of Albany and staid there that night, and the day following we got within eight miles of the city; but the weather being boisterous and stormy and the snow deep we staid here all night, and next day being the 4th of second month, 1758 we entered into the city, but I can truly say that I entered therein in much heaviness of spirit, and was ready to fear that it would be said of me, who has required this at thy hand?

Under this awful fear, I walked up and down the city until towards the evening, when a still voice run through me which I had sometimes heard on the road *Be still, be still.* When I was fearing lest I should bring dishonour to truth considering how I left home and how insensibly I had been led along, and dare not turn back, notwithstanding I expected when I came out, to have returned home in a few weeks. Under this trouble of mind a secret voice ran through me, *Be still, be still.* This sweet voice I strove as much as possible to obey, and found great peace in it; being favoured with a sense and sight that the Lord opened our way before us, and that we were in the way of our duty, and when my mind was freely given up, and my feet in the path that the Lord my God

2nd month

would have me to go, I never lay down in sweeter peace, since I had a knowledge of good and evil.

We had several meetings in this city; one on the 5th at the court house and another on the 6th in the city hall. These were small meetings by reason of the coldness of the weather and coldness of heart in the people who were more afraid of hazarding their bodies than their souls, and seemed more ashamed to be seen as serving God than the devil and the world, which occasions thin meetings and hard work therein.

After the last mentioned meeting we returned to our lodgings and dined; after dinner we had a meeting in the fort in this city, having obtained General Abercrombe's[34] permission therefore; and the next day, which was the 7th of the month we entered the town of Schenectady wherein we were all strangers, and it seemed a hard and great cross to the flesh, yea so heavy to my heart and mind that I entered it with tears, and my spirit mourned over it, but notwithstanding it was a close undertaking in that season of the year, the weather being cold and the snow between three and four feet deep, yet the Lord made way for us, opened the hearts of the people so that they behaved very kind to us, and our landlady told us she wondered how we could bear to travel in such cold weather; it must be for some extraordinary thing. Yes replied I, It is for the Lord's sake.

Having refreshed ourselves a little, my dear Friends went out to see if we could obtain a meeting in this town but it seemed much harder to persuade people in this place to serve the Lord than the enemy; especially the citizens, if the tree is to be known by its fruit. However we obtained four meetings here, one of which was held in the tavern where we put up. This meeting was chiefly composed of soldiers who behaved very solid and were desirous we should have more meetings among them, but we not being provided to stay longer we took our leave of them who tenderly wished us well, and that the Lord might be with us and prosper our journey.

Notwithstanding I had strong desires to visit Fort Edward, yet we thought necessity would oblige us to turn towards home. But God who never forgets his own seed though their lots may be cast as it were in Sodom and Egypt, provided a way for us to go unlooked for and unexpected. For just as we were about to get on horseback an old acquaintance of mine came in, who had not heard of us until a few minutes before. He was glad to see us and desired us to stay another night. I told him it was so expensive that we could not if we intended to get home. He desired us not to straiten ourselves on that account, for he would help us to what we wanted.

Here I saw all excuses were turned out, which brought a great weight and trembling on me, and also on some of my dear companions; when I had to renewedly to see that the Lord's tender regard was to the poor spirits in prison, and that it was his mind and will that his everlasting gospel should be preached to them for their encouragement and the re-newing of their strength. Also that the wicked and rebel-lious should be warned that in the day of account they might be left without excuse. Thus the Lord provided for us, and we set forward though we did not feel quite easy in going away that night. But considering our circumstances we thought it prudent to make what speed we could; though many have made more haste than good speed; which seemed our case at that time. Being sensible that no man ever spent time or money better than in the service of an almighty and merciful God, I often said in the secret of my heart while on this journey, if I had fifty pounds I would freely spend it, O Lord, in thy service; yea, I would stay at every place where thou might send me until my heart should be made quite easy for thou art good above all.

From Schenectady we returned to Albany and the 10th of month we set out for Fort Edward, where we were kindly received. After dining with an officer, a namesake of mine, myself and companions having been invited to drink tea with the colonel, Captain Gordon, with divers other officers. Though I did not practice drinking tea, yet found a freedom to go and see them, which we did. We had seen Captain Gordon the day before at Fort New George, who behaved very kind to us, at which place we had a large and solid meeting. When we entered the room where the colonel and his friends were assembled they all rose up paying their compliments to us, but my mind was kept quiet and still, hoping to have some service for the Lord among

them, which so fell out, for when our Friends who had been out to appoint a meeting returned and informed us that the people were gathering, the company rose up to go; but my heart being filled with the father's love, who would that all should be saved, I requested them, if it was no offense to sit down a few minutes, as I had a few words to deliver to them to which Captain Gordon replied, it's no offense, we are all willing to hear what you have to say. This ended I hope I may say to good satisfaction.

Then went from the fort to an island, where we met about 500 or 600 people and all things considered a solid good meeting. The minds of the people seemed so gathered down that they stood as if they knew not how to part. After meeting, divers, both officers and others spoke kindly to us; and Major Rogers very kindly invited us to his dining room where he had prepared tea, coffee, chocolate, and other things to treat us with, and having provided lodging for us, he accompanied us thereunto, and ordered his waiting man to see that we had every thing we wanted. Thus the Lord made these rovers kind to his poor pilgrims.

Next day we returned to the fort, and breakfasted with Captain Gordon and several others who had engaged us the day before. After breakfast we strove to have a meeting in the fort, but could not, only in the officers' room, where we had a little opportunity, and having done what we could, we took our leave, but I can truly say it was with pain of heart, seeing and feeling that our meeting had been too much in secret. For my good guide gave me to believe it ought to have been in the middle of the fort, there being several hungry souls therein who were not allowed to come to meeting, and a tender hearted man in the fort said, there were many therein who would be glad to hear the gospel preached, and when we took our leave of him he said to us, Your visit has been very acceptable to many here. Farewell, and may the Lord

God go with you and prosper your journey.

From this place we travelled to Fort New George. The sun being down and the weather cold we staid there that night, and had another sweet meeting there. I have reason to believe the Lord has a seed in that company. Their kindness to us was very great. O that God in mercy may be pleased to gather them out from among the dross and set their feet on the banks of deliverance where they may worship him with freedom of heart.

Next morning we went to another fort, at a place called Stillwater, where we went into the captain's room. He welcomed us to the place, ordered us dinner and behaved very kind. After dinner we mentioned our business and desired to have a meeting, and consulted him where it would be best to hold it. He said, in his room and went himself and called in the soldiers. They seeming shy so he spoke cheerful to them and said, Come forward my lads, which they did until the room was full, the captain and they all stood; which mark of respect I kindly acknowledged to them, when the captain replied, you are heartily welcome, its only our duty.

From thence we returned towards Albany and lodged at a young man's house where we had hay for our beds. The next day we got to Albany to dinner, in the afternoon set out towards home, but it was with regret of mind, and I had not travelled far before a great weight of trouble and silence fell upon me so that I thought I could freely have given almost any thing to have been back there again. For I was made sensible I had bent too soon towards home, looking too often on my own weakness, and wanting to lay off that sharp cross of travelling among the army and ill behaved rough inhabitants, the last of whom behaved worse to us than the army, particularly the priests and deacons who strove to hinder us from having meetings.

Thus we travelled on about eighty miles to the settlement of Friends. But oh! alas! home was hid from me and I knew not what to do. Our creatures were much fatigued and our money gone, so that I thought I must go home, if it was groveling through the dark. But thinking on this wise a day or two I grew very sick throughout my whole body insomuch that I thought I must die. Thus I lay very ill when divers Friends came to see me and had a meeting with me. In this meeting my heart was much broken down fearing I should lose favour with the Lord. But after this meeting a dear Friend came and kneeling down by the bedside and said, Dear Friend, if thou hast a mind to go back again don't let it trouble thee, for I see a way can be provided for thee to go. I told him I feared it would be too much trouble. He replied, No Don't thou be concerned about that, and so bid me farewell. In that instant my heart got easy and settled down in peace; then I grew better, and next day went to meeting, where I was favoured to speak a few things in the praise of my righteous master who never leaves nor forsakes those that put their trust in him. Eternal glory be given to his ever worthy and glorious name, has my soul renewed cause to say. From this meeting we went home with Widow Moore and her son. In the evening several Friends coming in, after a little solid conversation we fell in silence which at the time I seemed in no wise to desire, being weak in body and poor in spirit. Yet I thought if the Master has commanded this silence, it's my duty to submit; and after weighing the matters and finding freedom to join therewith, I observed we were in two rooms which did not fit quite easy on my mind, as one would hold us; then I told the Friends if they desired to wait in silence it would be most proper for us all to fit in one room, to which they agreed, and we joined companies, then I sat in a sweet cheerful frame of mind until it pleased my Master to strike me with these words, Formality never did me any good. With this all my senses were awakened and my judgment renewedly informed to set forth what it was that gives true peace, and makes us valiant for the Lord and his Truth upon the earth. A night to be remembered, a time sealed in the sight of God, who in a little time manifested his care towards us poor pilgrims: For as we were returning to the Friend's house where we had a meeting the day before one sleigh overset and the horses ran against our sleigh, broke it to pieces and jumped in upon us. But we received but very little hurt considering the danger we were in. Everlasting praises be given to the name of the Lord forever.

Next day we prepared to return again to that painful city of Albany; painful one it has been to me for many months. Our dear Friends at Nine Partners were very kind in fitting us out for our journey, Yea they seemed if they could not do enough for us:— May all praises be given to the author of all good, Things in this part of the country being unreasonably dear, those Friends provided us with many necessaries, and our horses being much fatigued Friends kept them in order to recruit them; and Jacob Watson, a young man who came from England, lent us his.

3rd month

And oh the first of the third month we set forward towards Albany again and on the second we breakfasted at the place where my poor distressed son was; and on the third we entered that wicked city Albany over which my spirit groaned and was smitten with a fear that they would not repent notwithstanding all the warnings they had had, and the deepening storms which seemed to hang over them, and the many that had heretofore fallen on their borders until their houses were laid in ashes and their streets ran down with blood. This awful fear on their accounts made my heart, flesh and bones to tremble the most part of one day before we obtained any meetings, our Friends being gone to appoint one, which they did in a new barrack built for the accommodation of the army.

This meeting was so very large that the people could not near all hear what was said, which induced us to appoint another meeting in the same place. These meetings were large and still and there appeared a great openness in the people to hear us. The same day we had a large meeting in the city hall, but this meeting was very much disturbed by some graceless persons and illbred children whose parents were, in the main to blame. It having pleased the Lord in these meetings to favour me with strength to speak pretty clear for the cause of truth, I began to conclude now I may go towards home, and so went to bed and slept very sweetly, but awakening with the day, a weight fell on me again so that I could not look towards home, and as I dwelt quietly under the weight I felt my mind drawn up the city which I followed until we came to the batteau carpenters. The captain thereof (being a Friend's son) had before been at one meeting with us; we told him our business, which both he and divers of the men were glad of, and soon contrived for us to have a meeting which was large and satisfactory, not only Friends but others also, who had an ear to hear. After this meeting my soul rejoiced, having had the company of several of the citizens at this meeting, which I had greatly desired, and when this meeting concluded my heart was so animated with unspeakable joy, that I was ready to say, surely now I am clear of this city. But this joy soon passed away, and I felt a check and caution not to rejoice too soon; then I resigned myself to the will of the Lord, and my mind rested in sweet peace. My poor tabernacle being weak and weary I went early to bed when my righteous master gave me sweet rest. But the work not being done, He, to spare my wearied mind and body, was pleased to lay the weight upon my dear brethren who accompanied me, so that the next day they took great pains to gather their fellow creatures together and we had a large meeting of about six or seven hundred persons; and notwithstanding many behaved more like brutes than Christians, yet the Lord gave me power and strength to speak to the under-standings of some who had an ear to hear.

Then my mind became settled and I rested in sweet peace. After this meeting my heart being filled with joy I again be-gan to look towards home, hoping to be set free. But as soon as I looked on my fellow travellers who travelled with me in spirit as well as in body I saw their countenances were sad. Then was I commanded to be still that I might see what more would be required of us. My dear tender companions were so low they durst not say any thing at that time concerning more meetings, yet could not be easy to leave the city. Then my mind rested on a place in the street, which I had often before had in my view. And when I mentioned it to my Friends and my female companion, Ann Matthews,[35] an-swered me and said, that is the place I have this morning been thinking. Then she accompanied me, and we walked up and down the streets to feel after the work where the Master would command a meeting to be held. And I found he pointed to that place which I had many times in my view before, but I looked so much on my own weakness, that I dare not speak thereof, until it pleased him who knows best how to carry on his own work to lay a weight on these tender youths so that they dare not move. Then I mentioned this place to them, where we obtained one of the largest, or how-ever I think, one of the best meetings we had in all this jour-ney. Thus the Lord is pleased in mercy to show his tried servants that the greater the cross the sweeter the crown. This meeting ended much to my satisfaction, and I felt the great weight under which I had travelled many months, re-moved, and the light broke towards home, which I was very ready to join with. But looking on my two young Friends I saw the sweet air had not quite cleared all the clouds from off their countenances. They told me, they had a mind to the upper end of the city, which I did not at first unite with, but seeing they could not readily give it up, after some solid thoughts thereon, I said to them if you have a mind to go, go and peace go with you. Then they walked up the town to a place before mentioned where several of our Friends's sons were at work; there they appointed another meeting which was large and ended well. This closed our labours in the city of Albany; and on the 7th of the third month, 1758, we left it; when the Lord blessed me with that peace that surpasses the understanding of man, agreeable to a promise he gave me many months before, if I would visit this part of America, the prospect whereof seemed like death to me, I being a simple woman, and so many hundreds of the roughest of mankind residing in those parts. But blessed be the name of the Lord, he supported me, and bore me up above the frothy and lofty spirit of man, for which high favour and unspeakable mercy I desire ever to be thankful, and have great cause to encourage all, who may have it on their minds to visit those parts, to go, for there are many tender hearts and many poor spirits in prison thereaway, who rejoiced to hear the free gift of God to man declared, and opening the prison door to their poor captive souls, the sound of which caused a spiritual baptism and living water to issue out of their rocky hearts. The last mentioned day we rode thirty miles on the ice, on the north river and about four miles by land, then stopped at Cloverick where my captive son was billeted. I had more comfort at this time with my poor captive son than I ever had, since he had the misfortune to enlist in the army.

THE JOURNAL OF ANN MOORE

PART III

The 9th of the month, we got to a settlement of Friends who received us with love and tenderness. Here we staid four days and had three meetings; then went to Oblong and had three meetings there. From thence, accompanied by several Friends, we travelled towards New York, lodged at Samuel Field's and had one meeting in his house; and notwithstanding there seemed an openness in the people to receive truth's testimony, yet it was a heavy time to me; but I was not insensible of the cause; having, the year before, been in those parts, and passed by a small meeting, which I was striving to do again. This caused my spirit to pass through deep baptisms, yet I could not give up, until the weight fell on my tender female companion, who stopped her creature and said, Where are we going? I replied, where I would go if I could. Then she answered, I seem so heavy, I know not how to proceed further. After some more solid conversation, we concluded to go to that meeting; when we freely gave up, the weight was removed off my spirit; and notwithstanding the roads were rough and hilly, yet it was made easy to me. In the evening we arrived at Nehemiah Merritt's, and next day had a meeting at his house; near the conclusion thereof, came a minister so called, who, after meeting he wanted to dispute with me, but I did not feel free to say much to him, believing he wanted to trap me with words, hoping to lay waste what I had that day delivered. He began with saying, Good woman, I desire to know the foundation of the doctrine you delivered today. I then asked him if he did not hear? He replied, I was so unfortunate as not to come until the meeting was almost ended. I did not answer him immediately but he urging

321

1 John. 2:27

me to it, I looked at him and said, I believe thou knows more than thou lives up to, and if thou would live agreeable to what is made known to thee, thou need not ask me nor no one else. For as the apostle said, "ye have no need that any man teach you but as this anointing teaches you all things and brings all things to your remembrance." Then he asked me, if we believed in the gospel of Christ? to which I replied be sure we do, that is well known by all that know us. No, answered he, some of you do not. Then I told him, they are not of us. They are called so, said he. I replied that may be, they are not all of Israel that were called so, neither are they all Friends who are called so. Finding him more in form than substance, I desired our Friends to prepare for going, we having to ride ten or twelve miles that evening, and the people having surrounded us so that we could not move. The man of the house desired him to drop his discourse that the people might withdraw, as he wanted room to set things for us to refresh ourselves with; and when we took our leave I said to the Priest, if thou are not satisfied thou may come and hear for thyself. I can't do that, said he, for I am to do tomorrow as you intend, to preach to the people. I then said to him, I neither know nor promise anybody to preach to them, it is as the Lord pleases, therefore I dare not make any such promise. This ended our discourse, and we proceeded on our journey. In the evening we arrived at Moses Powell's at Chappaqua, and next day attended a meeting there and a heavy one it was. From thence we went to William Cornell's and dined, in the evening went to his father, Joshua Cornell's and lodged. Next day were at a meeting at Ryewood, which was a good solid meeting. From thence to Benedict Carpenter's and lodged, where one of our companions, Benjamin Shotwell, left us. In the evening several persons came in expecting a meeting, but my body being weak I did not readily join therewith; yet the Friend of the house informed me there was an ancient woman in another room, who came with earnest desires to have a meeting. Then I felt freedom to join them, and had to believe this meeting was appointed by a secret hand, yes, the true light manifested it was, and I did not witness a clearer opening in all my travels in the north, though often highly favoured from on high.

From this place we went to John Stephenson's at Mamaroneck (who with his family were very glad to see us, and we them) where we staid two nights and attended one meeting, which was close and heavy. The first night after we got to John Stephenson's, I was made sensible some further service would be required of me on the borders of New England, which brought great weight on my mind, having before proposed to attend one meeting more, which was appointed in New York government, and then to proceed towards home. But not being easy to pursue my journey as I before proposed, I freely resigned myself up to him who had given me the power to run through a troop and leap over a wall, blessed be his name.

Having thus resigned my mind to the secret hand of wisdom and power, who desires all men may be saved, I acquainted my dear companions therewith, who were always willing to assist me to the utmost of their power. They encouraged me to go and clear myself, that I might return home in peace. Leaving our horses at the above mentioned Friends, we rode in chairs to the meeting appointed at West Chester and in the evening returned to John Stephenson's. Next day accompanied by several Friends, went to Middlesex in Connecticut, where a few newly convinced Friends dwelt. The wife of one of those Friends not being able to attend meetings I felt a desire to visit her, which I mentioned to my Friends, but the Friend living about a mile from our lodgings, and the evening being far spent, we deferred our visit until next morning, when several Friends went with me. I rode in great poverty of spirit and remained so, until one of my dear companions spoke to the woman. Then I was struck with a glance of the Father's love, which kindled and spread in my bosom, until it overflowed in sweet love to those tender lambs who are striving to follow the flocks of Christ's companions, who are gone before them. This sitting with this tender Friend ended greatly to our satisfaction. From thence we went to a Friend's house about four miles from Stanford town, where Friends had appointed a meeting at the eleventh hour. This meeting was satisfactory, many people attended and behaved well. After this meeting we refreshed ourselves and rode to the abovementioned town an evening meeting having been appointed there, which was very large, but it not being convenient for all who were assembled to get within sight of me occasioned some disturbance; they crowding against each one another, a soldier drew his sword, but being spoke to put it up without doing any harm. Divers in this meeting were attentive and seemed well satisfied and kindly invited us to their houses to lodge, of which we accepted, the town being crowded with soldiers, there was but very little room at the inn. So that we all (except Benjamin Parvin) lodged at private houses. Soon after I had gone to bed, I heard a great disturbance at the inn where I supposed several of our Friends were gone to sup. Hearing such a great noise struck my heart with pain lest some of my dear Friends who had kindly accompanied me, should be wounded or killed by some of the drunken soldiers. This anguish of heart and pain of mind continuing several hours, caused me to look over all I had done, but I did not find any condemnation; yet concluded this pain of heart could not be for nought and that if they were well I should be tried some other way, and so it turned out.

Next morning finding my Friends well, we got ready and set forward towards another meeting we had appointed and went cheerfully on about two miles when a soldier with a drawn sword in his hand ran fiercely after us, and coming up to some of us ordered us to stop, and waving his sword asked us if we were Quakers. We told him we were and queried with him, what was the matter? and told him if he wanted us to return to the town we were willing. He then said I warrant you shall go, we don't like Quakers. They won't fight for the king. His running with his drawn sword by my creature frightened her, and rendered her uneasy, which made me strive to join the other Friends, thinking he would let a woman pass, but as soon as he saw me, he ran towards me, waving his sword, and swearing he could cut off my head if I did not stand still. My creature being frightened, jumped up so fiercely, that my Friends thought she would have thrown me, but recovering myself I looked around and saw another soldier coming, of whom I inquired if he knew what the other man wanted. He said, he did not know. Then he caught hold of him, and desired us go on; but he soon broke loose and ran after us again, when he fell down, the other took hold of him, carried him back, and we went on.

But thinking what it could mean brought a heaviness over me, and under some solid thoughts thereon it sprung fresh

in my mind some words that had been dropped the evening before, which are as follows: "No joy, nor peace in this world is to be compared with a redemption from the world, the flesh, and the wicked one. Those who witnessed this

Isa 2:4

done in them and for them, know by experience the time is come, when swords should be beat into plow shares and spears into pruning hooks and not to learn war any more." And though a thousand enemies should be on one hand and ten thousand on the other, yet they are not dismayed for the fear of death is taken from before their eyes. Something on this wise having been delivered I believed that they had a mind to try if we would fight. Then we went on to the place where the meeting was appointed and a large, solid one it was.

3rd month

On the 25th of third month we left New England and returned towards New York, lodged at William Mott's; next day went to Mamaroneck Meeting, and staid that night at John Stephenson's, the day following went to New York and staid there two days, and attended one meeting. On the thirtieth day of the month, we crossed the bay and came to Benjamin Shotwell's at Rahway, where we staid that night. By this time we had rode one thousand and sixty-five miles and had visited eighty-three meetings. Next day were at a meeting at Plainfield, lodged at Elijah Pound's. And the first of

4th month

the fourth month we travelled to Jacob Birdsall's at Amwell and lodged that night, where they have an appointed meeting once a month; and we happening to be there on that day, staid, and attended their meeting which was good and solid. After this meeting we crossed the River Delaware, and lodged at David Kinsey's. Next day were at Buckingham Monthly Meeting, which was large and good, wherein three couples declared their intentions of marriage, one of whom was a granddaughter of Doctor Watson. From this meeting we went home with John Fell, father of the above mentioned young woman, where we dined and in the evening came to Doctor John Watson's and lodged. Next day attended Wrightstown monthly meeting wherein we renewedly witnessed a being baptized with the saving baptism, and drinking of that cup of ancient love which gathered us to be a people. O, that we may always live near this holy fountain which washes away all the spots of the earth, and fits us for God's Holy Kingdom. From this meeting we went to the widow Chapman's and dined, from thence to Amos Strickland's and lodged. Next day attended the Falls Meeting, and notwithstanding part of it was close and heavy yet it pleased God to give us a taste of his ancient love, for which favour my heart was made to bow with the living and bless his holy name who is eternally worthy forevermore.

The day following we went to Middletown, or Neshaminy monthly meeting which was large and close, deep travelling therein for the poor servants; yet it pleased the Lord who is ever good and merciful to all who put their trust in him, to arise and scatter the clouds for a little season causing the living water to run, to the refreshing of Zion's poor travellers; for which his eternal glorious name was blessed, praised, and glorified, who is worthy thereof now and forever.

At this meeting my dear companion Ann Matthews was taken with a fever and ague and a meeting being appointed next day at Bristol I was obliged to go and leave her; which was a great cross to me, she having been made very near to me in my deep exercises and travels in the north, but she being with divers of her near relations whom I expected would be as kind to her as I could, made it easier to me to leave her, hoping to see her again in a few days, I went with several Friends on the 7th of the month to Bristol, and attended the appointed meeting; and on the 8th in the company with Joseph White,[36] and several other Friends entered on a visit to Friends' families in Bristol, and on the 9th, in company with Phebe Titus[37] and some other Friends, went to Mt. Holly meeting and in the evening were at a meeting in Burlington, after which crossed the river to Enion Williams's, who with his wife came to Burlington to meet us. On the 10th with the before-mentioned Friends I again entered on a visit to families in Bristol; and on the 11th we finished, and on the 12th accompanied by the same Friends I went to a meeting at Trenton. I had hard deep travelling in these meetings and families, there being a great declension in my native land of Pennsylvania. Oh! Pennsylvania how art thy pillars fallen.

From the last mentioned meeting I went to Thomas Yardley's, where I found my young and tender companion, Ann Matthews, a little recruited.

On the 13th went to Makefield meeting and on the 14th to Plumstead, which was large and solid. From thence went home with the widow Fell to her son-in-law's, Benjamin Fell's,[38] where we dined and lodged that night, the widow being a cousin of my poor deceased mother. On the 15th the widow Fell and one of her sons went with me to Edmund Kinsey's [39] who was in a declining condition of body, but alive in spirit. This day Benjamin Parvin, the young Friend who had accompanied me through the north parts of America, left me and proceeded towards home by way of the Great Swamp in company with our esteemed Friend, Phebe Titus, and my dear companion Ann Matthews being separated from me by sickness, I felt stripped and lonesome, and looking strongly towards home, my heart grew heavy and my eyes were wet with tears and thus feeling lonely and heavy I walked into an orchard to vent my heart when my endeared spouse met me, and comforted my mind, saying to me Were they not with thee until thou come among thy near and dear friends? O Yes, said I. My endeared Spouse, thou art ever good, kind and merciful to me and it was thy love that made them so near to me, and induced them to venture their lives to accompany me, thy poor handmaid. O that thou would bless them, and my poor babes at home, and conduct us safe to our habitations. After this, my heart rested in sweet peace as though he had answered. Then I returned into the house where divers of my old acquaintance near and dear friends were come to see me. Next morning with melting tears I took leave of dear worthy Edmund Kinsey, who had been made a blessing to me in my young and tender years; and when we parted, he said, I must now take my final leave of thee, my dear friend, never expecting to see thee again. Farewell and may the great Jehovah, the Prince of peace (who was with us in the beginning) continue with us and preserve us safe to the end of time. And may meet with him in that place where sorrow and tears shall cease, and we never more be parted. Then I told him I united therewith, and we parted in great love and tenderness, under a renewed sense of that love and peace that surpasses the understanding of man.

From Rahway to Buckingham we rode 150 miles, and visited eleven meetings. On the 16th I went to Buckingham meeting, which was a large good meeting of about four hundred people. By this time I had visited all the meetings in Bucks County, Buckingham and Bristol each twice—also Bristol Friends in their families. From Buckingham Meeting I went home with Doctor John Watson, and staid that night, who had lent me his riding horse for two weeks and took care of mine, during that time which I esteemed a favour, and hope he will receive his reward, and all such who bear a tender regard to the servants and handmaidens of the Lord, for they that give a cup of cold water for his name's sake shall not lose [sic] their reward.

I left Buckingham, the 17th and on the 18th went with several Friends to visit Agnes Penquite,[40] an ancient worthy, of near if not quite a hundred years old. During our conversation with her, notwithstanding she was childish, she said some sensible things to us recommending us to mind the living God in all our undertakings for he is Good. Then she expressed a desire to be released from this world, saying, I am a great deal of trouble to my friends, and I fear I shall live a great while longer, do pray God to take me. After this we sat waiting on the Lord and were blessed with a sweet season. Here in much love and tenderness, I parted with several of my dear friends, then went with Mary Buckman and Joseph Hampton to Byberry, and called on the way to see a sick friend, who was brought up in the same house with myself, I thought him near to leave time and to enter into eternity; but feared he had not thought enough thereon in the day of his youth, which is a great pity indeed, that any of us poor mortals should neglect this great work, and leave that till the last that ought be done first. Time being but a moment compared to an endless eternity; and the joys of this world not worthy to be named against the joys of God's salvation.

From this house we went to see the Friend who brought me up from a child. I sat and conversed a little with him, not expecting to see him again, he being seventy years old or upwards. Then went out and walked in the fields, where the Lord in mercy met with me in my tender years for I greatly loved to see the place, where the God of my life had many times fed me.

From this Friend's we went to Byberry, lodged at John Worthington's, on the 19th went to their meeting, which was sweet and comfortable; lodged that night at William Walmsley's.[41] On the 20th went to Abington and had a good solid meeting, there were divers of my dear Friends invited me home with them, we being very glad to see each other; but as I could not go with more than one of them I went with Joshua Morris, son of Morris Morris,[42] and on the 21st went to Horsham meeting, toward the close whereof, Friends were invited to the burial of the wife of Peter Titus. From this meeting I returned home again with Joshua Morris and staid that night, he having taken me to this meeting in his chaise (myself and creature being much wearied) which I esteemed a brotherly act, and hope he will have his reward. On the 22nd at the request of divers Friends, I attended the above mentioned burial.

Notwithstanding my being at Byberry, Abington, and Horsham Meetings, likewise the burial was rather compulsion than a free will offering, not intending it, had my companion been able to go on; but as she could not, and their week day meetings came in course one after the other, I felt a desire to attend them. Nevertheless it pleased my ever blessed Master in each of those seasons, to meet with me, and blessed me with the incomes of his love, until my cup overflowed, whereby his flock was watered, yea we drank together of the fountain of living water, and gave him the praise, who is God over all, blessed for ever.

After the before mentioned burial, Joshua Morris accompanied me to Anthony Morris's in Philadelphia, who was very glad to see me, and I them.[43]

On the 23rd attended three meetings in the city, where I met that worthy servant of the Lord, Samuel Spavold,[44] I was at the Bank Street Meeting House, both morning and afternoon, which were sweet comfortable meetings, and in the evening I went to the Meeting House in High Street, where we had a large good meeting. Divers of the military men came to the door of the Meeting House and seemed to give good attention. On the 24th I attended the select meeting which was solid and comfortable. In the evening my dear and tender companion Ann Matthews came to me, which gave me great joy to see her restored to so good a state of health as to be able to go with me towards home, which I greatly desired, she having travelled faithfully with me in the service of Truth through the Northern Parts of America in a severe winter season, which made me strongly desirous that the Lord in mercy might raise her once more to see her tender parents and dear fatherless children, one of whom she weaned when we set out on this journey.

On the 25th we had two meetings more in Philadelphia,

one at the Meeting House and one at our Friend Anthony Morris's. This morning the young Friend who had travelled with us came to my lodgings, and was at those meetings with us, which were parting meetings for this time with my dear Friends in this city, likewise this tender family, the heads of which are like parents to me and their children like brothers and sisters. In the evening with much love and tenderness, we took leave of them, and set out towards home accompanied by the before mentioned young Friend and Thomas Lightfoot. Lodged this night at Samuel Howell's[45] who received us in much love. On the 26th I visited our ancient Friend, Grace Lloyd, and Jane Hoskins,[46] then returned to our lodging and provided to go on, travelled to the head of

northeast and lodged at Nathan Baker's, that night; and the next day being the 27th of the 4th month, 1758. Ann Matthew's creature being much tired, Thomas Lightfoot staid with her at a Friend's house, and the young Friend accompanied me to my outward habitation, and next day they came to us.

Finding my family well caused me to look back and consider how the holy one of Israel had, in his condescending mercy, preserved and blessed me in my going out and in my returning home, and mercifully preserved my family in my absence which caused me to return thanksgiving to him as I had many times done on the highway in this manner: Thou art good above all things, O righteous God! who art a repairer of breaches and restorer of paths for thine to walk in; all praises, honour and thanksgiving be ascribed to thy worthy and glorious name, now and forever more. Thus ended this journey.

On the 30th I attended our quarterly meeting, which was held about four miles from my home where I met many dear Friends, who were glad to see me, and I them. It pleased the Lord at this time to own us, by overshadowing of his ancient love under which our acquaintance was again renewed to the praises of thy worthy name, who is God over all blessed forever. I think it is worthy of remark, that the Christian conduct of those dear young Friends who accompanied me home, with some others from Pennsylvania in our quarterly meeting of business caused some who were members thereof to bless God, on their accounts. A high favour indeed, to be enabled so to answer the end of our creation, as to cause the great name of the Lord to be blessed by those that behold us. All praises be to the Lord God and the Lamb forever. O may the dear youth, be encouraged to live in humility, for it's the humble the Lord delights in, teaches of his ways and guides in judgment.

PINE STREET MEETING HOUSE, PHILADELPHIA, BUILT 1753

BANK STREET MEETING HOUSE, PHILADELPHIA, BUILT C. 1683

THE JOURNAL OF ANN MOORE

PART IV

Of her visiting some meetings of Friends in Maryland and Virginia in 1760

It rests with weight upon my mind to give my dear children a relation of this short journey and the vision I had the night before I left home. You are acquainted with my great and deep exercises on some of your accounts; being much blamed by some and others mocking and seeming to rejoice at the anguish of my poor afflicted heart, which made me conclude it would avail nothing for me to go this journey, as I could not rule my own family, nor persuade my Friends at home to walk orderly, what good could I do abroad? Thus the unwearied enemy, who knew my weak side, got in at unawares, and laid me so low I concluded to send word to my sister, Jane Nailer,[47] (who I expected would accompany me,) that I could not go; and under this conclusion I went to bed very sick both in body and mind, so that my life, the world, and all the enjoyments therein were no comfort to me; but like a mournful widow, or poor fatherless child, I wept, saying in the secret of my heart, O Lord! help me and undertake my cause. Thus committing my cause to the Lord, I fell into a doze, and saw in a vision toward the southwest, the appearance of a woman in the clouds, larger than anyone I had ever before seen. From her shoulders downwards the clouds were black, and over her head was a cloud as red as blood, and her face which was towards me, was likewise red. She had a large sword in her hand, which she waved at me, looking with a majestic sternness. This sight I thought I showed to a young man who seemed much surprised; but I desired him not to be afraid, for she could not hurt him. Then she waved the sword at me again; which gave me such a sudden shock, that I awoke with great dread on my spirit, and cried out in the secret of my heart, O Lord! what doth this mean? When the following interpretation was secretly suggested to my mind: This woman is thy great weakness, under which thou so often falls. The sword which she waved at thee, is that destroying spirit which casts people into melancholy, and unfits them for the service of God or man. And if thou submits to this spirit thou wilt fall, and thy blood will be on thy own head. Then in humble submission to the Lord, I resigned myself up to go, though all men might despise me. And all doubts and fears being removed, a strong zeal was raised in my heart for the cause of the Lord on the earth, and I clearly saw the design of the subtle serpent, who, when he can't raise up, strives to cast us into despair.

1st month

The Lord having thus opened my eyes, I set out on the 29th of 1st month, 1760, accompanied by my sister, Jane Nailer. We rode this day twenty miles alone, crossed the great falls, some part through the water, and the other part on the ice, our good Shepherd conducting us safe. Next day we were favoured at meeting with the sweet incomes of the love of the Lord, which renewed my strength in him, and enabled me to go cheerfully on, and I felt the Lord's blessed presence on the road. The day following we had a sweet comfortable meeting at Yates Plummer's. Next day we attended Sandy Spring meeting which was solid, yet deep and heavy was the work therein. The succeeding day being the 7th of the week, we past part of it among our dear and tender Friends at Sandy Spring. In the evening went to Richard Snowden's and lodged. Next day we were at Indian Spring meeting which was sweet and comfortable; from thence we went to Samuel Water's and in the evening to the widow Plummer's, where we had a heavenly and blessed opportunity. This widow had lately buried her husband, who died on the road about two miles and a half from his house, as he was returning from a store, where he had been to purchase things for a family of slaves under his care. He left the store well, as to any thing they knew, and it was supposed he found himself unwell, got off his horse, and lay down a few steps out of the road, having put both his gloves into one hand. He appeared as though he had departed in a sweet sleep; and having been a kind husband, a loving, exemplary father, friend, and neighbour, and having lived beloved, he died lamented. After passing one night with this widow and her fatherless children, she and her daughter Rachel, also William Ballenger, accompanied us to West River Quarterly Meeting, which held three days.

I feel most easy to make some remarks on the concluding meeting there, in which Robert Pleasants[48] and Mary Hill accomplished their marriage, having had the night before, a clear sight what would be the state of this meeting; and though it may be thought by some very simple to observe the visions of the night season; yet when the Lord in Mercy is pleased to reveal his secrets to me, either by day or night, I think them worth observing, and being truly thankful for, with every other of his mercies, which are manifold indeed.

The night above mentioned, when in bed, I saw in a vision that this would be a close trying meeting as also we should be favoured therein before we parted. I seemed as one of the service, and thought my master sent me with a little boy to get some yeast to raise the bread, as we travelled I saw a yellow woman sitting by the way side, whom I asked where she came from? She answered, she had been in captivity; and after querying her, why she did not go on, and not sit by the way side, we left her and went to the place where we were to get the yeast; it was a narrow passage through which we were to creep, the sight of which at first daunted me, thinking it was too small for us to go through. But as I stood viewing it,

I felt my faith increase and grow strong; so that I said to the lad who was with me, if thou will go before I will follow thee. So through we went and got our yeast, and returning found the woman still sitting by the way side; when I said to her, what art thou still here? Why don't thou go on? seeing thou hast got so far out of captivity? She answered, I am weary, and want to rest. We then left her, and went home, when I thought it was night and I in bed, and that my Master called me to get up; but not seeming well I delayed it, when he called a second time, saying, it is late: with that I looked out, and saw the suns and stars shine so bright that I said, I never see the like before, the sun and stars to shine at noon day. While I thus admired, I was called the third time; then I rose up and got on my horse, when immediately a man being by, on a strong horse, he with violence jumped at mine, and laid one foot on my horses neck, and his mouth against my face, as though he would have taken it therein. But my stepping nimbly on the side of a new strong horse I was soon out of his reach, and desired the owner of the horse to rein him another way. Thus was the vision; and here follows the interpretation:

I went to this meeting much in the state of a poor woman I had seen on the road though not desirous to remain content therewith; and having entered the meeting in great poverty of spirit, under which I sat a considerable while, concluded it would end a poor dull meeting; when suddenly this language arose in my mind, Hast thou forgotten the shining of the sun and the stars? I answered in secret, nay, but it seemeth as if neither would shine here today. We sat long in this state, when I said in my mind, I wonder the brethren don't break up the meeting, my vision having passed out of my mind after those thoughts had passed through it. I felt a divine motion, but it seemed so weak, I did not dare to move, until I felt the third time, with it came with such awakening power I thought it not safe to resist; when I rose up at the command of my Lord and Master, I felt the power of darkness smite me in such a manner, that I said in the secret of my heart, O Lord! if thou don't rise I cannot stand; and blessed for ever be his adorable name, he was pleased to arise and disperse the clouds of thick darkness and a blessed sweet comfortable time it was, and the meeting ended well.

As I sat during the signing of the certificate I had to remember my vision, and how I had seen the sun and stars shine at noonday; and I was called to rise three times, and when I rose and got on my creature, signifying my strength, that dark spirit sitting by the way side, that loves to take up a rest by the way, smote at me with all its power. But oh! that new building the spirit of Truth, that is ever new and powerful and supports above all the powers of darkness, bore me up, and gave me the victory. Thus I saw that spirit which had rose up against me as a horse, which is one of the strongest creatures, reigned back and must join the regions of darkness

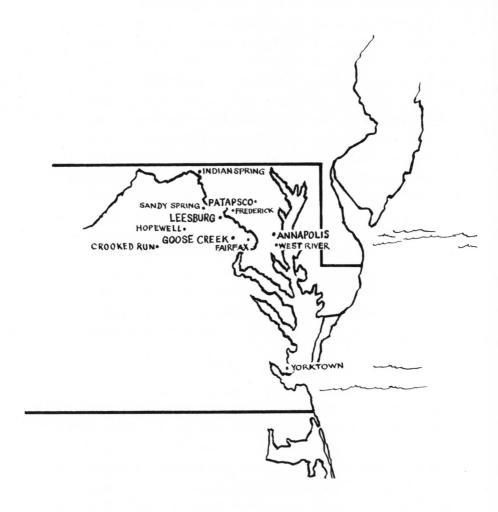

PLACES ANN MOORE VISITED IN MARYLAND AND VIRGINIA

and the foolish world, that loves ease and pleasure more than the Lord, because his cross is to them as a two-edged sword.[49]

From this meeting we went to Joseph Cowman's and lodged. Next day visited Richard Moore, grandson to that worthy Friend, Samuel Preston,[50] who deceased at Philadelphia, with whom he had lived some time in his young and tender years; but he had too much neglected his counsel, which he had to repent of, and often was ready to think his sins were so great that he should be forsaken both of the Lord, and his people, expressing himself that he sinned against knowledge, having known better and weeping said our visit was an inexpressible satisfaction to him. And notwithstanding he was so tender, there was something in that place that seemed hard and would not fall upon the rock that it might be broken upon which I fear the rocks will fall and grind to powder.

From this place we went to Joseph Hill's, in sight of Annapolis, and had a meeting there. I was in great fear dread of going to this house; having had a hard meeting there some little time before, which threw me into great dread of mind; and in this abased state of mind, I entered under that roof, having all the pomp and grandeur of this world put under foot, so that they were as nothing in my sight. But my poor sister seemed much cast down with the haughty looks of some of who were there, and perceiving the anguish of her heart, I prepared to go to bed that she might be out of the sight thereof, she being led to admire what we came there for. But soon after we were seated in their meeting the next day, the awful power of the living, everlasting God arose, which takes away the fear of man, and brings down every high look, which set my poor afflicted sister above them all, and enabled her to give God the thanks, and humbly to beseech him, that he might be pleased to appear for our help, and the honour of his ever blessed and powerful name. And he who was a hearer

John 15:14

341

of prayer, answered the supplication of her heart, and arose with great power and glory in his clouds, to the stopping of the mouths of gainsayers, and causing confession to be made, that they had not done whatsoever he had commanded them, therefore they were not his Friends, which was queried of them. For our dear Lord and Savior said, ye are my friends if ye do whatsoever I command you and some were made, through the power of truth, to confess they indeed had not done what he the Lord had commanded them wherefore they were worthy to be called His friends, and under a sense thereof they wept sorely, and my dear sister, who had never before been so far from home in the service of truth, seeing beyond what she had ever before done, said O! who would not be a servant to the Lord, who is so good. I never saw the like nor never experienced such sweet comfort.

This is to encourage you, my dear children, to be faithful to the appearance of the saving grace of our Lord and Savior, that he may be with you in the deeps, to bear you up as he has done my poor soul, to whom be everlasting praise forever.

From this place we returned towards home, and were again at Indian Spring meeting, it being in the way, which was a sweet, good meeting. From thence went home with Yates Plummer, and staid that night. Next day got home, and found our families reasonably well. But I soon saw the storms and troubles were not over; but rose higher and higher, so that high winds and floods of affliction washed me from all outward dependence, and from the love of every thing but the Lord, and his blessed truth. Then a journey which had long, at times, laid before me revived, and I said, O Lord! if thou wilt be pleased to go with me, I will go when and where thou pleases; for my life is bitter to me, and I would rather die than live in the manner I now do. And as I was travelling to Deer Creek meeting alone, which is about forty miles, this long journey was renewed on my mind, and resting with great weight, wrought a true willingness in me to go when and where the Lord pleased. When I got to Deer Creek meeting, I there met with a Friend under the same concern, with whom my spirit united, and I felt more secret joy and solid satisfaction than for some months before, and the God of my life having suffered me to be tried various ways, until my mind and love was drawn from all visible things, and fixed wholly and alone upon him. And notwithstanding I had for some time had in view a visit to Carolina, as also to Virginia, but feeling myself released from Carolina, I set out on the 22nd of the 5th month, in order to visit some meetings in Virginia, taking Patapsco, Forrest, Pipe Creek, Bush Creek, and Monoquesy by the way, then on to Virginia and were at four meetings at Fairfax, also visited Goose Creek and Pott's meeting, likewise had one meeting at Leesburg in Loudoun county, the 2nd of 6th month, to good satisfaction. After which, accompanied by the widow Rachel Hollingsworth[51] and Mahlon Janney, attended Crooked Run meeting, and from thence to Hopewell meeting, as also a meeting at the widow Lupton's, and on my return home, visited Fairfax meeting again, from thence came home, and found my family well.

5th month

6th month

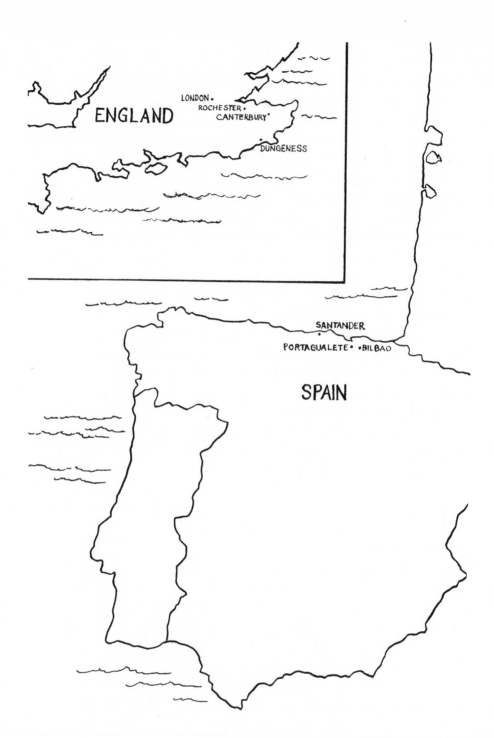

PLACES ANN MOORE VISITED IN SPAIN

THE JOURNAL OF ANN MOORE

PART V

A Narrative of Ann Moore's Voyage to Great Britain in 1760 & 1761; her Captivity by the French, Landing In Spain, arrival in England and England being at this time at War with France and Spain,

Feeling a religious concern to visit my brethren in old England, and having obtained the concurrence of Friends at the preceding Yearly Meeting; I came to Philadelphia the 1st of 12th month, 1760, and on the 24th of same, embarked on board a ship bound for London; divers Friends accompanied me to the vessel, where we were blessed with a sweet heavenly meeting, and marked in much love and tenderness.[52]

12th month

This day we sailed to Reedy Island and on the 26th got to the capes where our pilot left us. Soon after the wind rose high with hard rain and hail, which continued near three weeks and as soon as the ship began to toss and roll about my kind shipmate, William Henry,[53] and myself grew very sick; but having youth on his side he began to recruit in about two weeks, but I remained exceeding sick almost six weeks, not digesting my victuals kindly, until three days before we landed in Spain. This storm was so great that it seemed as if we should unavoidably be swallowed by the waves; but it pleased the great and gracious hand to preserve us therefrom, which was cause of getting but little on our way.

I have a desire to leave my children a hint of God's love to me, during this calm, preparing me for a trying time which was approaching, giving me a secret sign in some visions of the night season, of what I should meet with and that he would provide for me and preserve me safe, which is as follows: About a week before the French took us I saw in a vision in the night, our ship run aground having lost all her men but one, and he was near falling over when I caught him by the hand and said to him Take care, or thou will be down, for the ship is broken.

Then I thought after we had discoursed about the other men being gone and wondering where they were gone, we walked out the ship, and as we travelled, some fierce dogs ran out of their dens after us, as though they would devour us. Then I looked simply on them and said, Go back, Are you not ashamed? when they returned to their dens, looking much ashamed; after some time they came out again and fondled on us.

The next night after I saw the ship run aground, I dreamt I was a travelling and saw a comely young woman sitting on a road with two pails full of large ripe grapes; one pail was larger than the other, and the vines full all around her. She spoke to me and said, the little pail is for thee, which I expected, and thought they were the largest and sweetest that I had ever seen or tasted.

Then I awoke, and going again to sleep, had the same dream a second time. The night following this dream about the grapes, I saw in a vision a large company and much hurrying. But I felt my mind quiet and easy; and looking about me I saw a large apple tree fuller of ripe fruit than ever I had seen before. Then I thought the owner bid me take what I would, but I seemed loath to meddle with it and one limb being fuller than the others, he told me I should have what was on that; and so shook them into my lap; after which I saw my tenant and his wife, and observing a louse on each of them surprised me, and awakened a fear less I should get some, a fear which I awoke and solidly considering what it could mean, and being under deep travail of spirit, had to look at the vision of our ship running around when it arose in my mind that we should be taken, and the sweet fruit I believe pretended some favour I should receive, but the lice on my tenant and his wife I thought denoted poverty, and warning me to be careful of what I might be favoured with in time of need.

After the before-mentioned calm, the wind rose and we sailed pleasantly on until we came within two or three days' sail of the Land's End of England. The captain and the ship's company seemed very cheerful but my mind was sorely afflicted, being certain that we should meet with some sore trial, yet said but little about it, having a few days before hinted to them my belief that we should be taken; when they laughed at me to scorn. But soon after the scene changed, for as they were merry, laughing and joking, on a sudden one of the men cried out, Yonder, I see a ship, which struck them with amazement; and the captain and crew immediately put on their best clothes. The anguish leaving me and I grew easy, but I told them I believed it to be a French ship, though I felt easier than I had been for several days, to which my shipmate, William Henry, replied, so do I, yes I do believe as you that its a French ship. Then I thought I would follow the captain's example, and put on some of the best of my clothes, but when I attempted it I lost all power and seemed as though I should have fainted. Then I looked them up, and said, If they take part they must take all, for I cannot put any of them on, and turning into my lodging room I sat down alone, querying in my mind what could be the matter. When the language passed secretly through me, They that will lose their lives for my sake shall save them. Then I gave all up, as though I never had owned them, not expecting to keep any of them, and felt sweet peace.

Matt.10:39

By this time, the French privateer drew nigh to us, when our captain distributed his money, and threw some of it in my lap, yet would not believe it was a French ship that was pursuing us, until she came so near to us, that one of our men who spoke French said, he was certain of it: immediately after, they fired a cannon and hailed us; and our vessel not laying to as soon as the French wanted, they fired a second time; and soon after came on board our ship with drawn swords in their hands, as though they meant to kill all before them; tearing down the compass and looking glass, and hurried our captain, mate, and several others on board their vessel; taking several chests and trunks with them. This was the 29th of the 1st month 1761, and on the 30th they came on board our ship again, fearing we should be retaken and our captain being with them, he came to my cabin and spoke to me; when I looked out and casting my eye simply on them, one that spoke English moved his hat, and said your servant madam, and looked as sheepish as I thought the dogs did. Our poor captain desired them to be kind to me, which they were considering, the nature of the case, far beyond what I expected.

1st month

Now as our captain stood by me, he privately put more money into my hand and desired me if I could keep it to lodge it in some Friends' hands in London. Then I thought of the small pails of grapes, I dreamed I received of the women on the road, and herein it was fulfilled; for though he gave me but a little of what he had, yet that little proved exceeding good, as I thought the grapes were which I remembered with thankfulness. After this we sailed in company with them, until the 6th of the 2nd month, when they permitted William Henry, George Mason,[54] myself, and two other persons to land in Spain at a town calls Lastres; then I thought my vision of the apple tree was fulfilled; for I believed had I been able to have gone about and gathered all I had in the ship the French captain would have let me take them; for when he saw the mate (who was a pilfering little thief) open my trunk of clothes, and take out a green apron, he took the

2nd month

trunk from him and gave it to me, desiring me to take my clothes out of my trunks, and put them in a chest, which he had appropriated for William Henry, George Mason, and myself; to take our things ashore in; but mine almost filled it up, and the mate having got George Mason's key would not let him have it, as that he had nothing but what he had hid; but mine were thrown into my lap, as I thought the apples were; and having given some of them up, as though I never had owned them, I received them of the captain as a free gift, which increased by faith, and confidence in my ever Blessed Guide. And when we were landed, I was led to consider the love of the Lord, in discovering secretly to me in the shades of night his tender mercy and fatherly care over me who was, at this time despised by some as a poor creature. But that I leave and rejoice in the Lord God of my Life, who took particular care of me. Oh that my dear children may choose him for their chief joy and then he will never leave nor forsake them, for he is not a God afar off but a God and Saviour nigh at hand in every needful time, to all who put their whole trust in him. Glory, honour and praise be to his worthy name forever. Amen.

The night we were taken, the wind shifting and blowing against them they could not carry us into a land of bondage, so that I had daily cause to bless the Lord, for his manifold mercies to us poor captives. And though we were landed among a people of strange language, yet in the town called Lastres we found a man who spoke some English, and assisted us to hire us mules to carry our things and for me to ride, I being very greatly weakened by sea sickness. We agreed to pay a man twenty dollars for himself and two mules, to conduct us about seventy miles to the town of Santindero [possibly Santander]; and as he insisted on our paying him half the money before we set out, and not having dollars we gave him a doubloon when William Henry desired him to give us the change. But he would not understand but kept replying aye, aye, five more when we come to Santindero; and thus being paid he went with us about twenty miles and then turned back in the night, and left us to do as we could.

But William Henry understanding a little of the French language, informed our landlady how we were treated; when she went and brought home another man who spoke some English, through whose assistance we agreed with her husband to let their sons go with us, which they cheerfully did, and when they left us, we paid them more than we had agreed to, which made the poor lads skip for joy, and hugging the English Friend in their arms and gave us many thanks, and we had reason to believe they never had received such wages before, for we learned in travelling in that country, that men had but one shilling a day for themselves and one for a mule, and we had paid them above a dollar a day, besides their victuals.

From that place we went near forty miles by water to the town of Castero, which made us very sick, and I, not being able to go on staid with the two seamen at Castero, and William Henry and George Mason proceeded to Bilboa. I continued very sick almost two days, not having any person with me who could make the people understand what I wanted, and the wind was too high to follow them by water as they expected, neither could we make them understand to change our money to pay our reckoning, nor hire mules, to go to them by land, until the high wind drove a ship into harbour, and the captain speaking English kindly changed our money, and agreed with a woman to go with us to Bilboa, where we met our companions, with many others who had been taken captive as we were; two of whom were cast on the Spanish shore without money and the English Friend knowing the owners of the ship they were taken in promised them they should not want while he could help them; this introduced them into our company, but they telling the Friend they could get money on a bill, he took no further care about them, but took his passage and left them in company with William Henry and myself; but when they made trial, they could not get any, but hung on us, which was very disagreeable, as they swore greatly. The English Friend wanted William Henry to leave me and go with him, but he told him he would not, saying considering she is sick and the errand she is on, were I to leave her, I should be ashamed to look her Friends in the face, and though I am not of their Society, I love that people.

2nd month

It was the 14th of the 2nd month when I got to Bilboa,

where we staid until the 26th, when we sailed about nine miles to Portagillet [Portagualete], a town at the entrance of the sea where we were to clean out, and had our men been lively and active like some other nations, we might have put out to sea the day following, but they neglecting that opportunity, the wind changed, and we were detained about a month; and as I could not bear that the two seamen before mentioned suffer, they continuing to depend on me, I supported them with William Henry and myself about three weeks out of the money I had saved; when finding four half crowns a day lessened my money very fast, I grew uneasy, remembering the caution given me in the night season, and told William Henry, I would let him have as long as I had any to spare, but as I had been warned before our ship was taken to be careful of the favours I might receive, and those two seamen might do something to get themselves bread, but I could not; and desired him to inform them of our circumstances, which he did when they seemed much troubled, but I told them I could not help it. I had done what I could and they must go to the English consul, and lay their case before him which they did and told him if he would not assist them they must enter into the King of Spain's service, for they could not perish. Then he gave them six pence a day, and a guinea to pay their passage to England, which the King of Great Britain allows all his subjects who may be taken by the French and cast on that shore.

The 29th of the 2nd month, the wind changing fair for us to sail we got ready, the captain, his wife, and our company, all excepting myself seemed glad, and hurried to go on board the ship. But my mind was so exercised and oppressed, I knew not what to do, secretly wishing if the Lord had any thing for me to do before we should go on board the vessel, that we might be prevented without my mentioning it, and so it happened, for though several vessels had sailed, that day, yet when the pilot tried the bar it wanted four inches and a half more water before our ship could cross and when this news was brought, it bowed my heart before the Lord, with earnest desires to know his will concerning me; saying in my heart, I am willing to go wherever thou may choose to send me rather than loose my sweet peace, though they cannot understand me. Then I was answered that there are some at Bilboa that can understand thee, and also thou shall meet with a trial at sea. And as I sat low before the Lord, secretly waiting to see how I must move, being alone, it passed through my mind with sweetness, if thou will write to some in Bilboa, I will excuse thee, and preserve thee safe at sea. Then did my soul enjoy a peace beyond expression, and I sat down and wrote just what was conveyed to me, which was as follows:

In the pure love of the Lord do I write these things to thee Edward Doren,[55] and to the rest of thy countrymen in Bilboa, and all who desire rest to their never dying souls, there and thereaway. I have felt under the awful fear of Almighty God, a warning to you dear souls which I must leave with you, whether you hear or forebear, I shall be clear in the day of account. I have been made sensible in this time of my sojourning in this land, that you too generally put too much trust in outward performances, not minding the free gift of God in you as you ought to do. Christ within the hope of glory, it being the spirit of truth which the Father sent to lead into all Truth; which heavenly treasure we are blessed with in our earthen vessels. Therefore in the dread and fear of Almighty God, before whom I must daily give an account of my stewardship, do I warn you before it be too late to cease to do evil and learn to do well; that you may save your souls alive. For the holy spirit of the Lord Jesus is grieved and vexed because of swearing, lying, drunkenesses, and the many abominations that are in this world. Therefore, repent, repent before it be too late for we have no long continuance here. The desire of my heart is that these lines may be received in the same love in which I have wrote them. So that God over all may be glorified and our poor souls saved. These are from one who wishes the present and eternal felicity of all mankind. Farewell, Ann Moore. Written at Portagillet in Spain, the 29th of the 3rd month, 1761.

I have a desire to leave a hint of some solid discourse I had with a Roman priest when in Spain which was as follows.

Being at my lodging, reading the New Testament, he came with divers others into the room where I was sitting, when I rose up and spoke to them and putting my Testament under my arm, walked out into another room where our landlady was. He soon after followed me with four or five of his acquaintance and spoke civilly to me, asking me divers questions respecting our being taken, and likewise about my native land. When I civilly answered him, he looked at me like one amazed said, pray, ma'm, are you a Quaker? I replied yes, and pray, said he, what is your errand to England? Are you not a preacher among the Quakers, and going for that purpose? I answered, Yes, to visit my Friends in the love of Truth is my errand and I have no other. He then stood silent a little time and said, is it, indeed? I replied yes; then he asked me if we believed the New Testament. I answered, to be sure we do, Here it is under my arm. Is it? said he in a kind of surprise and took it and looked in it a little while and returned it to me, saying, Why it is, indeed, and what do you think of that passage our Savior spoke to Peter and said to him, "Thou art Peter, thou art a rock, and on this rock I will build my church and the gates of hell shall not prevail against it. I give unto thee the keys of heaven and what thou binds on earth shall

Matt. 16:18

be bound in heaven," saying again what think you of this? I then said to him, young man, as my lot is cast here through war I desire not to offend any man, but if thou will permit me to speak my sentiment without taking offense I will answer thee, but if not, I shall be silent. He replied as did some of the others, O, no offense in the least, we love to hear you talk. I then said the passage thou mentioned is not the Scripture text. A youth who was present answered, aye, but he can show you it in a little book he has at home. That may be, I said, and many more things of man's projecting but not sound Scripture. Then I repeated the text and told him he might, if he pleased, read it himself. Then before mentioned youth replied, Aye but he may not read the Scriptures. I told him I was sorry for it that a minister should not read the Scriptures. He then asked me what I thought the rock was and the key that was promised to Peter? I then told him it was my real belief the rock meant was Christ and the key his

Holy Spirit which are one, which opens and no man can shut and shuts and no man can open. What this spirit binds on earth will be bound in heaven for it is in us and with us all the days of our visitation, bearing testimony against every appearance of evil. This is the rock and foundation which God has laid and another foundation can no man lay than that which is already laid; if thou will mind this no man can deceive thee. Peter was a servant, as thou and I are, if we are so but Christ is the way to the Father. He, the lip of truth that cannot lie, has declared it. Then he replied though you do believe in Christ you cannot be right for there is but two ways, right and wrong and you must be wrong because you do not submit to the ordinances of Mother Church. I queried him, what the ordinance of the true Church of Christ were? He said the baptism and the Lord's supper. I asked him, what constituted the Lord's supper? He answered bread and wine. The before mentioned youth seemed then elevated, replied they cannot be right, for if a man lives forty years and dies without submitting to the ordinance of the church he won't go to heaven nor hell but to limbo. My spirit despising his nonsense, I made him no answer but said to the priest who was a civil man, after some other solid discourse, as we are engaged in discourse which concerns our everlasting welfare, I will now tell thee what I think is the baptism and the Lord's supper which we ought to be acquainted with: To know the power of the Lord, to subdue the will of the flesh and strengthen us to suffer patiently whatever he may permit to be tried with for his name's sake, and to draw us from all outward dependence to worship him in spirit and in truth as we do profess to do, and all who worship him in spirit and in truth, they know a supping with Him and He with them, they are made acquainted with the saving baptism, the true ordinance of the Church of Christ, and are willing to submit to it, remembering Christ said, "Ye are my friends if ye do whatsoever I command you." And I desire thee to consider in time if outward baptism and taking of bread and wine would do those men in the other room (whom I daily seeing going to perform some of the ordinances thou mentioned) swear, drink and fiddle and dance as they do? With this he seemed much daunted and turned very pale many times: but the afore-mentioned youth replied, That is only diversion. After some more solid discourse with the priest, I said to him, I request the favour of thee, as thou has so strongly pleaded for Peter to be the rock, to tell me, thy real belief, whether Christ or Peter is the author of our soul's salvation? O Christ, to be sure, said he. Then I answered, I hoped no man would be offended at my preferring our Lord and Master above all his servants. O, by no means, he said, and after some more con-versation we parted in peace. During the remainder of my stay there he often desired to be remembered to me, and wished me a prosperous journey and that God might bless me in my undertaking.

I am induced from the divine sweetness the Lord blessed me with when we parted to leave the above hints of our con-versation, for the encouragement of all the Lord's servants who may read this to own him before men, that so they may witness to him to own them in time of need.

I have also a desire to mention another trial I afterwards met with: it being our lots to be cast in Spain in the time of lent, where we continued until it was over, and towards the conclusion, came on their procession of the host, the images of our Saviour, their saints the apostles and the Virgin Mary through the streets and on the parade by the seaside, before the window of the room where I lodged, they erected an altar on which they placed the coffin that contained the im-age of our Saviour, and stood round it with the rest of the images fixed on great square tables borne up on men's shoul-ders. While they were erecting the altar, the power of the

357

Lord was upon me in such a manner that I trembled as one in a strong ague and a cry ran through my heart, O Lord, let them see as thou has let my poor soul see, that Christ within is the hope of the saints' glory, which became so close and heavy, I began greatly to fear that if I did not proclaim this which so powerfully ran through my heart, I should lose favour with the Lord; and great indeed was my distress, yea more than pen or tongue can declare, and my cries to the Lord were, O Lord! what can I do, I fear that I shall not stand, nor be strong enough to go through this great work, and so bring dishonour to thy cause and confusion of face on my dear friends; and then it would be better I had never been born; besides they cannot understand me. In this awful state I remained upwards of two hours until all fear of what man could do was taken away. Then beholding my hands which looked like one prepared for the grave, I went to the fire, and sat down alone, my companions being gone to another town there was no soul for me to speak to or ask counsel of. Thus I sat resigned to the will of the Lord, my God, waiting for him to point out to me, where He would have me go, whether to the church, or to the place where they had erected the altar. I had not sat long before I sensibly felt the will was accepted for the deed, as was the ram instead of Isaac. Glory, honour, and praise to the Lord God and the Lamb forever and ever. Thus did my soul sing His praise in secret, and being bowed low before him, my joy as far exceeded the declaration of pen or tongue as my baptism and sorrow before had done. A day of days not easily to be forgot. Yea, I have thought like letters engraven in a rock not easily to be erased. O! praises, thanksgiving and glory to the Lord God and the Lamb, forever and ever, Amen, Saith my soul and more.

Gen. 22:13

I have wrote the above that my dear children may see what the high and holy one who inhabits eternity, has done for their mother that they may be engaged to be inward with him, who is and ever was a present help to all his depending children: for O sweet Lord and Savior, he gave me power at that time to resign my life, and also my dear children, expecting my life would be taken for the testimony I should have to bear. May my dear children remember this, and believe the word of the Lord who said, Whoever will lose his life for my sake shall find it. And all he requires of his creation man is to resign the whole heart, then he lets us see that he is a God of order and requires no more of us than He will give us ability to perform. But a tried people will the Lord our God have under which trials we are sometimes laid so low, that we feel according to our measure, as our dear Saviour did, when He said, I have a baptism to be baptized with. O how am I straitened until it be accomplished, but glory to his worthy name he went through faithfully and now sits in glory and honour, which will be the end of all His faithful servants who sell all and follow him.

Matt. 10:39

Matt. 20:22

On the 3rd of the 3rd month, 1761, we sailed out of the Kingdom of Spain and as it had secretly appeared to me that we should meet with some difficulty at sea, so it happened, for on the 3rd of the 4th month we met the English fleet, who hailed us, and commanded our captain to speak with their admiral, which obliged us to turn our ship, and made our captain and several of his men angry and uneasy: this brought a deep concern on my mind, lest it should cause those with whom we were confined, to use us ill, being as deeply concerned for my kind shipmate William Henry who had patiently waited for me, as for myself. But as he whose word is yea and amen forever, had shown me in my deep distress that if I would write to some in Bilboa, I should go in peace, and he would preserve us safe at sea, He manifested his power and wrought our deliverance; for in the evening the fleet tacked about towards England again which made our ship's company look something pleasanter, and next day about

3rd month

4th month

twelve o'clock, some men came in a boat as we thought from the admiral and coming on board our ship, enquired where we were bound, our captain's name, and divers other things and then left us, and I thought, as soon as [they] could have related to the Admiral what they had enquired about, they fired two cannon, drew into rank, and then tacked about and sailed away. But we kept our course, though in much fear, they having put English men on board of divers of ships that sailed out of Spain when we did; and made them sail with them until they got within sight of the town they were going to take; and we feared lest when they should perceive we kept our course, they should send a ship and put men on board of us; and one vessel did seem to bear down towards us several hours, which made William Henry, our captain, and the rest of our ship's company very uneasy.

But my heart was deeply engaged all that time to that divine hand who could order all things for the best, that if it was his blessed will to deliver us. Then he was pleased to give me the answer of peace, and in a few minutes after, we heard a cannon fired in the fleet which was then out of sight and immediately the ship tacked about and followed the fleet. Then my tender shipmate called very cheerfully to me and said, come Friend Moore, we are once more delivered. I answered him saying I thank God and wish we may all be truly thankful; for I do look upon it to be the Lord's great mercy to us.

After this we sailed very pleasantly along and arrived on the British shore at a place called Dungeness, in Kent County the 11th of 4th month, 1761. From thence William Chell, a Friend, accompanied me to a town about three miles off; and having sent my trunk by water to London, we hired a carriage and went to Canterbury, where my shipmate, William Henry, and I parted. He took coach for London and I staid with an intention to visit the meetings in the Kent County, but being very poorly with a cold, I staid one week at George

Sims's and on the 20th of the month he and Benjamin Beale[56] accompanied me to Benjamin's house, whose wife went with us to most of the meetings in that county which were small and close heavy work therein.

On the 29th we went to Canterbury, to the before mentioned Friend's house. I staid their weekday meetings and then his sister accompanied me to Rochester where divers of my dear Friends from London met us, the sight of whom rejoiced my heart and a blessed heavenly meeting we were favoured with which renewed my strength, to return thanksgiving and praise to the great name of the Lord, my God, who had been graciously pleased to send His guardian angel to conduct me safe by sea and by land.

From Rochester I went on to London the 4th of 5th month, 1761, when I had the first sight of that great city London, where I was kindly received by my dear Friends. My tender and loving Friend, John Hunt,[57] not being quite well, could not meet me at Rochester, but as soon as I came to London, he came to John Townsend's[58] to see me and kindly invited me to make his house my home when in that city; which kind offer I accepted, and went with him to their morning meeting which was sweet and comfortable; after which he and Mary Weston returned with me to John Townsend's where my things were that I sent by water from Dungeness. John Hunt then went home and sent his wife to conduct me to their house.

5th month

Having attended the Yearly Meeting at London, I left it the 21st of 5th month, in company with several Friends, and went into the counties of Suffolk and Essex to visit the Seed therein. Rode that day about thirty miles to John Griffith's where we staid that night. Next day attended their meeting, which was sweet and comfortable. From thence to Colchester Quarterly meeting, and then on to Woodbridge Quarterly meeting where I received a comfortable letter from my true

Ann Moore

and sympathizing Friend, Joseph White[59] which came in a needful time, when I was ready to think I was forgot by all my old acquaintances, having just before met with some deep sorrow for not standing faithful to the testimony of truth manifested in my own heart, whereunto, if we were all faithful, we should not deceive ourselves nor others but should shine brighter than now we do. And though this for which I was so nearly tried, was but a small thing, yet if we are not faithful in a little, more will not be committed to our trust.

I have wrote these things for my dear children to read when I am gone to my resting place, and my advice to them is to be careful to obey that of God in their own hearts, then will they lay down in peace, and none can make them afraid.

9th month After visiting divers counties, I returned to London and staid a few days; and on the 29th of 9th month 1761, I set out towards Beverly [Beverley] Quarterly Meeting, intending to have taken it in my way to some meetings I had omitted in Norfolk; but my mind growing exceedingly uneasy lest I should go wrong, I waited on the Lord, in lowness of spirit much pain of mind, until he was pleased to reveal His will concerning me, which was to leave those few meetings before-mentioned and go to Harford [Hertford] Quarterly meeting and then through Buckinghamshire to London and Bristol, and I should go home in peace and He would preserve me safe at sea.

4th month And on the 9th of the 4th month, 1762, I embarked for Philadelphia, where I arrived the 26th of 5th month with great *5th month* joy, it being a high favour, in such perilous times, to pass safe.

And blessed be the name of the Lord, who according to his gracious promise, preserved me safe at sea, and blessed me with sweet peace thereon, which accompanied my home, *6th month* where I arrived the 5th day of the 6th month, 1762, with true and everlasting peace, and found my family well. Blessed be the delivering arm of our God forever and ever.

362

THE JOURNAL OF ANN MOORE

PART VI

In the 64th year of my age and 14th of 3rd month, 1775, I having in my mind for many months to visit some meetings in York County and having a minute of my Friends of the monthly meeting whereonto I belong signifying their unity therewith, so on the fourteenth day of the third month, 1775, I left my outward habitation and set out towards Pipe Creek and had a meeting in Winchester town with the few Friends therein and divers of the townspeople and several of Pipe Creek Friends who came in the fellowship of the gospel to meet me and I think I may say were divinely favoured. I went home from thence with my daughter and her son Thomas Farquhar and staid there one day and on the seventeenth I went to the preparative meeting at Pipe Creek and next day to the monthly meeting at the same place and after meeting set forward for Menallen meeting and rode fifteen miles that evening and lodged at a very kind man's house that night and the next day, it being the first day of the week and eighteenth of the month we went to that meeting and after meeting went home with James McGreen who married an acquaintance of mine. From there we went to the Huntingdon meeting the nineteenth of the month. The same day my Friends that accompanied me from Pipe Creek returned towards home and I came the next day to Warrington meeting. These were for the most part favoured meetings. I dined at Joseph Elgin's and in the evening went to William Willis's and William Chanley's wife accompanied me there and next day to York meeting, it being the twenty-second of them. That day I crossed the ferry at Wright's and next day with two other Friends went on towards Philadelphia, one turned another way to see his parents and I and William Corsey went to Warwick Miller's and staid that night and next day set forward on our way to the Spring meeting and when the meeting was over and not finding my mind easy to go home without going to Bucks County unto which motion I submitted and on the twenty-ninth I with Samuel Hopkins[60] and other people went to Germantown meeting which was a solid good meeting. I staid that night at John Jones's in Germantown and the young Friend Samuel and others returned back to Philadelphia where they dwelt and on the thirtieth I went to Abington Meeting. This was also a favoured meeting at which there was a burial spoke of one Margaret Mason, the wife of Benjamin Mason, who ate her dinner well and before night was a corpse. O! what need we have to be ready for our final change not knowing how near that awful messenger is to summonsing us to our final home. After this meeting we went to our Friend [Jacob] Lippincott and dined and after dinner went with him and his wife to see her father who had been blind some years and my companion had something on her mind to drop onto him which she delivered with tender regard and desire for his eternal happiness. From thence went to Samuel Tompkins where we staid that night and had a sweet opportunity with his mother who lay sick. Her children were there, and the next morning my companion, Margaret Porter,[61] feeling something on her mind to say to her unto which she submitted and rose up and went to the bedside and delivered what was committed to her and I stepped to the bed to take my leave of her and son and saw that the few words she had to deliver to her had taken deep hold on her mind which gave me some satisfaction of mind for I knew her to be a woman in her youth to be pretty high minded and drawn much to the things of the world.

From then we went to Horsham meeting the thirty-first day of the third month seventeen hundred and seventy-five.

From thence we went to Buckingham the first of fourth *4th month*
month and the next day being the seventh day of the week
we went to see the widow Fell and her daughter-in-law who
was a widow also. We had a sweet opportunity with these
widows and the next day we went to Plumstead meeting and
I called by the way to see my daughter-in-law who was poorly
both in body and mind.

The third of the fourth month we were at Buckingham
meeting. It was their monthly meeting and I thought in the
main it was a favoured meeting though I felt the seed lay low.
The fourth we were at Wrightstown monthly meeting, the
fifth we were at the Falls monthly meeting at which there
was six couples passed the meeting. In these meetings I felt
the seed very low yet the Lord in his mercy was pleased to
open to us renewedly the way of life eternal for the honour of
his own holy name and for the renewing of the strength of
his people whose hands were ready to hang down, blessed be
his worthy name for evermore, Amen.[62]

The sixth I was at Middletown monthly meeting. This
was a favoured meeting. The seventh we went from thence
to Newtown meeting in the court house and I think it was a
day of visitation to the place and Friends thereaway. The
night we were at the house I was brought up in and had a
meeting in the esteemed Friend's house who brought me up
from a child and I had reason to believe it was a day of visitation to them, his son and grandchildren and divers others.

Then we went to Byberry and on the ninth of the month
were at their meeting. After meeting I went to Philadelphia
and called by the way to visit the widow Dalton who was in
great distress for one of her daughter's husbands was very much
out of his head. We had a seasonable time with this widow
not only on his account but divers young people being there
were exceedingly reached and broken into tenderness, this is
the Lord's work and forever blessed be his name.

365

We went from thence and at Frankfort my companion who went with me through Bucks County left me and went home, she lived near Germantown. I with my two young Friends, James Thornton's[63] son and son-in-law, arrived at the city before dark. Next day being the second day of the week, I went to the morning meeting. This was a sweet meeting indeed to me and after meeting I went to Israel Pemberton's and dined with one of the English Friends, Mary Lever,[64] and after dinner Samuel Howell's[65] wife came there with whom I went and visited a daughter of Caleb Copley who lay in the consumption and very low therein and a heavenly sweet opportunity with her and her husband and tender children and divers other Friends. We went also to see a daughter of Mary Harvey's, the wife of John Ellet's who had newly lain in, with whom we staid a little while and then I went with Samuel Howell's wife to his house and spent some time in reading over the names of the Friends who came from Europe to visit the Seed in America.

And in the evening I went to Deborah Morris's[66] and had a heavenly opportunity with her and her aunt and several other Friends. Thus ended this blessed day. Next day I staid the week day meeting and a good meeting it was. After meeting I went to Wilmington and staid two days and then I went on again towards home and got to Nottingham to Joseph Haines's and staid all night. Job Harvey[67] and his son came there with me, then returned home and Joseph Haines came to the river with me and I desired him to return and not put himself to any further trouble, for I knew the way very well which he did and I crossed the river and went to William Coxe's. The sixteenth of the month I went with him and some of his children to Deer Creek meeting. This was a favoured meeting from thence I went home with the aforesaid Friend and dined, then set forwards to home and came that evening to William Cook's and staid that night

and on the seventeenth of fourth month 1775, I came home   *4th month*
and through divine favour found my family well.

P. S. I may note that my dear Friends were made uncommonly near and dear to my life as thought it would be the last sight I should have of some of them which I think it will. And so it was for divers of my old acquaintances were taken away out of time and I never saw them more, our seasoned and worthy Friend Sarah Morris,[68] Isaac Anders, Thomas Gill and many more.

> The righteous are taken away and no man layeth it
> to heart.

THE JOURNAL OF ANN MOORE

PART VII

A Journal of Ann Moore's Travels through some parts of Pennsylvania and also some parts of the Province of New York in 1778.

Having had drawings in my mind for some considerable time past to visit parts of Pennsylvania, and also some parts of the Province of New York, and having acquainted my Friends therewith, and obtained their approbation and certificate; I left home on the 4th of 5th month, 1778, accompanied by Alice Jackson[69] and Benjamin Hough,[70] who, with divers other Friends, had attended our Quarterly meeting; whose labours of love among us were truly serviceable. The day following we rode twenty miles, notwithstanding I was weak in body, and attended an appointed meeting at Little Falls, and from thence to John Smith's and dined, and in the afternoon to William Coxe's and lodged. Next day went to Deer Creek meeting, and dined at James Rigby's[71]: after which we crossed the Susquehanna, and rode to Joseph Haines but his house being filled with light-horse men[72], we went to George Churchman's[73] and lodged; and from thence to Nathan Yarnall's,[74] and attended their select and Quarterly meetings, as also their youth's meeting, which was held at Providence, the last of which, though pretty large and divinely favoured, would have been larger, only for the burial of Micajah Speakman's[75] daughter at Concord, at the same time, which a large number of Friends and others attended, and we were informed it was a favoured, solid, good meeting, which seemed a token of her happy change. After the youth's meeting, we dined at Benjamin Sharpless's and returned to

5th month

368

Nathan Yarnall's and lodged. Next day, being very poorly, I rested myself, while my companions and the family went to their   week-day meeting; after which Nathan Yarnall accompanied us to William Harvey's, where we lodged that night. Next day we attended Kennett monthly meeting, and lodged at Caleb Pierce's whose wife had been confined to her bed eight years, unable to turn herself. Next day we had a comfortable time with her, then visited Samuel Levis's wife, who had lain very sick and lame with the rheumatism six or seven months, with whom myself and divers other Friends had a heavenly, sweet meeting, worthy of our awful remembrance. From thence we went to Thomas Woodwards and lodged; next day were at the Quarterly Meeting at London Grove, which was very large, and held part of three days, and much labour and travail of spirit was witnessed therein, for the good ordering of the church.

From this meeting, myself and two companions proceeded for Bucks County. Stopped at Isaac Massey's, who accompanied us across the Schuylkill, above the camp. Lodged that night at Israel Jacob's; went with them to their week-day meeting, returned and lodged at Israel Jacob's. and next day being first-day, his wife went with us to North Wales meeting: and from thence to Abington, and lodged at William Hallowell's and next day attended their monthly meeting. After which, we proceeded to Buckingham Quarterly meeting, which held part of three days. It was large, and in good degree favoured with divine sweetness. From this meeting we went home with the Widow Scarborough and staid one night, the next day, the 30th of the 5th month, we crossed the river Delaware; and as times seemed difficult, Samuel Smith,[76] John Balderston,[77] and George Michener,[78] accompanied us to Kingwood, and on our way there we dined at Harmen Hester's about eleven miles from Lott's Ferry, had one meeting at Kingwood, after which the above-mentioned

Friends returned home, and myself and companions staid and lodged at Joseph Drinker's,[79] and from thence to Joseph Moore's. Next day had a meeting there with the family and a few of the neighbours. These last mentioned meetings caused me often to think, as I sat in silence, how the priests formerly stood with their feet in the bottom of Jordan, having none but the Lord to look to for power and strength, to stand for his honour and the encouragement of the people. But blessed be the adorable name of our God, who, in his own time, by his light and life-giving presence, broke through the thick clouds of darkness, to the setting forth of his great mercy and tender regard to mankind, in sending his beloved Son, our saviour and redeemer, a light into the world; and those meetings ended in prayer and thanksgiving to the God of all our mercies, who is worthy thereof, now and forever. Amen.

6th month   The weather being wet, we staid two nights at Joseph Moore's, and the 3rd of the 6th month attended the week-day meeting at Plainfield, from thence we proceeded to Joseph Shotwell's at Rahway, and on the 5th had a refreshing meeting there, after which returned to Joseph Shotwell, and dined: in the evening accompanied by several other Friends, visited their neighbours, Thomas Dobson and family, who had left New York in a time of battle. After some friendly conversation, a silence ensued, and we were favoured with the descendings of the heavenly Father's love, to whom thanksgiving and praises were returned, who is worthy thereof, now and forever.

I felt my mind drawn towards New York, but the way seemed so shut up, that we thought we must leave it, and return towards home. But some of our tender Friends at Rahway taking it under their weighty consideration, and thinking it best for us to make trial, we went with divers other Friends to General Wayne, at Elizabethtown; who, after reading our certificates and conversing with us, granted us leave, but thought it best for us to defer it until the middle of the week following; so we returned to Rahway, and next day, being the first of the week, we attended their meeting, and on second day, visited an ancient Friend who had been blind many years, which was a favoured opportunity. Lodged at Benjamin Shotwell's; and next day, in company with some other Friends, had a comfortable sitting in his family. On fourth day attended their meeting, and then proceeded to Elizabethtown. and staid at our kind Friend Joseph Stackhouse's. Next day, accompanied by Joseph and Henry Shotwell, we set forward towards New York, stopped and lodged at Ann Lizzearls, a kind widow, and from thence to Powle's Hook, intending to cross the North River to New York; but the colonel not being willing, we went to Bergen Point and lodged. Two of our company went to a general on Staten Island and got a pass, and the next day, being the 13th of the month, we crossed to New York, and the 14th, being the first of the week, we were at their morning and afternoon meetings, which were divinely favoured. Our dear Friends in this city received us with much love and tenderness. On the 15th, I visited some of my old acquaintance, and in the evening, accompanied by Henry Haydock's wife, visited Samuel Brown's wife, who was indisposed and unable to go to meeting. Divers Friends coming in, we were favoured together with a refreshing season, greatly to my satisfaction, having renewedly to see the tender regard of our heavenly Father, whose works praise him.

The 16th we prepared to go to Long Island, and just as we were going to set off, the divine power seized me, and made my flesh and bones to tremble and a voice passed through me, saying, "The poor servants have not been favoured with the crumbs which fall from their master's table," so that I did not dare to go until I sat down with the family, and handed forth the crumbs which were committed to my trust; and having thus relieved myself, we left New York, and proceeded to Newtown on Long Island. The 17th attended the meeting at Newtown after which we set forward towards Flushing; lodged at Isaac Underhill's and on the 18th were at Flushing Meeting, which was held at Matthew Franklin's; the meeting house being made a hospital for soldiers. After this meeting we went to Ann Field's, a widow, who had that day buried her son; a large number of Friends and others being there, we sat down together and were favoured; yea it was a time in which God's mercy in sending his Son a light into the world, a light to lighten the Gentiles, and the glory of his people were spoken to, and this blessed atonement which was sufficient for the fall was recommended to the people as the only way to life and salvation.

This opportunity concluded with prayer and thanksgiving to Almighty God who is worthy forever. From thence we went to Joseph Pearsall's and the 19th attended their meeting at Cowneck, and returned to Joseph Pearsoll's, and dined; then went to Thomas Seaman's and stayed there until the 21st, then went to Westbury meeting, and from thence to Samuel Willis's and on the 22nd had a meeting at Oyster Bay, and lodged at Jacob Bowne's; the 23rd went to Matinicock meeting, visited a lame Friend on the way, from whence we returned to Westbury; and the 24th attended the monthly meeting there. These were all large meetings and divinely favoured. From Westbury we went to William Seaman's at Jericho and lodged. The 25th we attended Secatogue meeting in which we were favoured. From this meeting we returned to Henry Whitson's and the 26th went to their meeting at Bethpage, after which we rode to John Mott's near Jerusalem and lodged. The 27th we had a comfortable meeting at the widow Mott's; and when most of the people were gone, I felt the heavenly Father's love to draw my mind to sit down a little while with these tender Friends, when he was pleased to bless us with the lifting up of his light and lifegiving presence, under which, humble petitions were put up for his people, who would that he should reign; as also that he might be pleased, if consistent with his Divine will, to preserve his people wherever they be, let their name to religion be whatsoever it may; and likewise that he, who in mercy had opened the way for us to visit his churches in those parts, might be pleased, in the riches of his mercy, to permit us to return home in safety, to the praise of his own glorious and powerful name. Thus ended this awful and hearttendering time, in praise and thanksgiving to him who is God over all, blessed forever, Amen.

From this place we set out for Newtown again; lodged at Benjamin Douty's and next day attended their monthly meeting and on the 2d of the 7th month, 1778, returned to New *7th month* York, and the weather being unusually warm, our kind Friends requested us to stay until it should moderate, to which we agreed, and staid there until the 9th, having attended their meetings on first day, we intended to leave that city on 2nd day, but were prevented from crossing the ferry by a number of the army crossing, who came from Philadelphia, so that we staid there until the 9th when we came towards Rahway, lodged on the way at Ann Lizzearl's, and next day got to Benjamin Shotwell's at Rahway, who had accompanied us through New York, and Long Island, and kindly lent myself and companion his horse and chaise to ride in. I had been very sick for several days before I came there, where I staid one day, then went to his brother Joseph Shotwell's, and the weather continuing hot, and I very poorly, we staid two days; when Benjamin Shotwell took me in a chaise (as I continued very weak) to Plainfield meeting; from whence he and his daughter accompanied us to Joseph Horner's. Next day they returned home and we went to Stony Brook meeting, which was a good meeting, as was also that at Plainfield. Leaving

Stony Brook the 14th, we crossed the river Delaware to Pennsylvania, and next day went to the Falls meeting; after which we went to the widow Kirkbride's, at the Four lanes end, to the burial of her grandson, whose parents deceased some time before. This widow had but one son living, who had buried his son the day before; and seeing the father, mother, and grandmother, weeping over these dear innocent babes, it arose in my mind to desire them to dry up their tears, and consider their happy state, and that we must be converted and become as little children before we can enter the kingdom of heaven; as also their happiness in being gone where the wicked cease from troubling, and the weary are at rest. Thus I was led to drop a few words of healing to the mourners, as also warning to the youth, which was a relief to my mind, and I hope to the mourners likewise.

From Middletown we went to Makefield meeting, where Rachel Hunt and her uncle Isaac Clark, who had accompanied us from Stony Brook, left us and returned home, and we proceeded to John Watson's at Wrightstown, and dined; in the evening rode to Thomas Watson's at Buckingham. Next day Thomas Watson accompanied us to see an ancient Friend of about eighty years of age, who by a fall was so disabled she could not sit up. We sat down with her to wait on the divine Father of mercies, who was pleased to favour us with his ancient gathering love, to our refreshment, to whom alone be all praise. From thence I went to see my cousin, Sarah Day, a sorrowful widow, who had but a little time before buried her husband, and was much oppressed by the times, and far advanced in years: one of her sons lived with her, the rest of her children being married. After the above mentioned visit, I returned to Thomas Watson's, thinking to proceed homewards next day; but feeling myself stopped, I waited to see which way my never failing guide would direct me; and as I kept my eye steady to the light, my way was opened to

Buckingham, Plumstead, Horsham, and Byberry; to all which I went, and had a meeting at each place, which were divinely favoured. The 28th of the month, proceeded towards home; stopped at Abington monthly meeting, and Germantown week-day meeting; this last was a favoured meeting. After which my cousin, Joseph Spencer, took me in his chaise to Philadelphia, and an acquaintance rode my horse, which was a great favour to me, I being aged and weak in body. I staid and attended the Quarterly meeting at Philadelphia, and also the week-day meeting at Pine Street: after which, I dined and had my lodging at Deborah Morris's and prepared to set out towards home; and divers Friends being present, we sat down awhile to wait on the Lord, who was pleased to bless us together, so that we parted in much love and tenderness; and I may say, I never in all my visits to that city, left it in greater peace of mind than at that time; having been favoured with many blessed opportunities during the Quarterly Meeting there. May the great name of our God be praised, now and forever.

After the above-mentioned sitting at my lodgings, which was the 5th of the 8th month, 1778, accompanied by divers *8th month* Friends, we proceeded to Wilmington, Hockesson, and New Garden meetings, which were comfortable meetings. The Friends who came with us from the city intended to leave us at New Garden, which was the place of my tender companion's residence; but they not feeling easy so to do, they and my companion went with me to Rumford Dawes's[80] who kindly accompanied us to my son-in-law's, M. P., taking meetings by the way, particularly East and West Nottingham, and Little Britain;—then crossed the river Susquehanna to Deer Creek Meeting, and to my son-in-law's above mentioned, where we all staid one night; and next morning before we parted, we were blessed with a sweet opportunity, and the mercy of Almighty God appeared so great to me, his

375

Ann Moore

poor handmaiden, as caused my spirit to bow, and return praises and thanksgiving to him who is worthy forever— Amen.

8th month   The 15th of 8th month, I returned home in that peace which surpasseth the understanding of man;—and found my family well.

THE JOURNAL OF ANN MOORE

Notes - Introduction

1. Walter Moore was born the 22nd 2 mo. (April), 1693 (old style) and died 13th day of 8th month, 1782. His children by the first marriage were Thomas and Sarah. *Records*, Baltimore Yearly Meeting.

2. Introduction to "Ann Moore's Journal," *Friends Miscellany* vol. 4, no. 7: 289-292. In her *Journal* she speaks of visiting the house in which she grew up in Newtown, Pennsylvania. Buckingham Monthly Meeting *Minutes* for 1-1-1738 record her acceptance into membership. A certificate of transfer to Fairfax Monthly Meeting, dated 7-4-1746, identifies her as a recorded minister of Middletown Meeting, Bucks County. Microfilm, Friends Historical Library,(hereafter cited as FHL), Swarthmore College.

3. Elizabeth Moore (Prosser); Rachel Moore (Price); Ann Moore Jr. (Price); John Moore; and Mary Moore (Griffith). *Records*, Baltimore Yearly Meeting.

4. *Minutes*, Fairfax Monthly Meeting, 7-4-1746; 12-27-1747; 2-30-1748; 8-29-1748; and 12-20-1753. *Minutes*, Gunpowder Monthly Meeting, 1-23-1754. Microfilm, FHL.

5. *Minutes*, Gunpowder Meeting, 1-22-1754; 8-25-1756; 11-23-1857. FHL.

6. Ann Moore to Israel Pemberton, 4-12-1763. Pemberton Papers, vol. 16: 69. Historical Society of Pennsylvania (hereafter cited as HSP).

Notes - Part I

7. Ruth Holland was a member of Gunpowder Meeting.

8. Mary Janney with her husband Amos Janney moved to Virginia and established a meeting at Fairfax in 1741. *Hopewell Friends History* (Strasburg, Virginia: Shenandoah Publishing House, 1936), 69.

9. William Matthews (1732-1792), a traveling minister, visited most of the meetings in the American colonies and in 1783 traveled to England, Ireland, Scotland, and Wales with John Pemberton. DQB.

10. John Wright, father of Susanna Wright, operated and established Wright's Ferry in 1727. The Wrights were well-to-do and well-educated, which may account for Ann Moore's feelings. Please see Elizabeth Hudson's *Journal*, Part VI, note 83.

11. For Jane Hoskins, please see Elizabeth Hudson's *Journal*, Part I, note 10.

12. Susanna Churchman Brown (1701-1790), born in Nottingham, Pennsylvania was a sister of John Churchman, a traveling minister and journal writer. Susanna married William Brown in 1728. Both traveled widely in the ministry. DQB.

13. John Cornell (1717-1781), the son of Richard and Hannah Thorne Cornell, was born at Cowneck, Long Island, but moved to Scarsdale about 1725. Thomas Cornell, *Adam and Anne Mott* (Poughkeepsie, 1890), 363.

14. For Esther White, please see Elizabeth Hudson's *Journal*, Part VI, 75. Grace Fisher was a minister of Philadelphia Yearly Meeting. In 1754 she traveled with Catherine Phillips in Bucks County. DQB.

15. Thomas Wight and John Rutty, *A History of Progress of the People Called Quakers in Ireland* (Dublin, 1751).

16. Joseph Irish and David Hoag were members of Oblong Meeting; Allen Moore of Oswego. *Records*, Oblong Monthly Meeting.

17. John Campbell, Earl of Loudoun, a commander of the British forces. *Dictionary of National Biography* (London: Oxford University Press, 1927), 828.

18. William Mott of Mamaroneck Meeting was a traveling minister. Attending New Garden Monthly Meeting in 1765, he became ill and died. *Collection of Memorials concerning Divers Deceased Ministers and Others of the people called Quakers, in Pennsylvania, New Jersey and Parts Adjacent* (Philadelphia, 1824).

19. Joseph Delaplaine (1725-1799) was a minister of New York Monthly Meeting. DQB.

20. Joseph Shotwell was the husband of Sarah Shotwell, a minister. DQB.

21. James Nayler (1618?-1660), prominent in the birth of the Society of Friends, was led astray by the praise of followers and allowed himself to be persuaded to ride into the city of Bristol on a donkey as though he were himself Jesus Christ. He was punished for this heresy which also angered George Fox and other Quaker leaders. This incident may have been a factor leading to the establishment of formal Quaker meetings to oversee the conduct of members. DQB.

22. Richard Lundy, II (1692-1772) was an elder whose home was much used for entertaining traveling Friends. DQB.

23. Samuel Large (1688-1765) was a traveling minister of Kingwood, New Jersey, Monthly Meeting. DQB.

24. John Watson was a Quaker doctor of Bucks County. *The Diary of Elizabeth Drinker*, edited by Elaine Forman Crane (Boston: Northeastern University Press, 1991), vol. 3:371.

25. Edward Stabler (?-1785) from York, England, had settled first in Philadelphia, then Virginia. In 1756 he wrote a letter to General George Washington protesting the taking of seven Quakers into the army by force. (It is possible that one of these was Ann Moore's stepson.) DQB.

26. Joshua Pusey (1714-1760), an elder at London Grove Meeting, was known for his hospitality. *Transcript of Records,* Nottingham Meeting by Williard Heiss.

Notes - Part II

27. John Everitt moved from Nottingham, Pennsylvania, to Pipe Creek, Maryland in 1737. His son Isaac was a traveling minister. DQB.

26. Alexander Underwood (1688-1767) was a recorded minister of Warrington Meeting in Pennsylvania. He traveled in the ministry in North Carolina. DQB.

29. William Penn, "No Cross, No Crown" in *Selected Works of William Penn* (New York: Praus Reprints, 1971).

30. William Edwards (1712-1764) was a minister of Abington and later Richland Meeting. *The Friend,* vol. 33:148.

31. Morris Morris (1677-1764) was born in Wales, emigrated to Bucks County, and married Susanna Heath who became Susanna Morris (1682–1755), whose *Journal* is reprinted in this anthology. Morris Morris was an elder in the Society of Friends. DQB.

32. Traveling Friends usually stated where they felt led to go and the certificate was written accordingly.

33. Benjamin Parvin (1727- ?), born and educated in Ireland, came to live in Bucks County, Pennsylvania. He was a surveyor, and often accompanied traveling ministers on their journeys, including John Woolman. DQB.

34. James Abercrombe (1706-1759) had replaced the Earl of Loudoun as commander of the British troops. *Cyclopedia of American Biography,* vol. 1 (New York: James White, 1898), 8.

35. Ann Matthews was a member of Gunpowder Meeting. *Transcripts,* Baltimore Yearly Meeting.

Notes - Part III

36. Joseph White (1712-1777), an American traveling minister, visited England, Ireland, and some parts of Wales between 1758 and 1761. DQB.

37. Phebe Titus was a member of New York Monthly Meeting, evidently traveling in the ministry. William Wade Hinshaw, *Encyclopedia of American Quaker Genealogy, vol. III, New York City and Long Island* (Ann Arbor, Michigan: Edwards Brothers, 1940), 454.

38. Benjamin Fell (1703- 1758), a minister, belonged to Buckingham Meeting. He was the son of Joseph Fell, born in Cumberland, England. Benjamin became an elder in Buckingham Monthly Meeting, and died in 1758. John Smith, "The Lives of the Ministers of the Gospels among the People called Quakers," unpublished MMS, 1770, vol. 1:176.

39. Edmund Kinsey (1683-1759) was a recorded minister of Buckingham Monthly Meeting. DQB.

40. Agnes Penquite arrived in Bucks County in 1686, and was a minister for over seventy years. She died 20th of 11th month, 1758, close to the age of 100. John Smith, "The Lives of the Ministers of the Gospels among the People called Quakers," unpublished MMS, 1770, vol. 2: 648.

41. William Walmsley (1709–1773) was a farmer, clerk, elder, and overseer in Byberry Meeting. *The Diary of Elizabeth Drinker,* vol. 1, edited by Elaine Forman Crane (Boston: Northeastern University Press, 1991),19.

42. Joshua Morris was also the son of Susanna Heath Morris.

43. Anthony Morris, III (1682-1763) was a prominent member of the Society of Friends and was a wealthy brewer and landholder. In 1738 he served as mayor of Philadelphia. He was the father of fourteen children, one of whom, Anthony Morris,

Jr. (young Anthony Morris) married Elizabeth Hudson in 1752. His house on Second and Arch Streets in Philadelphia was known as the Mansion House, and housed many traveling ministers. DQB.

44. For Samuel Spavold, please see Elizabeth Hudson's *Journal*, Part IV, note 50.

45. Samuel Howell (1719-1780) was a wealthy Philadelphia hatter who moved from Chester to Philadelphia in 1758. Later he became a member of the Pennsylvania Assembly. Crane, *Drinker*, 31.

46. For Grace Lloyd, please see Elizabeth Hudson's *Journal*, Part VI, note 84. For Jane Hoskins please see Elizabeth Hudson's *Journal*, Part I, note 10.

Notes - Part IV

47. Jane Naylor (Ann Moore spelled it Nailer) is listed in the Gunpowder Monthly Meeting Records. *Transcripts*, Baltimore, Yearly Meeting.

48. Robert Pleasants (1722?-1801), clerk of Henrico Monthly Meeting, Virginia, visited the banished Friends at Winchester, freed his slaves, and proposed the establishment of a free school for blacks. DQB.

49. This is a good example of the sort of interpretation Friends of this period put on their dreams.

50. Samuel Preston (1664-1743) was a traveling minister. DQB.

51. Rachel was probably the widow of Isaac Hollingsworth, a traveling minister of Virginia who died in 1759. John Smith, "The Lives of the Ministers of the Gospels among the People called Quakers," unpublished MMS, 1770, vol. 2: 145.

Notes - Part V

52. In the original manuscript, there are three additional para-
graphs describing Ann's disappointment when a companion
who was to have accompanied her on this voyage decided not
to go. Rachel Price evidently chose to leave this material out
of the copy she made.

53. William Henry (1729-1786), an American pioneer in steam
propulsion, was born in Chester, Pennsylvania. On this trip
to England he learned from James Watt about steam propulsion. He was not a Friend, but sympathetic. *Dictionary of
American Biography* (New York: Scribners, 1931), 560-561.

54. George Mason, an English Friend, was returning from a religious visit to the American Colonies. DQB.

55. Edward Doren was evidently the British consul.

56. Benjamin Beale was a Friend from Margate, the inventor of a
bathing machine. His wife, Elizabeth Beale, was a minister.
DQB.

57. For John Hunt, please see Elizabeth Hudson's *Journal*, Part VI,
note 64.

58. John Townsend (1725-1801) was a Quaker minister and a pew-
ter worker. He visited the United States after the American
Revolution. DQB.

59. For Joseph White, please see Ann Moore's *Journal*, Part III,
note 36.

Notes - Part VI

60. Samuel Hopkins (1743-1798) married Hannah Wilson in 1768
and moved to Maryland, but returned to Philadelphia and
became a member of the Northern District Monthly Meeting.
Crane, *Drinker*, 209.

61. Margaret Porter was a minister of Abington Monthly Meeting. In 1773 she obtained a certificate to travel in the ministry between Abington and New York. Microfilm *Minutes, Abington Monthly Meeting, 1765-1782.*

62. When Ann Moore writes that "Six . . . passed the meeting," she means that six couples were approved for marriage by this meeting.

63. James Thornton (1727-1794) was born in Buckinghamshire. He moved to Pennsylvania in 1750 and settled at Byberry. He was a traveling minister. DQB.

64. Mary Leaver (Ann Moore spelled it Lever) (1720-1789) was a traveling minister of Nottingham who traveled to the American colonies in 1773. *Piety Promoted ,* 9th Part (London: James Phillips, 1798), 172.

65. Samuel Howell (1719-1780) was a wealthy Quaker hatter and merchant. He married Ann Evans at Merion Meeting in 1745. Crane, *Drinker,* vol. 3: 132.

66. Deborah Morris (1724-1793) traveled to England with her aunt Sarah Morris in 1772-1773 and kept a diary of her travels. Henry J. Cadbury, *John Woolman in England, 1772* (London: Friends Historical Society, 1971), 12.

67. Job Harvey was the husband of Rebecca Owen Minshall Harvey, a traveling minister. John Smith, "The Lives of the Ministers of the Gospels among the People called Quakers," unpublished MMS, 1770, vol. 2: 113.

68. Sarah Morris (1703-1775) was a minister who traveled in Great Britain in 1772-1773. *Friends Library,* vol. 6: 478-479.

Notes - Part VII

69. Alice Jackson (?–1779) was a Quaker minister who traveled in New York and Pennsylvania. Crane, *Drinker,* vol. 3:319.

70. Benjamin Hough (1724-1803) traveled in the ministry and moved to Notthingham in 1771. Crane, *Drinker,* vol. 3:238.

71. James Rigbie (Ann Moore spells it Rigby) (1720-1790) became a minister of Deer Creek Monthly Meeting in 1749. DQB.

72. This reference to light horsemen, or cavalry, is one of Moore's few admissions to the existence of the Revolutionary War.

73. George Churchman (1730-1814) wrote a journal of his travels in the ministry from 1759-1813. DQB.

74. Nathan Yarnall was the first husband of Phebe Schofield Speakman (1738-1828) who was a traveling Quaker woman minister. "Ministering Friends," 7. QCHC.

75. Micajah Speakman married Phebe Schofield Yarnall in 1781. "Ministering Friends," Crane, *Drinker,* vol. 3:230.

76. Samuel Smith (1720-76) of Burlington, New Jersey, was a merchant and founder of the New Jersey Society for Helping the Indians. Crane, *Drinker,* vol. 3:195.

77. John Balderston (1740-1821) was a Quaker farmer in Solebury Township, Bucks County. Crane, *Drinker,* vol. 3.

78. George Michener (1747-1827) of Plumstead Monthly Meeting. Clarence V. Roberts, *Early Friends Families of Upper Bucks* (Philadelphia, Pennsylvania, 1925), 89.

79. Joseph Drinker (?–1809) was brother of Henry Drinker and a Philadelphia cooper. He married Hannah Hart in 1760 and they had ten children. Crane, *Drinker,* vol. 3:225.

80. Rumford Dawes was a Quaker merchant in partnership with brothers Jonathan and Abijah Dawes. Crane, *Drinker,* vol. 3.

INDEX

The editor wishes to thank Holley Webster of Swarthmore Monthly Meeting for her generous and faithful help in compiling the index.

Page numbers for place names on maps appear in italics.

Index

Index

Index

P

Pomfret [Pontefract] 205, *207*
Pontypool 246, *273*
Poole 95, 243, *273*
Port Isaac 97
Portagualete 352
Porter, Margaret 364
Pound, Elijah 326
Presbyterian 6, 18, 63, 136, 305
Preston, Samuel 341
Price, Rachel 21, 25
Providence 11, 85, 176, 266, 368
providence 130, 133, 137, 144,
    165, 176, 191, 194, 195,
    243, 245, 260, 271, 272
public houses 181–183, 252–253
public meetings 8, 18; in America,
    303, 309, 318–319; in Great
    Britain, 101, 196, 209, 211; in
    Ireland, 152, 154; in Wales,
    248–249, 251–252; with
    soldiers, 311, 314–315, 317
Pusey, Joshua 298
Puritan 2, 4, 5, 6, 14, 24

Q

Queens Ferry 180
quietism 14, 15, 64, 123, 164, 228–
    229, 304, 310

R

Raby 199
Radnor 111, *126*
Rahway 13, *126*, 137, 139, 140,
    297, 302, 303, 326, 329,
    370, 371, 373
Ranter 2
Ratcliff, James 83
Rathanagan 159
Rawdon 168, *170, 207*
Reading 73, 94, 102, 103, 161, 301

R

reasoner, the, 47, 115, 142; *see also*
    adversary, devil, and satan
Reays, Sarah Dixon 175
reconciliation between Friends 53–
    54
Red Ford 149
Reformation 24, 25, 29
reformation of Quakerism 7, 37, 88,
    101
Reverdon, Peter 112
Richabie, Mary 93
Richardson, John 61, 67, 206
Richland 37
Richmond 198, *207*
Ridgeway, Job 133
Rigbie, James 368
Ringwood 95, 233
Roberts, Ann 44
Rochester 361
Rockaway 302
Rogers, Major 314
Romsey 95, 233
Roscrea 157
Ross 155
Rotterdam 51, 52, 54, *57*
Roulofs, Eleanor 52
Row, Joseph 161ston 211, 214

S

sacraments, a Quaker view of 3,
    354–357
Saffron Walden *207, 213*
Salem 132
Salisbury 102
Sands, Joshua 307
Sandy Spring 289, 336
Sandwich 221, *273*
Santander 350
satan 83; *see also* adversary, devil,
    and the reasoner
Scarborough, John 298

S

Scarborough, the widow 369
Scarlet, John 85
Schooley, Samuel 302
Schooley, William 297
Seaman, Thomas 372
Seaman, William 372
Settle 168
Shap *170*, 171, 176
Sharpless, Isaac 162
Sheldon, Eleazar 131
Sherburn 99
Shields 199, *207*
Shipley 231, *273*
Shipley, Elizabeth 9, 25, 265,
    267, 271
Shipley, William 84
Shotton 199
Shotwell, Benjamin 297, 298,
    322, 326, 371, 373
Shotwell, John 136
Shotwell, Joseph 297, 370, 373
Shrewsbury 70, 88, *126*, 136,
    137, 138, 255
Sickside 184
Silver Springs 155
simplicity 6, 17, 237–239, 252
Sims, George 360
Skipton 168
slavery 4, 14
slaves 4, 14, 337
sleeping in meeting 232
Smith, James 301
Smith, Mary 234
Smith, Samuel
Smith, Theo 93
Snowden, Richard 336
Sodbury 257, *273*
soldiers
    of faith, 151, 188; encounters
    with, 152, 287, 296, 309,
    311, 315, 324, 325; hospital
    for, 372

S

Southampton 234
Spalding 165, *207*, *273*
Spavold, Samuel 204, 331
speaking to states or conditions of
    people, 79, 169, 171, 186, 189,
    198, 211, 235, 269
Speakman, Micajah 368
Spice Land 99
Squan 138
St. Albans *207*, 214
St. Margaret 218, *273*
Stabler, Edward 298
Stackhouse, Joseph 371
Stansted *207*, 212, 213
Stanton, Daniel 173
Staten Island 135, 371
Stephens, Elizabeth 131
Stephenson, John 297, 323,
    326
Stock 162
Stockport *170*, 189
Stockton 58, 199, *207*
Storrs, Joseph 67
Strickland, Amos 327
Strictland *170*, 171
strong drink 7, 88
Sullivan, Elizabeth 132, 135
Sulton 258
Summer, S. 133
Sunderland 56, 58, 199, *207*
Swaledale 198
Swansea 247, *273*
Swarthmore Hall *170*, 186

T

Talbot 255, *273*
Taunton 99, 100, 101
tavern 303, 304, 311
Taylor, Joseph 36, 19
Tenby 248, *273*

SCRIPTURE INDEX

Religious Language Index

The journals of the Quaker women ministers, Susanna Morris, Elizabeth Hudson, and Ann Moore, include rich, diverse names for God and the Lord. These traditional names occur so frequently in the text they are not indexed. Other forms of address for the power that moved these women are indexed below.

Index

Wilt Thou Go On My Errand?

was set in Goudy Old Style, a desktop computer typeface from the Adobe Type Library. In 1915, Frederick W. Goudy designed Gouldy Old Style, his twenty-fifth type face and his first for American Typefounders. One of the most popular typefaces ever produced, it is flexible for text and display. Its distinctive features include diamond-shaped dots on the i, the j, and punctuation marks; the upturned ear of the g; and the base of the e and the l. Several years later, in response to the overwhelming populariaty of Cooper Black, Langston Monotype commissioned Frederick Goudy to design heavy versions of Goudy Old Style. Goudy Heavy Face and Goudy Heavy Face Italic were released in 1925. Their huge success led to the addition of several other weights. Designers working for American Typefounders added additions to the family. In 1927 Morris Fuller Benton drew Goudy Extra Bold.

The book was composed on a Macintosh 610 using Aldus Pagemaker 5.0. Two thousand copies were printed in the United States of America by Thomson-Shore, Inc., Dexter. Michigan, in July 1994. It was printed on 60# Glatfelter Supple Opaque, an acid-free recycled paper from the Gladfelter Company.

Book Design by
Eva Fernandez Beehler and Rebecca Kratz Mays